# ARTIFICIAL INTELLIGENCE:
## Applications in the future of software engineering

# ELLIS HORWOOD SERIES IN ARTIFICIAL INTELLIGENCE

*Series Editor:* Professor JOHN CAMPBELL, University College, London

# ARTIFICIAL INTELLIGENCE:
## Applications in the future of software engineering

D. PARTRIDGE, Ph.D., B.S.
Computing Research Laboratory
New Mexico State University

**ELLIS HORWOOD LIMITED**
Publishers · Chichester

Halsted Press: a division of
**JOHN WILEY & SONS**
New York · Chichester · Brisbane · Toronto

First published in 1986 by
**ELLIS HORWOOD LIMITED**
Market Cross House, Cooper Street, Chichester, West Sussex, PO19
1EB, England

*The publisher's colophon is reproduced from James Gillison's drawing of the ancient Market Cross, Chichester.*

**Distributors:**

*Australia and New Zealand:*
Jacaranda-Wiley Ltd., Jacaranda Press,
JOHN WILEY & SONS INC.
GPO Box 859, Brisbane, Queensland 4001, Australia

*Canada:*
JOHN WILEY & SONS CANADA LIMITED
22 Worcester Road, Rexdale, Ontario, Canada

*Europe and Africa:*
JOHN WILEY & SONS LIMITED
Baffins Lane, Chichester, West Sussex, England

*North and South America and the rest of the world:*
Halsted Press: a division of
JOHN WILEY & SONS
605 Third Avenue, New York, NY 10158, USA

© 1986 D.A. Partridge/Ellis Horwood Limited

**British Library Cataloguing in Publication Data**
Partridge, D.A.
Artificial intelligence: applications in the future of software engineering. —
(Ellis Horwood series in artificial intelligence)
1. Computer software — Development
2. Artificial intelligence
I. Title
005.1'2    QA76.76.D47
**Library of Congress Card No.** 86–7171

ISBN 0–85312–735–0 (Ellis Horwood Limited)
ISBN 0–470–20315–3 (Halsted Press)

Printed in Great Britain by R.J. Acford, Chichester

# Contents

*for Azzie, Mischa, and Morgan*

# Preface

Artificial Intelligence (AI) has fascinated me for the last 15 years. I have been intrigued by the possibilities yet discouraged by the behaviour of (much of) the AI community. And now there is the widespread belief that AI has finally 'come good' and the casual computer users are about to reap the benefits in the form of smart computers.

I have attempted to clarify the situation by providing several different characterizations of the scope and limitations of current commercial AI. In addition, I have also delineated the fundamental problems that must be solved before we will see the full potential of AI in practical software. Lastly I have examined the conventional wisdom concerning these problems and presented my own views as to what the outcomes will be.

AI research has two major components: descriptions of extremely interesting ideas that are going to be implemented; and large programs that are shown to do a few interesting things. Neither component offers much of substance to the interested observer.

Unimplemented ideas are just that, and one is left to wonder about completeness, consistency, and practicality in general. Implementations on the other hand have to be accepted and judged largely on the basis of the few interesting behaviours claimed or demonstrated. Usable documentation is non-existent, the real scope and limitations of the program are anybody's guess. What exactly has been implemented, and what the implementation is supportive of, in general, must be taken from the implementor on faith.

AI is a behavioural science; it is based on the behaviour of programs. But it has not yet come to grips with the complexity of this medium in a way that can effectively support criticism, discussion, and rational argument — the requisites of scientific 'progress' are largely missing. Argument there is, to be sure, but it is all too often emotionally driven because rational bases are hard to find.

I feel that I should forewarn the reader that this book is not a manual for constructing AI software — it does not contain in depth demonstrations of

AI as practical software. It does not do so because I believe that the major benefits of AI as practical software are not yet realisable, and will not be for quite some time.

It is true that expert systems and natural language interfaces have made significant progress in this direction. But in-depth analyses and discussion of such systems abound; it did not seem worthwhile to reproduce any of them. More importantly, I take the view that current commercial AI products do not begin to demonstrate the full potential of AI, nor do they illustrate all of the awkward problems that still remain to be solved.

I have attempted to take a global view of the potential for AI in software engineering. I am looking to the future and thus the argument and discussion must of necessity be somewhat speculative and general. The details of current expert systems, for example, have little to say about the long-term possibilities of commercial AI. But the general characteristics of this class of software do give us pointers into the future. Therefore I have omitted the fine detail but attempted to extract and project from more general principles.

On finishing this book many questions will remain unanswered, especially if you were hoping to design and incrementally develop some practical application of AI immediately. Alas many questions do remain unanswered. I wish it could be otherwise — I'm not holding back with the answers for use in "AI and SE Rides Again", I can assure you of that.

I claim to be demonstrating how to apply AI to practical software but it would be wrong to pretend that many of the fundamental questions have adequate answers (or worse, to gloss over the problems themselves). By examining the unsolved problems I hope to have at least clarified their status — domain of relevance, relative importance, and current approaches to solutions.

Exposure of these problems has two main implications with respect to the potential for AI in practical software: first, it clarifies the limitations of current AI techniques and by so doing the software designer may have a better idea before he starts of what and how currently practical AI techniques may apply to the particular application contemplated.

Second, asking the right questions, at the right time, in the right context is an essential prerequisite for discovering some of the answers. I have posed so many unsolved problems within a comprehensive and coherent context, I think that I must have hit some of the above "rights" — in conjunction, I hope, with some of the fundamental obstacles in the path to utilizing the full potential of AI as practical software.

I wish to thank J. Mack Adams, Donna Hussain, and Roger Schvaneveldt for their comments on parts of this books, and Becky Koskela, Melissa Smartt, and Ken Paap who all read and commented on the entire manuscript, as did several anonymous readers. My editor also did an invaluable job both of questioning my more ill-supported assertions, and of transforming my pseudo-English into the real thing. The dozen or so students that have been repeatedly subjected to half-baked ideas in my AI classes during the last 18 months provided much valuable feedback. My thanks also go to the

Department of Computer Science and the Computing Research Laboratory both at New Mexico State University for providing the necessary working environment. Finally, Karen Cavert, aided by Stella Rodriguez, did sterling work transforming my ill-formed scrawlings into a machine-readable form.

The suggestions for improvement were many, all of which I took to heart; some stayed there, but most gave rise to changes in the book. In summary, this book contains one 'good thing', no kings (good or bad), many unmemorable dates, lots of problems (some with solutions), and a few overworked metaphors that I just could not bring myself to part with; naturally, the responsibility for everything is mine.

*Las Cruces, New Mexico*
*October 1985*

Derek Partridge

# 1

# An overview and a ground plan

Half of what you hear about AI is not true; the other half is not possible.

## 1.1 THE TIDAL WAVE OF AI

Something important is happening in the world of computer applications — in the domain of software engineering. It seems that a tidal wave of artificial intelligence (AI) is about to roll in and swamp the application of computers in every sphere.

The first wave is breaking into a multitude of expert systems, knowledge bases and natural language interfaces. The potential scope of AI in practical software is limitless.

The human user will be able to communicate with a computer system in English, if that is his preferred language, instead of having to first learn whatever formal, restrictive, and pedantically specified protocols that current computer systems insist on. Expert systems using knowledge bases will be cheaply available to offer all kinds of advice, from sophisticated expert opinion such as medical diagnosis, to more mundane, but apparently harder, assistance on say, planning a complex business trip. The quality of this advice will be far superior to that obtainable from the average human and may even offer a significant service to the human expert himself.

Thus an automatic medical diagnosis system such as MYCIN, a program that diagnoses blood infections, may be used by a human expert diagnostician with the same area of expertise. Human intelligence and computer intelligence are, and will most likely continue to be, different: the human excels at interrelating the components of a very broad range of knowledge while the computer's strong point is rigorous and relatively exhaustive search in a much more restricted collection of knowledge. Another promise of AI is for attaining new heights of necessary expertise as a result of mutual cooperation — human expertise and computer expertise working hand in hand on the problems to be solved.

The potential applications of AI are by no means restricted to expert systems but almost all AI applications will contain one or more knowledge bases. Whether it is a house cleaning robot or a computerized, customized tailoring service available in a local department store, they will each need to be expert within their application area, and expertise is knowledge based.

So the outlook is bright. We already have knowledge-based expert systems performing well in applications environments: R1 is configuring VAX computer systems for the Digital Equipment Corporation, PUFF is successfully diagnosing pulmonary dysfunctions at the Pacific Medical Center, etc. The initial problems have been conquered; it is only a matter of refining and honing techniques, and of scaling up into less restricted domains. Humanity will then be basking in the benefits of the information revolution, courtesy of the practical applications of AI.

It is also true that AI applications can be used to improve or degrade the quality of human life (and to some extent it is a matter of opinion anyway): consider the potential for automatic surveillance devices if automatic voice recognition and computer understanding becomes a practical reality. This is a difficult and important topic but not the one I want to deal with in depth in this book.

Are expert systems and natural language interfaces harbingers of things to come? Yes, and no. Yes, they are a first taste of the fruits of AI research in practical software, but not one that is smoothly extendible to the full potential of AI. They are not the leading edge of a much bigger wave following close behind but merely a preliminary ripple that will break. Substantial regrouping is necessary before the big wave can form.

Is general AI greater than the sum of the expert systems? Almost certainly, but is the difference largely quantitative, or is it fundamentally qualitative? Do we need just more of the same or do we need to add something totally different? I shall argue for this latter option.

Fig. 1.1 is a diagrammatic representation of the popular view of the expected invasion of software engineering by AI (1.1(a)), and a plan of the invasion as suggested in this book (1.1(b)).

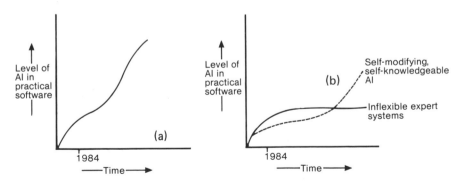

Fig. 1.1 — Possible routes for the progress of AI into practical software.

In Fig. 1.1(a) we are currently a little way up the slope with our expert systems and natural language interfaces. The way ahead is all uphill, steadily onwards, as we introduce more and more of AI into practical software.

In Fig. 1.1(b) the continuous line traces the progress of the currently practical AI techniques — non-adaptive, highly specific, largely inflexible systems. I believe that we can see the first signs in this levelling out in the importance of the "knowledge acquisition" problem and the resurgence of interest in machine learning after years of neglect — the knowledge bases that support expert systems are proving to be resistant to incremental upgrading, they are demanding an inordinate amount of high quality expertise and not performing that much better for it.

The dashed line in Fig. 1.1(b) represents my contention that work in AI must back down to first solve (to some reasonable degree) some basic problems, such as machine learning, and only then can the practical applications be built up to exploit the full potential of AI.

The reason for believing AI as practical software is not just about to happen has two bases:

(1) The research-based incremental AI program development paradigm does not produce programs that exhibit the necessary characteristics of practical software: comprehensibility, reliability, robustness, and maintainability.

(2) AI programs are not correct or incorrect; they are, at best, adequate. Adequacy is a complex, context-dependent quality that can be maintained in a variety of different contexts only by means of a sophisticated self-modifying capability (machine learning). The problems of self-adaptive programs are AI research topics, they are not ready for inclusion in practical software, and if they were included it would further aggravate problem (1) above.

To many software engineers, AI in software engineering is a solecism, to others it is already an established merger that works well. I hold neither of these views. I believe and will argue that although there is an inherent logistic dissonance between AI and software engineering there are also means of eliminating the incongruities and so producing a harmonious blend. Only then will the full potential of AI become available as practical software.

## 1.2  AN OVERVIEW

This book is intended to serve an immediate practical purpose — by describing general strategies for, and the current limitations of, incorporating AI in practical software — and it also aims at a long-term goal — to provide a rough paradigm to support the full potential of AI as practical software. This longer-term, theoretical goal does also, of course, serve a practical purpose: it provides the framework that can support and guide the development of individual projects. It is the total collection of such projects that will constitute the AI revolution in software engineering.

My plan is first to exhibit the essential incompatibilities between the program development paradigms of software engineering and of AI. The second part of the task is then to describe and illustrate general strategies for minimizing these incompatibilities. Finally from this somewhat piecemeal attempt at a reconciliation I sketch out a paradigm to support comprehensively the full potential of AI within the constraints necessary for practical software.

In Chapter 2 I have outlined a middle-of-the-road version of the software engineering program development paradigm. It is a well-known and well-accepted process yet it is useful to review it. This review also affords me the opportunity to place the emphases where they will be most useful for the subsequent contrast with the AI program development paradigm.

Chapter 3 is a whistle-stop tour of AI — nothing grand, nothing startling. But an introduction to AI is necessary even if you know both the facts and the folklore; you also need to know my biases and prejudices about this contentious topic — I have tried to make them explicit.

Having previewed AI as a subject, in Chapter 4 I turn to the problem of, what is the program development methodology of AI? I have tried to describe, justify, and further articulate the rudimentary run-debug-edit cycle. I have not presented an apologia for code hacking but taken the stance that the run-debug-edit cycle (if used correctly, and any procedure can be misused) is a valid technique and the best that we can hope for. This is not just an attempt to palliate a fundamentally flawed and inferior methodology; it is a demonstration that the run-debug-edit cycle is a process of necessity. I will argue that the process can be strengthened. Nevertheless it remains vulnerable partly because of the nature of AI problems and partly because of the current state of the art in machine-executable notations (i.e., programming languages).

In Chapters 5 and 6 I consider the specific technical problems associated with the task of making AI programs function as practical software products. I should say right away that for the purposes of this book, AI, unless otherwise qualified, is centred upon the construction and evaluation of computer programs. This is a somewhat parochial view; there is much AI and many AI researchers that have very little to do with computer programs. Let me briefly justify my current focus.

AI work that is not founded upon computer programs can be divided into two categories: about-to-be-implemented ideas, and implementation-independent studies. The first category contains ideas that are unimplemented because it is easier to play with such ideas, in conjunction with waves of the hand, than to subject them to the uncompromising logic of the computer. Such AI is usually "being implemented" or "nearly working" — and all too often it tends to remain that way for ideas typically progress much faster than programs.

The second category encompasses work such as philosophical studies which can be genuinely independent of any implementation or even class of implementation (for example, the class of hardware characteristic of modern digital computers). There is clearly a place for such program-free work in AI, although it should probably have implications for what can and cannot be achieved within certain classes of implementation.

To the first category I give the attention that it merits and the second also receives short shrift because my prime concern is explicitly with the current and future potential of AI as practical software. That is not to say that philosophical studies, for example, are irrelevant to the issues at hand. Such studies can have an important bearing as in say, the question of the necessity for machine learning in AI. When appropriate I make use of implementation-independent AI work. But when in Chapter 4 I characterize the methodology of AI, I am referring to program-centred AI for that is the topic that this book is addressing. Having said all that, I do also happen to believe that computer programs are a crucial feature of what makes AI, AI. It is what distinguishes it from philosophy, psychology, etc. Thus in my view programs should play at least a supporting role in all AI.

An AI program, a product of the run-debug-edit cycle, is not as it stands a suitable object for practical software applications. What degree and type of change is necessary? Is it a relatively simple transformation?; a more radical metamorphosis?; or a fundamental transmutation?

In Chapter 5 I argue that, dependent upon particular circumstances, the necessary changes may vary from simply the addition of documentation to a total redesign and recoding of the algorithm discovered. Wherever within this spectrum of possibilities that we settle there is an inescapable need to disinter the bones of a program: an implementation-independent and comprehensible infrastructure of the program — the de facto specification, or an underlying general principle, or just a succinct and thus comprehensible representation of what's going on in some part of the program.

Chapter 5 addresses both the trade-offs and the problems inherent in the various approaches to the problem of turning an AI program — a pile of code that behaves adequately — into practical software. A process fundamental to all approaches to this problem — the process of stepwise abstraction — is described and illustrated.

In Chapter 6 I deal with the incompatibilities between the two paradigms — the incremental, specification-development procedure necessary in AI does not readily yield programs with the requisite characteristics of practical software. Both software engineering and AI offer techniques, that if suitably extended, can contribute significantly to the minimization of the methodological discordances. The strategies described and illustrated are largely state-of-the-art, or close to it; they are also a somewhat piecemeal approach to the problem.

In the penultimate chapter I have attempted to draw all the threads together and sketch out at a high level a more comprehensive line of attack on the fundamental problem: how can we exploit the full potential of AI as practical software?

In addition Chapter 7 contains discussions of some of the other important questions that need to be aired but are secondary to the aims and objectives of this book. Such problems as the societal consequences of AI as practical software, and the always awkward moral questions in a discipline that is heavily funded from military sources.

Finally, in Chapter 8 I respond to a number of possible objections to the main theses, and I summarize what I claim to have done in this book.

Having reviewed the book and my own aims and aspirations concerning it, I shall now advance a fundamental contention that AI problems are a special class of problems, and advance arguments and examples to support it. At the same time I shall present a framework within which we can, throughout the rest of the book, more readily discuss the class of AI problems — that is, problems that are ill-structured in practice.

It may strike you as somewhat chimerical, if not just contradictory, to attempt to structure the essentially ill-structured. But provided we stop short of total structuring it can be done, and what is more, it certainly makes subsequent discussion a lot easier.

I am reminded of an analogous problem that could reduce the length of this book drastically, stated syllogistically:

All programmed problems are well structured.
AI problems are ill-structured.
Thus AI problems cannot be programmed, the set of AI programs must be empty.

If this is true my concern with AI as practical software also vanishes; AI can never be implemented.

Fortunately, there are several escape hatches from this conclusion; I shall use one of them.

One could argue that the minor premise is false: AI problems are just very complex and thus only appear to be ill-structured — I am not going to do that.

In fact I would be very inclined to go along with the conclusion if it were not for the existence of *H. sapiens*. If evolution had by chance sent him and her off to oblivion with the dinosaurs and sabre-toothed tigers attempted refutations would be on a very sticky wicket.

But as it is, man is here and is, presumably, a well-structured mechanism. He is also the exemplar of intelligence. We must then conclude that intelligence can be adequately implemented in a well-structured mechanism. And so there is definite hope that AI can be implemented in well-structured programming languages.

Clearly an AI research worker has got to get to this point; we all have our own arguments — this one is mine.

The foregoing was not just a pseudo-scientific diversion before we get down to reality, the nuts and bolts of our problem — in our case, the gotos and procedure calls of an AI program. It is a question of direct relevance to the problem at hand, for a belief in the full possibilities for AI is still largely an act of faith. We cannot be certain that AI is possible in practice or even in principle. And what about 'mechanical' super intelligence?: an even more open question.

The viewpoint taken in this book is that there are no good reasons for believing that the full potential of AI cannot be realized, in principle, but that there are a number of difficult and unsolved problems to be dealt with before we can be equally assured that it is also realizable in practice. The further, vital implication of this latter statement is that the final goal must be robust and reliable AI, not ephemeral and fragile systems that can survive only in research laboratories when cosseted by highly-skilled and dedicated research workers. So now we see yet another route to the problem of AI as practical software, let's get on and lay the groundwork for some answers.

## 1.3   THE CLASS OF AI PROBLEMS

Software engineering problems are a subset of AI problems: the subset of well-defined problems. Well-defined is not in fact sufficient to characterize the class of non-AI problems. Many complex games are well-defined; they are also AI problems — chess is one popular example.

The feature that makes such well-defined problems AI problems is that they are (or currently appear to be) both computationally intractable and too complex to be amenable to formal analysis. That is to say, although there is a simple and well-defined algorithm for playing perfect chess, time and space constraints totally preclude the possibility of ever successfully running this algorithm. Chess playing computers approximate the well-defined algorithm by using 'heuristic algorithms' (a phrase I am going to use in place of the more accurate but more cumbersome, 'algorithmic approximations to heuristics'; more on this in Chapter 3).

But because of the complexity of chess there is no formal, analytical measure of how well any given heuristic algorithm approximates the well-defined but intractable one. Chess is a problem that is well-defined in principle but ill-defined in practice. AI problems are then characterized by being ill-defined in practice, and this implies that they are also complex.

As an example of the difference between conventional software engineering problems and AI ones, consider the problem of managing personal finances. As a problem of computing the difference between total expenditure and total income it may be complex but it is analytically tractable. The necessary computation can be completely and precisely specified. Following the development of such a specification a solution can be implemented. When so viewed it is a conventional software engineering problem.

But if we view the problem as say, one of diagnosing in a non-trivial way why our financial position is as it is, or one of advising us as to how better manage our finances, then we are up against an AI problem. A complete and precise specification of the problem is no longer possible. What is an intelligent diagnosis? What is good advice? These are questions that cannot be answered completely and precisely, but most of us will be able to recognize bad and silly advice, especially if we try it out in the real world.

There are perhaps two general points of difference to bring out here: one of specification, and one of evaluation. First, although we can hold no hope that certain problems can be completely and precisely specified, we can nevertheless admit that such problems are very real and thus well worth attempting to solve to some extent. These problems are not scarce, quite the opposite I would contend. This type of problem is very much the stuff of which most of our everyday lives are composed.

Second, of potential solutions only the particularly poor ones are readily recognizable as such. The goodish attempts are difficult to rank relative to each other. Is one fairly sound diagnosis better than another? In general this is a difficult question. But, 'is this diagnosis poor?', is usually more readily answerable, especially if it can be tested against reality.

Closely associated with my claim that there is a class of AI problems that is distinct from software engineering problems, I shall further claim that AI system development is, and should remain, different from that of software engineering. I shall now make a first attempt to draw this distinction.

A major principle in software engineering holds that the specification of WHAT is to be done is the crux of the matter while HOW it is done is relatively unimportant. We can view AI as a reversal of these priorities. Consider the following definition of AI:

AI is a collection of algorithms that are computationally tractable, adequate approximations of intractably-specified problems.

Stated another way: the essence of AI is the finding of useful approximate implementations of the specifications of very hard problems — it is the HOW not the WHAT that is most important.

So, for example, I can provide a well-defined specification for the problem of chess (and to a lesser extent for, say, medical diagnosis). But all known algorithms are intractable. The AI task is to discover tractable and adequate approximations to the specification. Of course as I said above, usually nothing like a complete specification is available so clearly AI cannot hinge on specification like software engineering does. My point is that even if we could specify the AI problems satisfactorily, the correct implementations would all be intractable algorithms because of the vast (perhaps infinite) amounts of contextual information that would have to be considered to support 'correct' intelligent decisions. There is clearly more to AI than that; I shall amplify my claims in this demarcation dispute throughout the course of this book.

The complexity and ill-structure of typical AI problems means that, in order to evaluate how good an approximation a given program is, we have to run the program and observe its behaviour. AI problems are typically described and thus evaluated in a performance mode — that is, we can outline the sorts of things that the desired program should, and should not do.

Thus, it is known that a medical diagnosis expert system should generate certain classes of diagnoses for certain classes of symptoms. The way in which the diagnoses should be generated is an open question; it is one to be resolved by reproducing the required behaviour.

So potential solutions to AI problems must be specified in a machine-executable notation (i.e. a programming language) in order that they may be evaluated. Another complication is that AI problems are never really solved in some absolute sense and certainly not in the way that a software engineering problem can be solved with respect to its rigorous specification.

The best intelligent systems known, human beings, do not produce absolute solutions to the problems that require intelligence. None of us have absolutely solved the natural language communication problem, for example, what we (most of us) have done is adequately solved it.

An absolute solution implies that it could not be improved and that every other, different solution is inferior. Such judgements are just not meaningful with AI problems.

The best that we can realistically hope for is an adequate solution — and even that is neither easy to find nor easily recognizable. That is to say it can be difficult to decide whether one version of a program is more adequate than another version, and there is no sure way of knowing if a particular program is adequate or not.

The way to approach this adequacy evaluation is through inadequacies — we modify a program to remove inadequacies. When a program contains no glaring inadequacies then it is, in a very real sense, an adequate approximation. So it should be no surprise that AI programs do not tend to be models of structured programming; if you don't know where you are going with a pile of code, it's hardly surprising that you don't have a structured program when you get there.

The final obstacle that the AI program developer has to face is context dependencies: AI problem descriptions tend to be awkwardly context dependent.

When describing a natural language interface there will be numerous occasions when the adequate response to a particular query depends on the particular circumstances of the query itself including: the nature of the preceding dialogue, the skill of the particular system user, etc. — clearly a context-dependent situation. I shall return to the problem of context-sensitivity later.

Perhaps the most unlikely conclusion from the foregoing discussion is that AI is possible at all. As I've already said, maybe it isn't. But a lot of dedicated and talented people are bent on showing that it is both possible and practical in applications software.

I have made a fundamental claim that AI and traditional software engineering problems are different classes of problems. While it is true that progress with certain AI problems may well reduce them to traditional software engineering problems, and that restricted versions of AI problems may be successfully treated as traditional software engineering problems; a non-trivial set of AI problems will always remain.

I should like to make two points about this irreducible set:

(a) The problems that it contains are not amenable to computerization using the usual software engineering program development strategies.

(b) These residual problems are not just 'academic' problems that we can successfully ignore for all practical purposes. The modern equivalent of, 'how many angels will be able to sit comfortably on the head of a pin?', may well be in this set, but a lot of important practical problems are right there with it. Problems such as sophisticated natural-language communication, complex planning and decision making in the empirical world, etc. are in this set. Thus it contains many problems to which we are hoping to apply modern computer technology in an effort to enrich the quality of life (a disputable claim for computer technology and one that we shall return to in Chapter 7).

## 1.4 CONTEXT-SENSITIVITY AND AI PROBLEMS

I have so far classified AI problems as problems that are ill-structured in practice. A further dimension along which it is useful to partition our set of AI problems is with respect to the degree of context sensitivity that they exhibit. We can differentiate between AI problems (or components of AI problems) that are tightly-coupled, and those that are loosely-coupled, to their contexts.

Chess is a loosely-coupled problem: the next best move in a chess game is almost totally dependent on the current board configuration (although the best play does take psychological factors into account).

In expert systems, the diagnosis of a disease is almost totally dependent upon the patient's symptoms and test results. The analysis of a mass-spectrogram is also largely a context-free algorithm: it is not well-defined as to how best to do this analysis, but it is not dependent upon what samples were previously analysed, nor upon who the analysis is for. The foregoing are all AI problems that are only loosely-coupled to their context.

By way of contrast, high quality explanation of expert decisions is more highly context dependent. An explanation capability must be sensitive to who wants the explanation (a program maintenance engineer, a domain expert, or a novice user), and what they want it for; a sophisticated explanation component must be tightly-coupled to its context.

Natural-language systems, at a human level of natural language discourse, are even more saturated with tightly-coupled, context sensitivity. One can typically single out only extremely limited components of a natural language interface that are not, in reality, highly context dependent. An adequate response to a given query is typically dependent not only on who asked and why they asked, but also upon the semantics underlying the previous dialogue. In the words of Steiner (1975): "There are no closed circuits in natural language, no self-consistent axiomatic sets."

I can illustrate the difference between what I mean by loosely- and tightly-coupled context sensitivity by the use of an analogy from the plant world. The average plant is a system that is tightly-coupled to its context — roughly: earth, air, light,and water. If one digs up such a plant, in the continued absence of both earth and water, it typically dies, usually quite quickly. By way of contrast the average cactus is only loosely-coupled to its context. Mature cacti are almost context-free plants. Rip up a cactus and deprive it of earth and water for a few months. It will likely show no signs of the deprivation. It might even flower! These desert dwellers are not context-free organisms, but they are often capable of functioning for long periods independently of both earth and water; they exhibit a much more loosely-coupled context sensitivity than the average plant.

If one accepts this context-sensitivity viewpoint, then current practical AI software is just those AI problems (or components of AI problems) that are only loosely coupled to their contexts. The highly context-sensitive problems, like natural-language understanding, and components of AI problems, such as self-explaining in expert systems, are just the AI problems that are still firmly in the research domain — except for some very limited and rigidly constrained special cases.

Loosely and tightly-coupled context sensitivity seems to differentiate nicely between AI that is now potentially practical software, and AI that cannot yet be practical software. In addition, it ties in conveniently with the view that machine learning is a critical stumbling block. Complex context sensitivity must be tackled through mechanisms of self-modification — that is, machine learning. Machine learning or self-adaptivity is later developed as a key feature that must be tackled in order to exploit the full potential of AI as practical software.

It is not clear just how far we can go towards the production of intelligent software and yet avoid the most difficult aspects of AI problems (e.g. complex context sensitivity). The existence of useful expert systems and natural languages interfaces clearly argues that we can go some way down this particular road and be successful. The important, and as yet unanswered, question is: how far can we go? Is the end already in sight with knowledge bases that quickly become unmanageable and therefore cannot be further upgraded and extended? Or is the end a long way off and reachable through some simple and straightforward breakthroughs in machine learning? No one knows.

My viewpoint has already been stated. I should just like to add that even if the necessary progress is made in the above-described manner then the end result will be little different from the one that I am advocating. The big difference will be the efficiency with which the final result was achieved; a piecemeal approach that just attacks each current local limitation with little regard for the overall picture will be far less efficient than an approach that is globally directed by a comprehensive paradigm — even a paradigm that lacks fine detail and is somewhat incomplete. A rough general map is better than no map at all.

Let us now attempt to develop some structure for dealing with the class of AI problems.

## 1.5   A STRUCTURE FOR ILL-STRUCTURE: INCOMPLETELY SPECIFIED FUNCTIONS

AI problems are typically described in terms of behaviour: either the behaviour of a human when dealing with the problem, or the desired behaviour of the computer if the task is beyond the scope of human capability (such as, 3D VLSI design).

Thus for a natural language interface we describe a class of utterances that the program should generate in response to a certain class of input statements. For a proposed expert medical diagnosis system we can determine, from the expert diagnostician, the various input–output relationships associating sets of symptoms with certain diseases.

When there is no human expert in existence the problems are trickier in that we can only construct wish lists of input–output relationships and hope that it is possible to reproduce them mechanically. Thus in certain data-driven vision projects it is not at all certain that the features to be extracted from a class of input patterns are indeed extractable from those patterns in isolation. Humans can do this task but they also use a lot of extra information, context-free recognition is a mechanical possibility but not a human one.

Nevertheless the problem is not essentially different for our purposes. Such input–output descriptions of AI problems are, of course, functional descriptions. What is also probably obvious to the reader at this point is that the functional descriptions are never complete; AI problems can be characterized only in terms of incompletely specified functions (ISF).

'Never' might be too strong a word here. Consider for instance the problem of chess. A complete functional description might be: generate a win in every game. That seems like a complete enough description of the desired behaviour of our chess-playing program, at one level. But it is too high level to be of much practical use (rather like describing a natural-language interface as: generate an appropriate response for every input.) At a lower level we might describe the problem as: for each possible board configuration input, output the move that will be most beneficial with respect to the final outcome of the game.

Although the phrase "most beneficial" may be well-defined in principle, it cannot be exhaustively described in practice. We have to use heuristics that appear to produce the desired behaviour when subjected to an informal analysis. We have lost the ability to describe the program's complete behaviour once we attempt to refine our high-level and vague description down to a more specific and potentially implementable one. I shall return to this problem of levels of specification and implementations in Chapter 4 as it has an important bearing on the necessity for the run-debug-edit paradigm in AI.

So AI problems can be characterized in a functional manner, but the functional description is typically incomplete and context-sensitive. Given a certain class of inputs, human beings tend to produce a certain class of outputs, and the appropriateness of some outputs is dependent upon the context of the input. The classes of inputs and outputs, and the context dependencies can be complex, infinite, and only loosely circumscribable.

It is true that some software engineering problems do in reality have this same unhelpful structure when first encountered. Requirements analysis and the system designer's convictions as to what is feasible in practice soon chop the ill-structured problem down to a well-defined, manageable one. So what's the difference? Why can't AI do the same thing and adopt the tried-and-tested strategies of software engineering?

Some attempts at commercialization of AI do indeed do this, and then they become, for our purposes, conventional software engineering projects that use some AI-developed implementation techniques, such as production-rule knowledge bases.

The reason that AI cannot in general impose these rigid, a priori limitations on the problem and remain AI is that the purpose of utilizing AI in practical software is to upgrade the quality of performance of computers in just those applications in which conventional software cannot do a good enough job. The potential for 'smart' computers is dependent upon the successful application of ill-defined heuristics to large amounts of ill-defined knowledge under the constraint of complex and ill-defined context sensitivity. As soon as we start to define and limit these various quantities a priori the possibility of generating the desired quality of performance quickly evaporates.

The development of an adequate AI implementation is very much a process of exploration in an analytically-intractable space. During this exploration we learn about what sort of limitations can be exploited, and both when and how they can be exploited. As an example, consider the problem solving abilities of you and me — instances from the only known class of adequate approximations to intelligent problem solving. Let us suppose that I need to purchase a paintbrush. My solution to this problem will take into account: how I shall pay, what means of transport I shall use, where I shall go, what route I shall take, etc. I can probably neglect the weather (but not if I'm snowed in). I shall not consider the exact time of day (unless it is close to closing time, or the traffic rush hour). I shall not give much consideration as to what to wear (unless I am going on to a formal luncheon immediately afterwards). And so on, the point being that in order to reach some decision within a reasonable time I do have to neglect most potentially relevant sources of information, but at the same time I must be prepared to consider any of them as specific circumstances dictate. No rigid exclusion of any set of information sources is likely to yield intelligent decision making.

It is perhaps not too much of an overstatement to claim that intelligence is founded upon an ability to dynamically focus upon the most relevant information and to largely neglect the majority of potentially relevant information. Clearly this is a direct consequence of the tightly-coupled context sensitivity that is a typical feature of AI problems.

Limitations there must clearly be, but they are decided upon by what is found to be necessary to perform adequately and they must be dynamically modifiable, not rigidly fixed, in many cases. So the software engineering approach of rigid, a priori limitation of the problem will not work except for relatively well-understood (because of extensive AI research) and loosely context-coupled problems — technical expertise is currently the best example of such a class of problems.

Returning to AI problems that cannot be successfully treated as conventional software engineering problems, they are ISFs and they must be implemented as such. Ideally an implementation incrementally homes in on an adequate approximation. It also has to possess sufficient self-adaptive capabilities to retain its performance adequacy through both time and space.

We can usefully impose more structure on a problem description. We can divide the ISF into three components:

(i)  A set of well-defined, largely context-free, input-output relationships — the well-defined component.
(ii)  A set of context-dependent, input-output relationships — the context-sensitive component.
(iii)  A set of inappropriate or unforeseen possibilities — the unknown component.

As an example, consider the problem of constructing an intelligent natural-language interface for, say, banking transactions. The well-defined component of the ISF will contain relations such as:

input:  'When was the last withdrawal from my account?'
output:  give date of last withdrawal.

A whole host of such fairly well-defined and loosely context- sensitive input–output relationships can be identified — they will comprise the well-defined component of the ISF.

In addition there will be a set of more context-sensitive input–output relationships, such as:

input:  'Please explain my current balance?'
output:  An intelligent response must be based upon knowledge of the particular user and his account, the program's knowledge of its explanation capabilities *vis à vis* its knowledge of this user (e.g. can it offer a relatively standard response and work from there, or should it first try and refine the request by querying the user?), etc.

or even worse,

input:   'Tell me what I am doing wrong?'
output:  There is a host of possibilities dependent upon what the user was
         actually doing and what the system knows about what the user
         was doing and should be doing.

In order to describe this context-sensitive component of the ISF we need
to decide upon classes of alternative possibilities and potential strategies for
choosing among them.

Lastly there will be a component of the function that we know is non-
empty but we don't know much else about it. There will be many possible
inputs to this interface system that are so inappropriate (we believe) that an
intelligent, reasonable response is anybody's guess. For example:

input:   'Where is the best place to park my camel?'
output:  ?

We must also recognize that there are some input–output relationships,
which we have not foreseen, that ought to be in either the well-defined or the
context-sensitive component. So there is also a set of unforeseen relationships in this residual component of the function — I'll forgo the challenge of
providing you with an example of an input–output relationship that I have
not foreseen.

But as we shall see in Chapter 4 part of the process of incremental
development of AI programs consists of (or, can be viewed as) a steady
stream of elements popping out of this set of unforeseen relationships. And
it is important that we both recognize and prepare for this aspect of AI
program development.

So we have the possibility of characterizing AI problems in terms of a
three-component ISF. The point of this somewhat minimal structuring of
the ill-structured is that it provides some superstructure upon which we can
later build arguments about these elusive objects. In particular we will, in
Chapter 4, consider the incremental development of an AI program in terms
of developing the structure of an ISF. And finally, in Chapter 7, we shall find
that this structure is convenient for discussing the significance of context-
sensitivity and the role of machine learning in the development of the full
potential of AI.

## 1.6  CONVENTIONAL SOFTWARE ENGINEERING AND THE
FULL POTENTIAL OF AI

A basic theme of this book is that the full potential of AI cannot be realized
within the conventional paradigm for constructing practical software. So to
wind up this introduction I shall say a little about these two critical modifiers:
'conventional' applied to software engineering, and 'full potential' applied
to AI.

By conventional software engineering, I mean all of the varieties of the
general methodology described in the following chapter; conventional

software engineering is software engineering as it is widely understood today. I use the qualification 'conventional', particularly in the latter half of the book, in order to distinguish the accepted methodology from the augmented version that I suggest is necessary. Non-conventional software engineering is a paradigm that will yield practical software and yet allow exploitation of the full potential of AI. In the early part of the book especially, I drop the adjective 'conventional' whenever it seems to be clear that I am referring to the paradigm described in Chapter 2.

Loosely, the full potential of AI refers to the use of all of the potentially beneficial aspects of human intelligence (and perhaps improving on some of them) in the application of computers. More specifically, I shall argue that this full potential will be based upon sophisticated machine learning capabilities, which in turn will be based upon meta-knowledge — the computer must know what it knows and what it doesn't know, and be able to do something about it.

By way of contrast the current infiltration of software engineering by AI only represents a limited selection from the full range of what AI has potentially to offer. Roughly, we have implementations of loosely context-sensitive, analytically intractable, static, open problems. AI has so far introduced into practical software the notion of computer applications in areas that do not enjoy the luxury of correct and incorrect answers — as, for example, medical diagnosis.

As stated above these limited applications of AI have infiltrated practical software; that is to say, these AI features have been introduced into practical software without any major disruption of the conventional methodology. Such will not be the case when we attempt to move the full potential of AI into practical applications software. Indeed a number of informed observers have argued that the current limited applications of AI are already close to their limit within the current paradigm (e.g. Boden, 1984).

Having dug some foundations let's review the software engineering program development methodology; once we have that tied down we will be ready to delve into the mysteries of AI in contrast to those of software engineering.

# 2

# The general methodology of software engineering

If it can be completely specified it can be programmed;
if it can't be completely specified then you shouldn't
be attempting an implementation.

Apart from a somewhat superficial run through the general methodology of program development in software engineering, in this chapter I attempt to contrast the idealized scheme with the pragmatics of conventional software development. We shall see that the desired paradigm is somewhat illusory to the practising software designer. The ideal scenario for software design contrasts sharply with that of AI program development while the activities of the practising software engineer and of the AI program developer appear sufficiently similar to suggest that a future merger would not require much change on either side — practical software development and AI program development look like much the same thing.

If this were true then once again this book would appear to be finished shortly after the opening credits. To the astute reader, conscious of six more chapters just waiting to be read, there must be either a solution to this awkward similarity problem or else a very long conclusion and postscript.

I shall argue that this similarity is both superficial and incomplete in a number of critical respects. In general, we shall see examples of the principle that large quantitative differences do in effect produce differences in kind. Quantitative differences in problem characteristics such as degree of ill-structure, and degree to which a first problem specification is viewed as an approximation of a satisfactory implementation are examples of dimensions along which we shall see the dissimilarity emerge.

Practical software design is both an art and a science, although many talented researchers are trying to ensure that science gets the lion's share of the action. Gries' book entitled, *The Science of Programming* (Gries, 1981) is, as the author says, less a statement of the current situation and more a belief in what the future holds. A more rigorous program development paradigm, something like, formally Specify the problem, Prove completeness and consistency of the specification, Implement the specification, and finally Verify correctness (the SPIV paradigm after employing the acronymic reduction so beloved by the AI world), would accentuate the contrast with AI program development. But such is not the case, so I have more work to do to support my arguments.

Nevertheless, the very fact that smart and informed people disseminate a belief that the rigorous software development paradigm will one day extend to large-scale projects does indirectly support my argument of essential difference. For even in principle it is difficult to entertain a similar belief in the mechanization of intelligence. So, bearing all that in mind, let's have a look at the in-practice paradigm for software development. With respect to the subsequent contrast with AI, it is the worst case example.

Software engineering is the construction of computer programs to perform complete and rigorously-specified functions. The programs produced are intended for practical use. This entails that the programs are robust, reliable, and maintainable, and these requirements in turn entail that the products of software engineering are comprehensible.

There is a more or less general agreement that the complexity of the software engineering task is best tackled by a strict separation of the process into a sequence of distinct stages. Four such stages are: requirements, specification, design, and implementation — and this is the decomposition scheme that I shall use (although not quite in that order). In addition, it is highly desirable that validation of each of these stages is to some extent demonstrated; we need the above-listed desiderata of programs at every stage. Transparency to humans is thus of utmost importance throughout the software development process. Ease of generating informal demonstrations of completeness and consistency depends critically upon the transparency of the representations developed.

## 2.1   RIGOROUS SPECIFICATIONS

The starting point of a software engineering project is a process that we wish the computer to perform. But the most important part of a software engineering project is a rigorous specification of this process. The initial process description is typically an informal statement in English; it is thus likely to be vague, incomplete and ambiguous. It is clearly not desirable to implement a specification that contains these weaknesses; for different interpretations will lead to different implementations and hence programs that function differently. Programs are cluttered with problem-irrelevant, programming language idiosyncracies and tend to be largely incomprehensible objects considered as a whole. Deciding how and why a given program does not meet certain implications of a vague process specification is a course of action that we wish to avoid.

A key step in any software engineering project is then to settle upon a complete, rigorous specification of the process to be implemented. This is perhaps the most difficult, time-consuming and important step of all. It involves substantial interaction with the person, or persons, whose process is to be implemented. It often amounts to clarifying and completing the process statement adding necessary information — often information that the problem instigator had never realized was missing. It can also involve eliminating hitherto unperceived contradictions, and generating an explicit statement of the scope and limitations of the problem. In fact, at the less structured end of the software development spectrum we can usefully separate out a pre-specification stage, and this we will look at in the next section.

The basis of a software engineering project is thus a rigorous, and to some extent, demonstrably complete and correct, explicitly bounded problem. It is true that the extent to which the desiderata of this basis specification are formally proven tends to decrease from small, formally well-defined problems, such as the Euclidean algorithm (Dijkstra, 1976) to the rather more empirically-defined, larger-scale problems such as that of the operating system 0S360 (Brooks, 1975).

Giddings (1984) distinguishes three classes of conventional software: one domain independent class (DI software), and two domain dependent classes (both DD software) — experimental (DDEX software) and embedded (DDEM software). He blames much of the software crisis on the fact that development strategies focus on DI software, whereas such software is in fact quite rare.

He states the "DD software development is an empirical, ongoing proccss," and suggests that it is best tackled with the help of a problem-solving environment. This is a programming environment that contains subsystems to assist the human programmer in the programming task. For example, there might be a subsystem that automatically maintains and checks a cross-referenced index of all program identifiers. I also believe in the merits of such environments to assist in the task of DD software development (for most AI is DD), but our views as to what to aim for and how best to do it differ drastically — I shall return to this topic in Chapter 7.

Rigorous specifications tend to be functional; they specify what the system should do rather than how it should do it. It is here that we find our first important point of contrast with AI problems. The rigorous functional specification (RFS) of a software engineering problem may well be derived from an ISF, but once it is generated the original ISF can be largely forgotten. The software engineering program development paradigm does not pretend to try to implement an underlying ISF; it aims solely at a correct and complete implementation of the RFS.

Recourse to the underlying ISF only occurs if it is discovered, during the course of program design or implementation, that the basis RFS is incomplete, inconsistent, or inadequate. In other words, if the RFS cannot be implemented appropriately and satisfactorily then it may be modified, but such modifications are firm changes that provide a complete and well-defined set of constraints for the subsequent implementation.

Thus, although the process of software design and implementation, especially in its least formal manifestations, may involve repeated consideration of the underlying ISF, such backtracking is solely for the purpose of 'fixing-up' the RFS; and the RFS, in isolation, remains the sole target for implementation.

The RFS is the key object in software engineering; so where does it come from?

## 2.2   REQUIREMENTS

Sad to say the user who requires some computerized assistance does not usually (ever?) have a nice RFS to hand over to the software engineers. Even conventional computer users see their needs in terms of an ISF rather than an RFS.

An RFS is generated from the user's requirements by the organization that will implement the system, and these requirements stem from intangible user needs — an ISF. In a special issue on requirements of the IEEE Transactions on Software Engineering, the guest editor, Ross (1977), discusses the fundamental and ill-understood problem of requirements; it is, as he says, the "system-problem aspects that occur at the beginning, before a system is even specified, much less designed or built".

Ross also says that efforts aimed at solving the problems of software engineering have for too long been misplaced toward the system end of the scale. The real solution lies toward the human end of the scale. He is saying that requirements is a neglected area and if we could improve our abilities to generate firm requirements from the user's ISF then the subsequent stages of software development would not be so plagued with the necessity for backtracking and retro-fitting.

Ross & Schoman (1977) argue that requirements definition only provides complete boundary conditions for the subsequent design and implementation stages. "A problem well-stated is well on its way to a sound solution." They contrast this statement with "the obvious assertion that 'a problem unstated is a problem unsolved.' "

These slogans are sound advice for the software engineer but they do not apply so readily to AI. As we shall see, it's only after an AI problem has been adequately 'solved' that we are in any position to abstract a detailed statement of it. An analogous situation is that of a mathematician who insists on defining his terms before he starts and the AI programmer who will never get started if he attempts to do such a thing.

Minsky (1982), in the context of a discussion on the potential scope of AI, raises the point that formal definitions offer little promise for capturing the meanings of everyday common sense. A single rigid definition is fine for formalizing mathematics, he says, but it ignores a basic fact of real life: "what something means to me depends to some extent on everything else I know — and no one else knows just those things in just those ways." This is yet another instance of context-sensitivity compounding the problem of AI.

Minsky continues with the claim that the implications of ambiguity, inconsistency, and circularity (every meaning in a mind depends on all other meanings) certainly complicate our task but that they can be dealt with and we should not be terrified of them. The alternative, which attempts to reduce the study of minds (and by implication AI) to simple chains of definitions rather than messy webs of partial meanings, is an oversimplication that impoverishes the phenomenon under study — an impoverishment that is resistent to subsequent reversal and is thus not a useful route to a first approximation to an intelligent system.

The AI programmer must obviously have some loose problem statement and requirements but the point of the program development methodology of AI is to discover an adequate approximation which can then be well-stated. In fact there does seem to be more than a superficial similarity between the development of requirements in software engineering and the complete program development process in AI. Both start out with a ISF and both end up with a well-defined derivative by means of an iterative process involving the user environment. A major dissimilarity is that the software engineer also wants to be able to demonstrate that the requirements are both complete and consistent. It is not obvious that completeness and consistency will always have a clear meaning in AI.

This emphasis on the assessability of requirements is a natural result of applying the principle that the sooner you detect a problem the less trouble it is to correct — 'a stitch in time saves nine' is the domestic version. Boehm (1984) suggested that 100 is a more precise number as a factor for the cost savings when an error is removed at the requirements analysis stage rather than when the system is in operation. Ideally, the software engineer would like to be able to state the problem and justify the solution just once — right at the beginning — in the requirements definition.

This initial formalization of the requirements for the informally specified process or problem is really a refinement and development of the problem itself. The development of a formalized specification from an informal one —.real needs in a human social environment — is a non-trivial operation. It is also a critical operation since the formal specification is the keystone of a software engineering project. Any questions as to the appropriateness and accuracy of an implementation are settled *vis à vis* the RFS. Modifications of the process implemented are made in the formalized specification and then it is reimplemented.

The key role of formalized specification has given rise to the development of languages especially for both the formal statement of requirements and the subsequent RFS. These Problem Specification Languages (PSLs) are designed to be capable of formally specifying complex processes in a clear manner.

Some examples are: Structured Analysis (SA), a language for communicating ideas. SA contains 40 features that facilitate rigorous communication of requirements. In an effort to deal with their very large software engineering projects, TRW have developed a Software Requirements Engineering Methodology (SREM). They claim that one of the benefits is the clear distinction between requirements for processing, and design of processing, and that much of the activity in software development called 'functional design' is really a detailed definition of requirements. Both of these approaches and several others are discussed in the above-referenced IEEE special issue on requirements.

A number of formal languages were devised before the advent of computers (e.g. predicate calculus) and some of these notations are used to express requirements (and specifications) formally. The design and development of PSLs reflects the specialised set of criteria that requirements engineering or analysis brings to the fore.

The existence of a formal language within which to cast the requirements offers some necessary guidance for requirements analysis provided that the notation is not too restrictive; it must also be sufficient as a medium for expressing requirements conveniently and clearly. An appropriate notation is a valuable aid. Requirements analysis then becomes an iterative discussion constrained by reference to a formal schema. Again we shall see an analogy with the detection of inadequacies in the complete AI program development methodology.

In particular, the formal specification, based on a requirements analysis, should relate as closely as possible to both the original informal specification and the programming language implementation. The simplicity of these relationships will then simplify and so assist the necessary transformation between these three objects. These transformations are important and complex; any reduction in complexity is an important asset.

I shall not delve into the intricacies of a formal notation for requirements specification. These notations are neither generally applicable nor readily understandable without some prior study of the notation. Instead I shall provide a loose and superficial example, but one that will convey the flavour of requirements analysis. This will also lead us into a simple formal specification, and provide a basis for subsequent enhancements.

Consider the following functional specification of a primitive task for a hand–eye robot:

Locate, pick-up, and place a ball in a designated receptacle.

This specification falls far short of an RFS incorporating the boundary conditions generated by requirements analysis. Requirements should answer questions such as: 'Will the initial setup always contain exactly one ball?'; 'Can the hand reach to every possible ball location?'; 'Can the environment contain any obstacles?' etc.

All of these questions need to be put to the user and the answers must be checked for completeness and consistency. If there is a requirement that there may be more than one ball in the environment then some further requirement must also be specified, for example, 'should they all be picked up, or just one?'. 'If just one, does it matter which one?', etc.

The requirements that the nearest ball is picked up first, and that exactly one ball will always be present, are inconsistent. Not disastrously so, but such a state of affairs does seem to indicate some confusion and thus the user should be probed again on these points.

Fig. 2.1 illustrates two versions of an RFS for the hand–eye robot's pick-

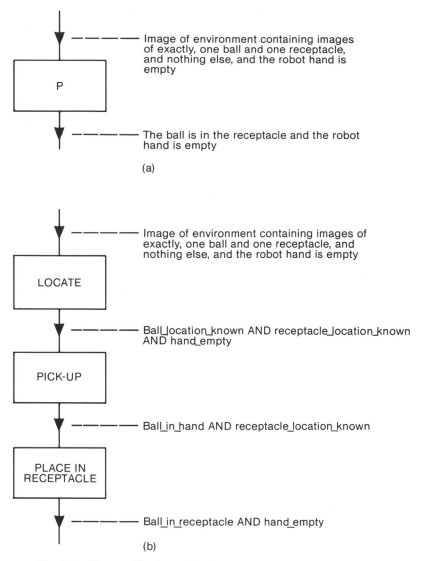

Fig. 2.1 — Two specifications of the hand–eye robot's pick-up-and-place task

up-and-place task. Fig. 2.1(a) specifies the function P such that for all input images consistent with the stated precondition the stated post condition will be satisfied: that is, if the robot's camera inputs an image with exactly one ball and one receptacle in it, the robot will perform the necessary actions to result in the ball being in the receptacle.

Fig. 2.1(b) specifies this task in more detail: it specifies that the robot will first locate the ball and the receptacle; it will next pick up the ball; and finally it will place the ball in the receptacle.

There are several additional points to notice about this example. First,

Fig. 2.1(b) is a more precise specification than that of Fig. 2.1(a), but Fig. 2.1(b) is also specifying the implementation to some extent. It specified that program P will be implemented as three consecutive subtasks: "locate", "pick-up", and "place in receptacle". As opposed to some alternative implementation of P. The robot's hand could, for example, grasp around randomly until it picked up the ball, it might then locate the receptacle and place the ball in it. This specification-implementation ambiguity is developed in Chapter 4 as part of the justification for the AI program development methodology.

Second, suppose the ball is initially in the receptacle? The precondition is still true and the post-condition will be satisfied in Fig. 2.1(b). But the robot will have picked the ball out of the receptacle and then put it back again. So the specification is correct with respect to this possibility, and it's neither inconsistent nor incomplete, but it is perhaps less than satisfactory — it's inefficient. Why? It all depends on the requirements, they are incomplete.

At the start of the task, can the ball be in the receptacle? That is what we need to know. If so, we can include a check to avoid the inefficiency; if not, we can add another clause to the precondition and no such check is then necessary.

An accurate and efficient design and implementation hinges on the specification which in turn relies on the requirements analysis.


## 2.3   DESIGN

With requirements analysis behind us and a rigorous specification in hand (not necessarily an RFS but the exact style of specification is not important), we are at the door of the design and subsequent stages; the rigorous specification is the touchstone that we use to assess the correctness of all subsequent development — in AI we do not have this luxury.

The rigorous specification defines exactly what is to be done; the task of the designer is to specify precisely how it can be done in a machine-independent and readily comprehensible manner. An opaque design is always a disaster; the sagacity of the implementation-independence quality of a design is a much more open question.

In this latter case the general rule is to aim for implementation-independent designs, especially in the early stages of high-level design. But particular circumstances, such as specialised hardware or extremely demanding time constraints (e.g. in the Ballistic Missile Defense system developed by TRW, there were very stringent timing constraints that the software had to meet or else it was useless), will mean that implementation considerations must infiltrate the design, perhaps to the highest levels. Software design methods run the gamut from well- to ill-defined. Precise methods may be available for well-understood, relatively simple, problems (such as designing a parser), but large-scale software design has to rely on heuristics and is thus at the ill-defined end of the scale.

The software designer selects and combines mechanisms that satisfy the specification. The choice of mechanisms to use is guided by a set of constraints. The most important constraint is the requirement that the design be readily comprehensible (apart from the constraint that it should be 'correct'; a problem I shall return to).

Comprehensibility is based upon perceptual clarity (the extent to which the organisation of the underlying algorithm is apparent in the chosen representation), so the perceptual clarity of a design is of paramount importance for two reasons: first, the recurring necessity for, at least, informal validation of the design; and second, as a prerequisite to modification of the design as dictated by subsequent events — errors, changed requirements, etc.

What makes a design transparent to humans? Obviously there is no simple and correct answer. The process of program design is a craft: an art just as much as a science. Technical expertise is required to master and make the best use of available algorithms and the formal notations used to represent them. But the process of design is also very much an art, whether the final product is a house, a home appliance, or a program.

Nevertheless, guidelines are available although they must be applied and combined with skill to produce the best results. Let's first look at a fundamental design strategy for cutting complexity down to manageable portions.

### 2.3.1 A modular hierarchy
In a paper entitled, "The Architecture of Complexity", Simon (1962) argues that the human ability to comprehend complex objects depends upon those objects possessing the property of "near decomposability". This property gives us a modular hierarchy as the structure of the complex object.

He further argues that the process of evolution will be liable to yield nearly-decomposable complex objects. This suggestion is particularly relevant with respect to efforts to implement intelligent activities. For intelligence is widely believed to be the product of evolution and hence it is reassuring to know that it is perhaps likely to be decomposable into a modular hierarchy. But although we thus have some reason to hope that intelligence is a modular phenomenon, we still have to find the modules. The modules generated by the process of evolution by no means have to correspond to any partitioning that has proved to be useful in modern science. I shall return to this important question in the following chapter.

From the architecture of complexity we can move to the complexity of architecture and the seminal work of Alexander (1964). He described a scheme for mastering the complexity of architectural design by building a modular hierarchy from the bottom up. That is, he suggested that we build a hierarchy to support the design process as a result of successive grouping and classification of an originally amorphous collection of "detailed requirements or misfit variables." So, for example, in the design of a simple kettle he lists 21 misfit variables such as: it must pour cleanly, it must not corrode in steamy kitchens, etc. He then groups these 21 variables into five categories, and then groups these five categories into just two: function and economics. Thus he ends up with a four-level hierarchy, which, as he says, enables the designer to grasp the problem all at once. I shall return to Alexander's work in Chapter 4 with respect to the evaluation of successive approximations in AI system development. For now we can just note that the amorphous collection of misfit variables that the designer works with is another example of a performance-mode 'definition' of an ISF.

Modularity is perhaps the single most important contributive factor to the perceptual clarity of a complex object. A modular structure is one that is composed of maximally independent substructures called modules. A further and closely related rule for attaining clarity is that the inter-module dependencies be explicitly specified, preferably within the modules themselves.

It is not usually possible to reduce a complex specification immediately into a large set of minimally interacting simple modules. It is more likely to reduce to a few minimally interacting less complex modules, but then these modules can often be modularized as well and so on until we do end up with a large set of simple modules. By decomposing complex modules into inter-acting sets of simpler modules we end up with a hierarchical structure: the final design is a hierarchy of minimally but explicity interacting modules. Fig. 2.2 is a schematic illustration of a three-level design. The rigorous

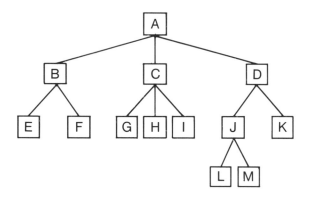

Fig. 2.2 — A modular hierarchy

specification of what the program should do is node A. This specification is decomposed and refined into three minimally-dependent subproblems: B, C, and D. Each of these subproblems is specified in terms of what must be done but at a finer level of detail than at node A.

In Fig. 2.3 we begin to develop a design for the robot pick-up-and-place task introduced earlier. The specification of the task in the root node of the diagram now contains some of the more obvious boundary conditions that might be generated from a requirements analysis. Successive levels in the design both break up the task and provide more detail as to what must be done.

The clarity of such a structure results from the fact that the design can be

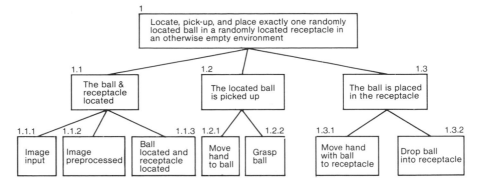

Fig. 2.3 — A few design steps for the robot's pick-up-and-place task

viewed and comprehended in a top-down manner. That is to say, an enquiry into some particular feature can be initiated by first consulting the relatively few, somewhat abstract, high-level modules to gain overall understanding of the program's structure (modules B, C and D of Fig. 2.2).

A knowledge of the general structure of the program is then used to guide the enquiry down through the hierarchical levels to the particular segment of code that is of interest (for example, from D through J to modules L and M in Fig. 2.2). Alternatively, comprehension of the function of a particular segment of code is aided by reference up through the modules that enclose it. A move upwards through the hierarchy clarifies the overall function within larger program modules (thus in Fig. 2.2, the details of module M may be more comprehensible when viewed as a subtask of J).

Rajlich (1985) claims that there are two basic orthogonal hierarchies for computer programs: the seniority hierarchy in which the organization is in layers; and the parent–child hierarchy wherein larger packages are decomposed into smaller subpackages. My examples in Figs. 2.2 and 2.3 are primarily illustrative of a seniority hierarchy (each level is in itself a complete description of the problem) which provides the intuitive basis for both top-down and bottom-up design strategies. A parent–child hierarchy, being orthogonal, can also be present in the resultant program if the design is implemented using say, a strategy of decomposition in which submodules are dependent upon only one higher-level module — their parent.

### 2.3.2 Design documentation

The bottom-level structures, the most detailed subproblem specifications that comprise the complete design are given by the sequence of modules E, F, G, H, I, L, M and K of Fig. 2.2. One might then ask, why keep the higher level modules? The answer is that they are the basis of the design documentation; they are also a natural product of a top-down design procedure which is explained below. For the moment the important point is that the higher level modules are a crucial aid to comprehending a program. The implication from this is that for maximum clarity a design should be accompanied by its documentation. The high-level modular decomposition is just one important facet of the subsidiary information that is fundamentally part of every piece of practical software — the basis of the design documentation. Clearly a program will run on a computer without its documentation thus it is not strictly part of the program. But in practice a program without documentation can quickly become effectively useless.

As mentioned earlier, program code and support documentation have an unfortunate tendency to become separated in space or time (that is, the code is modified but the documentation is not, so it documents some earlier version of the program). This problem suggests that a practical aid to program comprehension is to include documentation within the program listing. This is in general a good idea and is typically done by means of comment statements and indentation of the code, but the time-gap problem will still exist. Fig. 2.4 illustrates a typical code and documentation layout.

```
program A is performed
        process B is performed
                code for E;
                code for F;
        process C is performed
                code for G;
                code for H;
                code for I;
        process D is performed
                process J is performed
                        code for L;
                        code for M;
                code for K;
```

Fig. 2.4 a program containing the hierarchical design of Fig. 2.2

Brooks' (1975) extensive experience with large-scale software development leads him to the firm conclusion that design documentation should definitely be kept within the program, not as a separate document. This strategy, he states, will clearly minimize the chances of the eventual program and its design documentation being separated.

And as with most guidelines inappropriate usage may detract from overall clarity because of the resulting clutter. A careful path must be trodden between adding useful documentation to the program and cluttering it with inessentials.

### 2.3.3   Top-down design
I shall consider in more detail the top-down design method; it is perhaps the most popular method but it is by no means the only one. Freeman (1977) lists four further design methods: outside-in, inside-out, bottom-up, and most-

critical-component-first. He also states that a design method specifies three things:

(1) what decisions are to be made,
(2) how to make them, and
(3) in what order they should be made.

Within this framework we can examine top-down design. In top-down design we make those decisions that affect the greatest possible amount of the total design. We make decisions at the highest level first and then at successively lower levels. The order of decisions within levels is not specified in top-down design. Freeman states the general caveat of top-down design as: make decisions that take into account as many as possible of the relevant design goals and constraints and that restrict the set of alternatives for lower-level decisions as little as possible.

The design of an implementation is thus accomplished by a technique of successive divide-and-conquer. A complex problem is reduced to a small number maximally independent subproblems. The virtual independence of each subproblem then allows us to focus attention on one such module and, forgetting the rest, reduce it to a small number of maximally independent sub-subproblems and so on. The process of stepwise decomposition continues until the sub-problems obtained are sufficiently simple so as to be immediately codeable with little effort. Fig. 2.5 is a schematic illustration of the top-down design process that resulted in the modular hierarchy of Fig. 2.2.

Note that this technique naturally produces hierarchically-structured modular programs. The top-down design technique attempts to deal with the more general aspects of the problem first and gradually focuses down onto the details as we divide out smaller and smaller subproblems.

An implementation consists of an algorithm and some data structures. The design of complex data structures usually parallels that of the algorithm and uses the same techniques. A number of fully worked examples of algorithm and data structure design are given in Wirth (1973) and Coleman (1979).

In addition to separating and validating each individual stage in the overall process of software development it is also advantageous to institute checks at various points within an extended stage such as design. Top-down design is particularly amenable to such incremental development by means of level-by- level testing and integration of the design. Top-down coding and testing are then techniques used to guide and control the sometimes lengthy design stage from the first high-level design through the intermediate levels to the final detailed design.

Yourdon (1975) makes the general point about the feasibility of top-down design being critically reliant upon the prior existence of a rigorous specification; he says, "It is extremely difficult to develop an organized top-down design from incoherent, incomplete, disorganized specifications." Thus the top-down design method will not be readily applicable to AI problems. AI, lacking the luxury of rigorous specifications, must face the

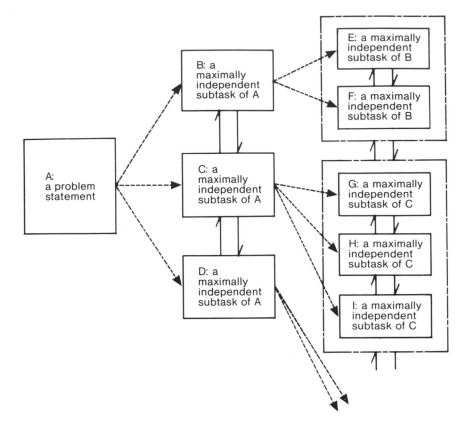

Fig. 2.5 — Two steps in a stepwise decomposition process

problem of design with respect to meagre, formal specifications; there is often no opportunity to establish the logical structure of the solution before decisions are made on detailed elements of the solution.

The major snags that tend to detract from the simplicity and success of the top-down stepwise refinement or decomposition technique stem from two sources: the interaction between modules, and constraints of the implementation environment.

A problem never decomposes into totally independent modules because then it would not really be one problem but several problems. Typically one module generates information that another module uses. This raises problems of both timing and compatibility. The information must be produced before it is used, and it must be structured in a manner acceptable to the receiving module. Each of these requirements seems to be obvious and hardly a formidable problem. But when multiplied manyfold in the context of a large number of interacting modules they constitute a serious problem. Their nuisance value is magnified by the very success of the stepwise decomposition technique: the power of divide-and-conquer design resides in the focusing of attention on small facets of the overall problem and disregarding the rest — this works very well, except where the module interaction occurs.

Timing constraints can be dealt with straightforwardly when implementing a simple sequential process. Although special techniques such as data flow analysis have been developed both to aid the design of processes that are not simple sequential, and to increase the efficiency of the implementations of sequential processes.

### 2.3.4   The interface problem

Module interaction in general is known as the interface problem. In a large software engineering project different people design and implement different modules. The independence of modules makes this possible. Our module designer is free to design and implement the internal structure of his module without regard to the other modules being designed. His only global concern is whether his module will receive and send information in a form that is correct for the modules that send to it and receive from it, respectively — we can call this the external view or interface of the module. Interface requirements imposed by the global context of the module within the overall design can in turn place constraints upon a module's internal structure. Thus a designer is free to design his module's internal structure only so far as is consistent with the interface requirements. Interface design is to some extent a prerequisite of module design.

The necessity to establish and continually check the compatibility of the interfaces between modules at all levels of design imposes a substantial communication burden within a software engineering group. In fact the time spent 'communicating' about the design (discussing possibilities and documenting decisions) far outweighs the time spent actually designing (estimates of a 9:1 ratio, communicating and designing respectively, are not uncommon).

The communication problem arises because a typical software engineering task is too large for a single person to cope with. Any design decisions that have inter-module repercussions must be transmitted to and discussed with all the (relevant) team members. It is only the strictly intra-module designing that can be done in isolation — even then the goal of overall consistency dictates that the same general design techniques are followed by each member of the team.

The Chief Programmer Team concept was introduced by IBM as a new approach to this problem. A super programmer does all of the design and implementation with the aid of a support team that documents and generally takes care of all of the peripheral support tasks. The analogy drawn is that of a surgeon who does all of the critical cutting and his support team who prepare the task, ensure that the necessary tools are on hand when required, and tidy up afterwards. The idea seems to work but you do need a super programmer. But having only one person worry about module interaction does not make the problem go away — it just localizes it.

An interface constraint on the modules specified in the design of Fig. 2.3 is that module 1.1.3 must generate the information that specifies the location of the ball in a form that is acceptable to module 1.2.1 At this high level of design we can decide that the ball's location will be specified by, say, a triple, (X,Y,Z), the cartesian coordinates of the centre of the ball. As the design becomes more refined we will also have to refine this interface specification to a more concrete representation until finally it becomes a language-specific data structure within the coded implementation — a LISP list, or a three field record in Pascal, for example.

### 2.3.5   Implementation environment constraints

The second and lesser drawback to the efficiency of top-down stepwise decomposition is due to the constraints imposed by the implementation environment. As a design is refined towards implementation-level detail the designer must take into account the idiosyncrasies of the target programming language (and perhaps also hardware). It is clearly desirable that the detailed design and the implementation environment (language plus supporting hardware and software) mesh smoothly together. Even at the highest levels of design it is wise to bear potential implementation environments in mind.

The last thing that we want after a long and exhaustive process of design is to find that it is fundamentally incompatible with the implementation environment. Shaving the corners off of square pegs in order to jam them into round holes is a procedure that we wish to avoid; and with some foresight it can be successfully avoided.

Having said that I should balance this view by stating that it is also highly desirable that an algorithm be designed independent of any implementation. Designing an algorithm is the difficult process, coding it into a particular programming language is relatively easy. Thus the difficult task should be accomplished once only in an implementation-independent manner; it can then serve as the basic algorithm for any number of codings into different particular languages. Once again we have a trade-off to manage: the clarity and efficiency of an algorithm tailored to a particular implementation environment versus the longer-term efficiency of designing one general algorithm that will be easily applicable (but probably less clearly and efficiently) to a range of implementations.

If we again return to the primitive robotics task of Fig. 2.3, examples of implementation environment constraints are easy to find. Module 1.1.2 of the design describes the subtask of preprocessing the input image to eliminate noise. At this high level of specification potential implementation environments have little impact. But once we refine module 1.1.2 and have to specify the noise-elimination algorithms and the general class of data structure for the input image (e.g. an array or a list) then we shall necessarily be favouring one implementation environment over another.

Such biasing of the design is largely unavoidable as we attempt to refine a design with successively more detail. We have to live with it and usually we can, but in this particular application (image processing) unfortunate design decisions can easily lead to disastrous implementations.

Image processing is a class of problems that are notorious for their ability to consume prodigious amounts of computational resources. Specialized hardware and software (typically offering parallel processing capabilities) are often necessary in order to process images within a reasonable time.

Thus further refinement of the robot's image processing tasks should most likely be constrained by the image processing capabilities available within specific target implementations; this will ensure computational efficiency in a critical subtask.

## 2.4  IMPLEMENTATION

With a detailed design that is complete and consistent (both within itself and with the problem specification) we are ready to transform it into a machine-executable form — a program. The detailed design must be implemented in a particular hardware-software environment. This is the stage of programming or coding and it is perhaps the most straightforward stage of all which is not to say that it is devoid of challenge and free of man-traps by any means.

The implementor selects and combines mechanisms that satisfy the detailed design. The choice of mechanisms to use is guided by a set of constraints: the most important of which is the requirement that the resulting program is readily comprehensible; a second constraint is the target programming language and the structures that it offers; and lastly, there are the timing and space constraints inherent in specific environments.

The perceptual clarity of a program is of paramount importance for two reasons: a large and complex program is never totally correct (a sad practical fact) and thus errors must be tracked down and removed; secondly, there is a continuing need to modify programs to meet changing requirements. These two tasks are the main components of software maintenance. Often programs are maintained in an environment that is far removed in both time and space from that in which they were designed and implemented. In the worst, but far from uncommon, case the program code itself is the only basis to work from: the supporting design documents have been lost or are no longer reliably descriptive of the much-modified program.

We shall return to the question of software maintenance later. For now the cursory introduction of this topic has served to underline the importance of perspicuousness as the most important characteristic of a well-designed program.

What makes the structure of a program comprehensible? As with design there is no simple and correct answer. A battery of rules that tend to clarify program structure are available. Structured programming is a common name for this farrago. But again these rules are just guidelines, and to produce the best results they must be applied with a proficiency founded on technical knowledge.

Absolute prohibition on the use of GOTO statements is an example of a useful guideline being distorted to provide an axiom. As such it does not always yield the desired result: on occasions the judicious use of a GOTO statement is the simplest and clearest implementation of certain constructs — as, for example, immediate exit of an environment when a certain error occurs.

Apart from expertise in utilizing the various options of the implementation language the programmer should also exploit graphical devices to add transparency to the code. Programming languages are one-dimensional notations. Algorithms are more easily visualized as two-dimensional objects (non-sequential algorithms might be better visualized in terms of higher-dimensionality representations).

The competent programmer can then exploit the two-dimensional nature of a page of code to let the underlying algorithm shine through. Clustering and indentation of the code are relatively common and straight-forward techniques for simulating a two-dimensional object with a one-dimensional notation. Fig. 2.4 is a two-dimensional layout that reflects the tree structure illustrated in Fig. 2.2. A general guideline for perspicuous programs is that the static structure of the code should reflect the dynamic structure of the algorithm that it specifies.

The underlying algorithm is, of course, the final product of the design stage. Thus we are integrating the machine-executable code and the precursory design. We should go somewhat further down this road. Bearing in mind Brooks' injunction about keeping documentation within the program, we should also integrate into our structure at least the bones of the higher levels of design, as illustrated in Fig. 2.4.

As we start to mix more and more of the higher levels into the code there is grave danger of falling foul of yet another guideline: don't clutter the program with redundant documentation. Fig. 2.6 is a program whose internal documentation is directly derived from the design of Fig. 2.3; it is over documented. It has been commented to excess. It would be a clearer and hence a better program if a fair proportion of the comments were omitted.

So once again our implementor is called upon to exercise his power of creative judgement. He must select and integrate just the right amount of just the right features of the design to illuminate and thereby facilitate understanding of the code.

Of course other supporting documentation may be kept alongside the program to be examined or ignored by program users. In the last two chapters we extend the computer's role from that of a passive repository for documentation to that of an active disseminator of selected aspects of this documentation.

As already mentioned Fig. 2.4 illustrates a program that displays the hierarchical design of Fig. 2.2. A simple list of the code statements would execute just as well on the computer (maybe more efficiently as it will not have to delete all of the spaces and comments). But as we all know, inducing

```
*a program to locate, pick-up, and place exactly one randomly located
ball in a randomly located receptacle in an otherwise empty
environment*
    **the ball and receptacle are located**
        ***image input***
        GET (IMAGE);
        ***Image preprocessed***
        CLEANUP (IMAGE);
        ***ball located and receptacle located***
            ****ball located****
            LOCATE (BALL, XBALL, YBALL);
            ****receptacle located****
            LOCATE (RECEPTACLE, XRECEP, YRECEP);
    **the located ball is picked up**
        ***move hand to ball***
        MOVE-HAND-TO (XBALL, YBALL);
        ***grasp ball***
        PICK-UP;
    **the ball is placed in the receptacle**
        ***move hand with ball to receptacle**
        MOVE-HAND-TO (XRECEP, YRECEP);
        ***drop ball into receptacle
        OPEN-HAND;
```

Fig. 2.6 — An over-commented program

the computer to accept ones coded offering is usually a lengthly process that
hinges critically upon human comprehension of the program.

Mention of the difficulties inherent in persuading the computer to
acknowledge the correctness of ones code brings us to the procedure
euphemistically styled, debugging.

### 2.4.1  Debugging

Throughout the foregoing sections I have assumed that the program
designed will be a correct implementation of the specification. Thus
although perceptual clarity was promoted as the most important program
characteristic, correctness was assumed. For clearly it is neither very
interesting, nor very useful, nor very challenging, to design incorrect
programs.

A surprising number of texts (e.g. Gries, 1981), especially those towards
the rigorous-proof end of the software-development spectrum, spare little
or no space for the topics of debugging, editing, and maintenance. But we
are committed to an inspection that is biased towards large-scale software;
an area where rigorous proofs are few and far between. So we must give full
consideration to these somewhat less-than-respectable practices. And this is
all to the eventual good for rigorous proofs of AI implementations occur

with much the same frequency as excluded middles in classical logic. In AI program development there is no question about the necessity of incremental modification.

Large and complex programs are never proven to be correct. The reliability of non-AI programs is better described as free from known error; and the value of that attribute is dependent upon how well the program has been scrutinized for errors. There is much work on proofs of program correctness and on reliable transformation of specifications to implementations. As yet, it has not produced techniques that are applicable to practical, large-scale software engineering, although the impact has been considerable in terms of increasing general awareness of the correctness problem. The statement that "testing only shows the presence of errors, not their absence", is only a half-truth but it does emphasize the basic weakness of the major software validation technique.

Nevertheless, executing a program with various test sets of data and analysis of the results is the route to reliable software — it is called debugging or software validation. A program is an implementation of a function. If a piece of software has any long-term usefulness then it is most likely a function with a very large range of input values. Testing must then be performed with only a small subset of the function's range. The reliability of a piece of software is to some extent dependent upon the quality of testing. Good testing hinges upon the selection of actual test data from the large set of possible test data.

As usual, only guidelines are available for steering the selection process. Boundary conditions are error-prone features of algorithms, so test data is chosen to probe the upper and lower limits of data values. This boundary probing should include both sides of the boundary — the barely legal and the barely illegal. Any particularly 'unusual' data values are tried, for example, zero in the range of integers. A test of all branch paths through the algorithm is another important goal for a set of test data. A good meta-level guideline is for a person other than the designer and implementor to devise and run the test data. Given the specifications the tester can select test data that will perhaps be free of the biases and unwarranted assumptions that the designer may have inadvertently built into his algorithm. It is true that the test data designer may bring his own biases into the picture but hopefully they will not be the same as those of the designer.

In addition to running cunningly devised sets of test data, this fundamentally dubious process of trying to ensure oneself that a program contains no errors can be supplemented in several ways.

For a start, if the program designer can suppress his conviction that he will get it right first time (usually a belief that is uncommonly resistant to negative reinforcement), he will design a battery of checks and traps into the program. Then every execution of the program must run the gauntlet of this logical minefield. Every successful execution of the program is guaranteed to be free of every problem that the designer foresaw.

Weinberg (1971) offers the suggestion that if programs are freely but arbitrarily bugged then the quality of the testing can be gauged from the percentage and types of these introduced bugs that were not discovered.

Finally, there are a number of software tools geared specifically to easing and automating the process of debugging. Yourdon (1975), for example, describes a Dynamic Debugging Techniques package, DDT (it kills bugs!).

This is our first mention of software tools — programs that are used to facilitate the development and management of other programs. It will not be the last; in fact the idea of software tools is developed and extended throughout this book until it eventually constitutes the major argument for a belief in the possibility of AI at its finest as practical software.

### 2.4.2  Editing

Detecting our mistakes, oversights, and more fundamental misconceptions — blithely known collectively as bugs — is only part of the problem, perhaps the easier part for conventional software (in AI, as we shall see, "correct" and "incorrect" can even be hard to distinguish). Having detected the presence of a bug two other problems follow:

    (i)  find it in the program; and
    (ii)  modify the program to eliminate it.

Both problems can be difficult and time-consuming, demanding perseverance, talent and inspiration from the system developer. Some bugs, like coding errors, may be hard to find and easy to fix. Others, like fundamental misconceptions may be easy to locate but hard to fix. All combinations are possible.

Again guidelines abound for locating bugs, including the defensive programming mentioned above. Software tools can speed up the process of homing in on a bug. Having located the logical wart, we must tackle the task of removing it. Again this is a two-part task:

    (a)  analyse the error; and
    (b)  design a modification to eliminate the error without introducing any new ones.

Analysis hinges upon comprehension of the program: both what it is supposed to do in general and in detail, and how it is supposed to be doing it. So, access to the design documentation as well as to the implementation is often an essential prerequisite to fixing a bug.

The actual fixing is, or should be, a process of design. The analysis process leads you to the highest level of design (even to specification) in which the error occurs. This level is then redesigned in the light of your new found knowledge, then refined down once more to a detailed design, and finally you reimplement and retest. We return to this editing process in the context of program maintenance below and again in Chapter 4 where we see it elevated to a starring role within the AI program development paradigm.

When testing is successfully completed, the program is debugged and we have (after some tidying up of loose ends) a finished product — a marketable piece of software or a deliverable product. The RFS "defines the meaning of program correctness; any program meeting the technical and documentation specifications will be deemed a satisfactory deliverable" (Tausworthe, 1977). This is the view at the more formal end of the practical software spectrum. Brooks (1975), pragmatic as ever, claims that a program delivers satisfaction of a user need rather than a tangible product — a state of affairs closely akin to that of AI. The big difference is that the software engineer has within his *modus operandi* the right to extract specific requirements and a subsequent RFS. And his further obligations do not go beyond design and implementation of the RFS. If, as Brooks claims, the practical reality is a back-and-forth interchange until you convince the user that the specific piece of software will pretty much satisfy his needs, then this is a criticism of the requirements analysis process. The problem can be localized and we can work on sharpening the requirements analysis process. In AI, the superficially similar problem of meeting intangible user needs is a fundamental and unavoidable feature of the process, rather than a weakness in some stage of the methodology.

Certainly some requirements analysis can and should be undertaken in an AI project. There is always some conventional software engineering in an AI project; it should be fully developed to assist in the management and control of the AI aspects (a general strategy that we will return to in Chapter 6). But in AI intangible human needs are part of the essence of the whole problem not a feature that can potentially be isolated and factored out by a process such as requirements analysis. Even in principle it is difficult to envisage the possibility of complete requirements analysis for AI problems. The software engineer not only has the principle at hand, he also has practical techniques that have been shown to be effective.

A second and related point of contrast concerns the fact that requirements analysis aims at defining the boundaries of a software engineering problem. Clearly an explicit, complete, and rigorous statement of the scope and limitations of the problem to be implemented is a valuable, perhaps invaluable, aspect of the RFS. Consider the problems of comprehensive testing if various aspects of the problem have ill-defined boundaries — such is the nature of AI problems.

A major problem in AI research is: what is the scope and limitations of a given AI program? We know some things that the program does adequately, and we know a much larger set of things that it does inadequately, but we don't know where the intervening boundaries are. In a research environment this is a nuisance; in a practical application environment it is intolerable. Scope and limitations are thus another obstacle to the development and marketing of AI software. Warnings to prospective AI software buyers are already surfacing, "caveat emptor" is the rule of purchase, it will be especially important for the buyer of AI software.

Having walked through and viewed the software-engineering, program-development, methodology in some detail, we can stand back and look at the process as a whole. Fig. 2.7 is a summary of the methodology that I have described.

Are we now finished? A deliverable piece of software has been con-

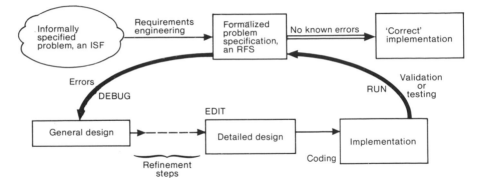

Fig. 2.7 — The program development process of software engineering

structed and installed in the application environment. Can we now forget it and move on to the next assignment? Perhaps we can, but we know for certain that for someone, if not for us, this piece of software, hot off the terminal, has just become an object of intense interest and long-term significance; I am thinking of the maintenance programmer.

## 2.5  MAINTENANCE

When a piece of software has been completed, including testing, and delivered for use, then the task of software maintenance begins. Maintenance has two facets: tracking down and removal of bugs that show up, and modifications to meet environmental changes.

A properly designed and implemented piece of software is a program and full documentation. Full documentation includes: requirements, specifications, a description of the design in general and in detail, and a description of the program, its structure and its use. Even the most well-designed program is typically not a very transparent object — well constructed documentation is. Furthermore, the documentation provides the all important global view of the structure implemented: the major structural components and their mutual interactions. This information is in the program, but it is so severely cluttered and spread out among programming language detail as to be effectively absent.

This global information is vital to both direct the search for the code that implements a specific subtask, and guide a proposed modification of the design and subsequent modification of the program code.

Notice that any modifications, whether to remove an error or to implement a change in the specifications, should be introduced at the highest possible level in the design. The modified design is then refined down to a new implementation. Small design changes may result in large code differences and vice versa. On no account is it wise to chop and change the code, and keep rerunning the program until the error disappears or the desired modification appears. In a large and complex program occasional short-term successes may result, but in the long term the only possibility is chaos.

Belady and Lehman have developed laws of program evolution (see Lehman & Belady, 1985), one of which states that an evolving program increases in complexity unless work is done to maintain or reduce the complexity. Brooks (1975) is more pessimistic. He states that program maintenance is an entropy-increasing process, and even when a system is subjected to the most highly skilled editing it is eventually doomed to a state of unfixable obsolescence. Current efforts to upgrade expert system software incrementally has yet to prove decisively that Brooks is wrong. Yet wrong he must be if the AI revolution in practical software is ever really to succeed. For incremental development is another fundamental component of the AI program development methodology.

By way of contrast Linger, Mills, & Witt (1979) claim that a rigorous design should survive its implementation, not be swamped by it, and provide a framework for the intellectual control of changes to the implementation as requirements change. Documentation modifications should accompany program modifications; more precisely, program modifications should follow design modifications.

In practice, as has been said before, programs tend to get separated from their documentation in both time and space. All too often maintenance is required for an effectively undocumented program. In this situation the only long-term solution is a reconstruction of the documentation.

The design (or a possible design) is abstracted from the program. A usable series of high-level descriptions of the program may be abstracted by successively neglecting and condensing the most detailed aspects of the description. There is no guarantee that the original design will be abstracted or that any two software maintenance people will abstract the same high-level descriptions of the program. What matters is that there are abstract descriptions, at varying levels of detail, free from implementation clutter. By virtue of their comprehensibility these descriptions can be used as scaffolding to support program maintenance.

Abstraction of underlying representations to facilitate comprehension of the program and thus support the maintenance of an undocumented program is a minor feature of the software engineering paradigm. It hardly gets a mention in most treatments of the software engineering process. In Chapter 5 we will take this insignificant process and raise its status to that of a major component of the effort to use the full potential of AI in practical software. The process of abstraction is developed and extended in a number of different directions in order to support various aspects of the proposed paradigm shift.

# 3

# Artificial intelligence: a potted travelogue

AI research is the process of finding adequate
tractable approximations to intractable algorithms.

What I am about to embark upon in this chapter might be comparable to a review of the science of astronomy about 30 years after Stone Henge was completed. Nevertheless it is useful to review the few decades of AI research to provide a background for the recent realization that commercial software engineering has a need to encroach heavily upon the domain of AI. So I shall attempt to provide some perspective even though the events may be too close to permit a sharp focus. Some would argue that this is an epoch, the end of the formative period in AI and the beginning of the utilitarian one. I think not. The formative era will continue for some time (perhaps becoming an aeon). The following chapter is thus also intended to highlight the problematic areas of AI that can as yet boast of no well-formed solutions. Subsequent chapters will then indicate why certain of these problems must be solved before AI will become a gusher of ideas for practical software.

The intent of this chapter is also to lead the uninitiated through the AI chronicle and thereby familiarize him or her with the liturgy of this mystic art. Opinions differ dramatically as to what if anything the craft of AI has contributed to the sum of human knowledge. The landmarks in one camp are seen as balderdash in another.

What is AI? Ask three practitioners and you're likely to get at least four different definitive statements. The researchers of AI are not usually noted for their reticence. In fact it's not much of an exaggeration to claim that there's no business like show business — unless it's AI. So beware of the oversell it is unhelpful in a research environment, but with respect to practical software it could be disastrous.

Having put the reader on the defensive (a fairly good place to be when starting into AI), I'll rush in with a few disclaimers and then we can proceed. This chapter is a personal view; but a conscious effort has been made at least to touch upon all of the major sects and heresies with particular regard to their likely potential importance in software applications.

I have avoided extensive referencing and instead added a bibliography to facilitate the follow-up of any aspects of particular interest to the reader.

## 3.1   AI AND DUBIOUS DIALOGUES

Are some of your best friends computers? A silly question? Maybe, after all your friends don't look like computers, they look like people. But what about the people you interact with over the telephone or by letter? The question is less silly now and likely to become a thoroughly serious one before the end of the century.

It is not at all uncommon now to entertain some doubts as to whether an apparently personalized letter is totally computer generated, or whether the party at the other end of a telephone line is a person or a recorded message. It is true that such doubts are usually short-lived, but AI as practical software will change that drastically. Ominous anecdotes already abound:

> The secretary who sought privacy to continue her dialogue with a computer simulation of a psychoanalyst.
>
> The Company Vice-President, who ordered an apparently obstreperous salesman to report to his office on Monday morning, had in fact been communicating with a natural language understanding computer program.

Computer programs that give rise to intelligent behaviour are artificial intelligence programs. Defining AI is probably a task beyond the scope of human intelligence, although the Turing Test is an interesting approach that we shall be considering. Let us say for the moment that AI is the development of computer programs that exhibit intelligent behaviour.

## 3.2   ILL-STRUCTURE APPEARS

A concept like AI, or even the word "intelligence" that cannot usefully be pinned down with mathematical precision, is an ill-structured concept. Ill-structured concepts are part and parcel of what makes AI different from software engineering.

Consider the following old linguistic chestnut; it makes the point with a minimum of fuss.

> Is it correct for a computer to translate, "The spirit is willing but the flesh is weak", into Russian as, "The vodka is good but the meat stinks"? — probably not, but it might be adequate, it depends upon

the context. Context-sensitivity is an important characteristic of intelligence and therefore of AI as well.

If a computerized, natural language interface for a financial data base is asked by a human, "who won the cup in 1983?", what is the correct answer? Is there a single correct answer? Are there any correct answers?

The average soccer-interested British male would probably assert that there is a single, correct answer, and it is, Everton, the soccer team that won the Football Association cup in 1983. But such a person has used, probably unconsciously, a complex set of implications to convert the ambiguous concept "the cup" into a well-structured one.

An American in 1983 is likely to interpret "the cup" as The Americas Cup for 12 metre yacht racing (they lost it for the first time after 132 years). At any rate it is highly unlikely that the U.S. interpretation would be the same as that of his trans-Atlantic counterpart. An American might well have a problem even with the general concept of winning cups — they tend to go in for bowls (and there's a nice ambiguity there).

## 3.3  ADEQUACY: THE CRITERION OF AI

What is the correct implication? Is there a correct implication? Is an answer based upon the most probable implication the correct answer? Deciding upon the correct implication, or if indeed there is a correct implication, is another context-dependent problem. Even worse, is the answer that the interrogator expects the correct answer? It is by no means unknown for apparently correct and accepted answers to be later proven false.

Back to reality: ill-structured concepts abound in the everyday lives of all of us. A consequence is that correctness is not a useful measure to apply; the criterion of AI is adequacy.

So what should our intelligent, natural language interface reply if it is to be judged as adequate? The most likely answer for a moderately intelligent program is something along the lines of, "Please rephrase your question, I was unable to understand it." A supersmart AI program, on the other hand, should perhaps recognize that the question is totally irrelevant to the financial data base it was designed to answer questions about. The most adequate answer might be, "Stop messing about and ask a sensible question," or "Stop wasting my valuable time, I've got more important things to do than answer idiotic questions like that!" — it all depends on the personality of the AI, or its human designer.

Finally a last observation on the frustrated financial data base: what would the following somewhat delayed answer signify? "Hm, Watford, I think. Would you like to query your account now?" Artificial intelligence — or the real thing? (A flawless imitation just like you and me.)

This last answer is, I think, the most impressive. It indicates that the answering system not only knows about other things other than the financial data base, but also it suggests a depth of understanding of human communication. It is courteous and leads the dialogue back to where it should be going within the given context.

## 3.4 THE TURING TEST

Breadth and depth of communication abilities seem to be strong indicators of intelligence. At the genesis of modern AI, the British mathematician, Alan Turing set up in 1950 the paradigm for deciding the question: can machines think? Turing's (1950) imitation game gives us the breadth and depth of conversational abilities as the probe for evaluating the intelligence of computer system. Despite many years of criticism the basic paradigm has endured: in essence, if in extended and unconstrained natural language communication a computer system is indistinguishable from a human being then that system possesses intelligence. Hence we have a definition, of sorts, of artificial intelligence.

Turing's choice of natural language as the means of scrutinizing a system for intelligence turns out to be quite apt. The underlying implication is that if a system is capable of chatting sensibly in prolonged and unrestricted discourse then the system is also capable of the other many and varied accoutrements of intelligence. The validity of the implication is a subject for endless debate.

But as we shall see soon, natural language is so persuasive an indicator of intelligence that in AI the test backfires on us repeatedly. Natural language is the nitroglycerine of cognitive science: handled carefully it is an immensely useful means of investigating intelligence, but injudicious handling all too often results in the ELIZA syndrome. Natural language and computers are an explosive combination.

## 3.5 THE ELIZA SYNDROME

Since 1950 there have been some weak claims (usually not by the system designers themselves) that some programs have passed the Turing Test. The most famous of these programs is ELIZA (Weizenbaum, 1965). Numerous introductions to AI offer a short and sensible dialogue between some human and the ELIZA program. A commonly encountered example of an ELIZA–human dialogue is the following (ELIZA's utterances are in capitals):

> Men are all alike.
> IN WHAT WAY
> They're always bugging us about something or other.
> CAN YOU THINK OF A SPECIFIC EXAMPLE
> Well, my boyfriend made me come here.
> YOUR BOYFRIEND MADE YOU COME HERE
> He says I'm depressed much of the time.
> I AM SORRY TO HEAR THAT YOU ARE DEPRESSED
> It's true. I am unhappy.
> DO YOU THINK COMING HERE WILL HELP YOU NOT TO BE UNHAPPY

I need some help, that much seems certain.
WHAT WOULD IT MEAN TO YOU IF YOU GOT SOME HELP
Perhaps I could learn to get along with my mother.
TELL ME MORE ABOUT YOUR FAMILY
My mother takes care of me.
WHO ELSE IN YOUR FAMILY TAKES CARE OF YOU
My father.
YOUR FATHER
You are like my father in some ways.
WHAT RESEMBLANCE DO YOU SEE
You are not very aggressive but I think you don't want me to notice that.
WHAT MAKES YOU THINK I AM NOT VERY AGGRESSIVE
You don't argue with me.
WHY DO YOU THINK I DON'T ARGUE WITH YOU
You are afraid of me.
DOES IT PLEASE YOU TO THINK I AM AFRAID OF YOU
My father is afraid of everybody.
WHAT ELSE COMES TO MIND WHEN YOU THINK OF YOUR FATHER
Bullies.
DOES THAT HAVE ANYTHING TO DO WITH THE FACT THAT YOUR BOYFRIEND MADE YOU COME HERE

And this persuasive snippet is supposed to buttress the claim that Turing's Test is about to be passed. Is machine intelligence just around the corner, if not already alive and well and living somewhere around MIT?

The answer is, no. It is true that certain AI programs are capable of an extended and sensible dialogue in English. And moreover it is a dialogue that carries significant information in both directions. A number of expert systems, such as the TEIRESIAS–MYCIN combination (a natural-language interface to an expert system, Davis & Lenat, 1982), fall into this category. But the range of sensible dialogue is extremely narrow and fragile. A fundamental feature of Turing's Test is that the dialogue should be broad ranging and robust.

The ELIZA program fails the Turing Test dismally on two critical counts: sensible dialogue is possible only for short periods and within very narrow constraints.

ELIZA is a very dangerous program. It is an active carrier of the computerized strain of the if-you-cannot-understand-it-you-have-to-believe-it disorder? This malady strikes fast when a computer is involved, especially in conjunction with an AI program.

"We cannot rectify this error in your account, the computer system does not permit it," is a statement with a sadly familiar ring about it. This remark and its many variants are likely to be an ever-increasing blight on our lives. Now if the computer itself tells you that something is, or is not, true, especially within the context of a seemingly intelligent dialogue, it tends to be accepted as gospel truth. (Computers only speak ex cathedra?) Joseph Weizenbaum, ELIZA's creator, was motivated to write a book just to counter the adverse effect that his program was having on casual computer users. A disturbingly large range of people insisted on investing the ELIZA program with intelligence despite all protestations to the contrary by Weizenbaum himself (see Weizenbaum, 1976).

Thus we have the ELIZA syndrome to guard against in AI: seemingly intelligent snippets of conversational dialogue or of problem solving ability are an almost irresistible basis for unwarranted grandiose assumptions as to underlying abilities and hence potential domains of application. The results of applying underpowered, or worse, totally inappropriate programs to societal problems could be catastrophic — if not cataclysmic.

## 3.6 THE MYTHOLOGY OF AI

### 3.6.1 The academic myth: intellectualism is the peak of intelligence

If we can simulate man's difficult intellectual achievements, like chess playing and theorem proving, then solutions to the simpler problems, like cleaning a house or working on a production line, will fall out along the way. Wrong! We are tackling the intellectually impressive but not the harder problems first.

Starting with the easiest examples is, of course, a legitimate way to proceed provided we do not present such examples as the ultimate goal of AI. Far from being the major peak of intelligence, intellectualism may be only one of the minor foothills. Furthermore it is a moot point as to whether any path up this foothill leads to the major peaks. A charge often levelled at AI researchers is that they are climbing trees as a first step towards reaching the Moon.

I shall later develop the argument that practical implementations of static and abstract intellectual problems have generated a false sense of optimism in the near-term potential for AI as commercial software.

Simon (1981), in an essay on the influence of automation on society, records the surprise of AI researchers when they realized that the intellectual aspects of intelligence were the easiest to simulate with a computer.

Consider the work-station operations in a factory production line: welding a fixed pattern of spot welds, or the checking of some component for standard defects. A simple mechanical task endlessly repeated. The biggest problem for a human performing such a menial task is boredom and consequent lack of attention.

Computers don't suffer from boredom, attention is one of their strong suits. Let's put together a computer, some sensory devices such as a camera and tactile sensors, and a program to integrate sensory and control information in a suitable way. We have an industrial robot. It will spot weld the precise pattern of welds all day (all night as well) without fatigue — a veritable super-menial; or is it? Something for nothing is a rare event in this particular Universe, so where's the catch?

### 3.6.1.1   *Reality is a web of ill-structured problems*

The light bulbs flicker along the assembly line and production grinds to a halt with robots screaming for help wherever they were using visual input.

A drive belt is adjusted causing a barely perceptible change in position of assembly components. Once again emergency lights are flashing for human help and the production line awaits a human solution to the crisis.

The above vignettes illustrate that every eventuality must be foreseen and explicitly programmed for within the robot — therein lies the catch. In the real world, every situation, however well constrained, hides a wealth of ill-structured problems. No robot designer can foresee and program solutions to every possible eventuality within the robot's environment, however impoverished and tightly controlled it might be.

We know that this problem is ill-structured but adequately solvable in practice; human beings do it all the time. How do they do it?

### 3.6.1.2   *The need for constant environmental monitoring*

Lack of single-minded attention is one part of the answer. Humans continually monitor their environment and can thus foresee or at least understand some resultant problem with their immediate task. If some earlier task in the production line is disrupted then a human operator will expect some subsequent disruption of his task. He may well even be able to predict the exact nature of the disruption he will face.

### 3.6.1.3   *The need for non-pertinent knowledge — lots of it*

The second component of this human success story is the experience or knowledge that can be brought to bear upon any problem. Some knowledge will be task-specific knowledge: such as the tendency for a particular component to fall over or have some defect. But in addition there will be general world knowledge: such as that curved surfaces tend to roll, and dropped objects tend to fall downwards.

This wealth of knowledge is the basis of successful adaptive behaviour, and such behaviour is the key to solving these ill-structured problems adequately. Traditionally we do not marvel at the knowledge-guided problem solving abilities of a menial worker, or to take that other much-maligned super problem solver, the housewife.

It is an indisputable fact that the cleaning of a house requires a larger, more diverse, and complex knowledge base than does the playing of international standard chess. Yet success in the latter pursuit is typically taken to be indicative of intelligence whilst the former is rated as a menial chore.

House cleaning is in fact a highly complex ill-structured problem. The first general house cleaning robots, which are not just around the corner, are likely to be either totally ineffectual or a dangerous liability. The ineffectual version will halt operations for user instructions for every toy, dog, cat, grand-dad snoozing in an easy chair, or other unforeseen perturbation of its expectations in the house. The higher risk version is likely to clean-up all such objects that it stumbles across.

### 3.6.2 The Spock myth: an artificial intelligence will not be impeded by human weaknesses such as emotions and non-logical reasoning

It is a common misconception that the cold, totally rational automaton will put us to shame as it slices logically through the problems of everyday life. *Star Trek's* favourite Vulcan is mythical in more than one sense.

Is human intelligence a local optimum, given the conditions of life on Earth? Or is it an evolutionary back alley, perhaps a dead-end? Is machine intelligence going to be the ruthless competitor dominating evolution's best effort as placental mammals quickly overran their marsupial counterparts in Australia? After several decades of feverish activity in AI research the answer is still not known; it is a question that only the passage of time will really answer, although there are a number of reasons to believe that evolution came close to the optimum with H. Sap. (see James & Partridge, 1973). This argument implies that human intelligence with all of its obvious weaknesses may be an optimum (within the constraints of the empirical world); it may be an upper bound on the possibilities for AI.

Hofstadter's (1979) dialogues with doubt suggest that human foibles such as love and hate might simply emerge as epiphenomena in any sufficiently complex system. Even if there was no attempt to program, say love, into a system, it might arise once the system reached a certain level of complexity — that is to say, we might be prepared to admit that the system appeared to act lovingly as a result of observing its behaviour. So, although an AI system designer would not purposely include the problematic features of human intelligence within a system, these features may just emerge as necessary side effects of intelligent behaviour. Much as AI would like to extract the sapiens without the homo (like a winkle from its shell), it is not at all obvious that the two are really separable.

## 3.7 THE GOALS OF AI RESEARCH

The cognitive science branch of AI seeks to throw light upon the nature of human intelligence, its scope and limitations, and how it works. Within this domain the computer is a tool for modelling theories of human intelligence. The cognitive scientist theorizes in terms of high level concepts: long-term and short-term memory, semantic mismatch detectors, semantic networks, etc. Such components have no obvious correspondence with anatomical features of the brain; they are high level abstractions rather closer to the behavioural characteristics that they seek to explain than to the organ from which the behaviour (presumably) arises.

By way of contrast, the brain modelling approach to AI theorizes and models in terms of units than can be related to brain structure: cell assemblies, neural networks, even individual neurons. The basic building blocks for the theory may now be directly observable, but piecing them together to explain observed behaviours represents a formidable problem. Consider explaining the details of a weather pattern in terms of inter-molecular interactions rather than temperature, pressure, prevailing winds, etc.

The lion's share of AI research does not ostensibly seek to answer any questions at all about human intelligence. The goal of this work is to emulate or surpass human performance of certain intelligent activities. The strongest link with human intelligence is that it represents a performance measure to strive for and then surpass.

This is also the domain of major interest for software engineers in as much as it is the AI domain of major practical success. Thus expert systems, it is claimed, can surpass human experts using, it seems, totally different mechanisms. But I would claim that despite the almost standard disclaimer to the contrary, some degree of structural correspondence between AI modules and hypothesized mechanisms of human intelligence is both a perceivable and a necessary feature of this work, especially within a software engineering application. As we shall see, comprehensibility is at a premium, and reasoning by analogy with one's own supposed thought processes is a necessary vehicle for realizing this goal. In the above-mentioned expert systems, for example, automatic explanation of the system's diagnoses (or whatever) in psychologically meaningful terms, rather than in terms of the implementation structures, is seen as an important problem. As a further and more specific example, Michie (1982) calls for a technique of "structured induction" to combat the inscrutability to man of the products of machine learning.

When we consider that cultural differences all too frequently block and distort mutual communication and understanding between instances of natural intelligence. Consider for a moment the likely problems between Mr. Average and an AI system designed on purely ad hoc principles (if such a thing is possible); the Grand Canyon might well look small by comparison with the chasm that would separate these two. Communication difficulties are a problem within the relatively homogeneous umbrella of human intelligence, we must beware of the potential for escalation of this problem when we introduce an artificial intelligence.

Next we must consider heuristics: a key concept in the realization of AI. A good heuristic is any strategy that works, and it is not explicitly linked to the mechanisms that humans apparently use. So at first glance the use of heuristics appears to deny the humanness claimed in the preceding paragraph, but as you will see the ultimate source of heuristics is inevitably human. The result is that an AI system is bound to display a certain humanness. (But see the section on machine learning which encompasses the potential for developing non-human heuristics.)

## 3.8   THE HEURISTIC APPROACH

If it feels good, do it. That injunction, although not quite accurate, is at the heart of AI as a heuristic art. More precisely, if it works, use it, is the principle behind heuristic programming.

A heuristic is a rule of thumb: a procedure that achieves a certain goal on an acceptable proportion of occasions. A heuristic to guide machine learning might be: a machine should learn only significant events. To incorporate a heuristic within a program we generate an algorithm to approximate it — a heuristic algorithm, in short. So an implementation of the above heuristic must include explicit code to approximate: what makes an event significant, what aspects of a significant event will be learned, etc. (an algorithmic approximation to this heuristic is examined in some detail in Section 5.4.2).

> A house-cleaning robot will require a heuristic such as: water plants when dry.

Now that appears to be a reasonable rule that will be appropriate most of the time with some notable exceptions, e.g. cacti and artificial plants. But although this statement of the heuristic would probably be sufficient if you were instructing a friend who was taking care of your house for a while, for the housecleaning robot it will need to be transformed into a precise, algorithmic rule.

Let us try for a more precise statement:

> Add water, in an amount appropriate for the size of the plant, to every plant whose soil has a relative moisture content less than some prespecified value.

That formulation would seem to explain what's wanted — or does it? Let me list some of the questions that would have to be answered before this heuristic attains the algorithmic specificity currently necessary in AI systems.

> What does "appropriate for" mean? — proportional to?
> If so, proportional to what? — size of plant?
> How do you measure size? — height?; estimated weight?; surface area of soil?; volume of soil?
> "Relative moisture content," — relative to what? — size of plant?; volume of soil?; surface area of soil?; depth of soil?
> Where do you measure the moisture content? — on soil surface?; $x$ inches below the surface?; the average of several arbitrary probes?

The questions are many, reasonable answers are legion, and correct answers are exceptional. But the questions must be paired with precise answers before we will obtain a machine executable version of the original heuristic. The selection of a particular set of necessarily somewhat arbitrary answers will result in a particular algorithmic approximation to our original heuristic. There are very many such algorithmic approximations, and very few ways to choose between them.

So a heuristic implemented in an AI program is more accurately viewed as one of many possible algorithmic approximations to the heuristic — but this is an exceedingly clumsy and pedantic phrase so I shall use instead the terms heuristic and heuristic algorithm.

The reader is, I hope, wondering why I can tell my friend to water the plants when dry but I must make a lot of extra decisions before I can tell my robot much the same thing — especially if, as I claim, there are no good reasons to believe that AI will suffer from any limitations that do not afflict RI (real intelligence).

The difference is just a question of time, and is due to the vast amount of knowledge that my friend can apply to understanding the heuristic as opposed to the paucity of such knowledge that a robot will have at his rubberized fingertips in the foreseeable future. My friend will (unconsciously) generate his own algorithmic approximation to the heuristic; it will be many years before we can trust a robot to do the same.

I can reasonably expect my friend's approximation to be acceptable to me because of the overall similarity between his applicable knowledge and mine, but I cannot be sure of it. Heuristics come with no guarantees. Then why do we use heuristics? Wouldn't some proven algorithm be better?

Proven algorithms would certainly be preferable but in AI they are unfortunately either hard to find or hopelessly inefficient. The use of a heuristic represents the best known solution procedure that will succeed, if it does succeed, within reasonable time and space constraints.

The space–time trade-offs here are not just microseconds, or even days or weeks. They may well run to centuries or the lifetime of the Universe! The search for efficient heuristics is well-motivated when the only known proven algorithm will take years to terminate. People just won't wait that long.

The game of chess provides a simple example. In principle, the best move to be made from a given board configuration is easily computed. We generate the full game tree down to all of the terminal win, lose, or draw, situations. Then a mini-max algorithm is applied to specify correctly the best move to make. Unfortunately both the space and time resources required to use this algorithm are impossible to meet.

The full game tree for an arbitrary board configuration in chess will in general more than overfill all existing computer memories. The time required for generating and processing it is of the order of the time that the Universe has been in existence. Clearly a heuristic is called for. In practice heuristics are used to estimate the relative goodness or badness of potential moves without generating the full game tree.

We need to be able to specify the best next move for all legal chess board configurations. All the guaranteed algorithms that can do this are still wild and free. Not a single specimen has been captured. But herds of heuristic algorithms roam more or less under control within the world's chess programs; they can tell you the next best move with an accuracy that varies from terrible to quite good (as measured by the competitive successes of programs that embody these heuristic algorithms). The nature of a heuristic is such that it comes with no warranty other than an empirically based assurance that it performs adequately.

It is sometimes possible to support a heuristic with a probability-based argument. But probabilities must be based upon analysis of the problem, and more often than not AI problems are analytically intractable. Analytic intractability, you will remember, is another characteristic of AI problems.

The guarantees, or lack of them, are one thing, but where does the heuristic come from in the first place? Contrary to my earlier suggestion, they are not usually to be found quietly grazing in an adjacent pasture just waiting to be led away and harnessed to an AI program; they typically have to be broken-in and domesticated before they perform adequately. But where are the wild ones to be found?

The sources are varied and ill-understood. Some heuristics are definitely plucked from the air (no different from many algorithms, of course). A common source of inspiration for heuristics is, not surprisingly, you and me — homo sapiens in general. I use me, and you use you; there's nothing like being close to the source. Introspection is a very convenient strategy, but it must be used with caution.

To return to the chess example, I can manufacture a first approximation to a best-move heuristic by introspection and rationalization of the strategies that I appear to use when playing chess. Typically the heuristic would be composed of components that compute first approximations to king threat, piece mobility, etc.

Given that my personal chess rating, as judged by performance measures, is probably approaching abysmal (from below), I am probably not a good source of high quality chess playing heuristics. Despite the loss of proximity to the source, a better strategy might be to plug into an expert chess player.

Tame experts are indeed a good source of heuristics. Unfortunately experts are no more expert at introspection than you or I. All indications are that they are full of expertise, replete with high quality heuristics, but how to pour them out of the expert and into a program is a problem that is receiving a lot of attention. Later, in the context of machine learning I shall describe several approaches to this transfer of expertise problem.

Provided that the first guess for a heuristic strategy focuses upon the significant dimensions of the problem domain then there is every chance that the heuristic can be tuned to adequacy by means of an iterative process. This tuning process may be totally automatic, in which case it is described in the section on machine learning; or it may be in essence the run-debug-edit paradigm, a man–machine symbiosis, and as such it is considered in detail in the following chapter on AI methodology.

The development of heuristics is a creative process, but like most creativity, the perspiratory aspects of development and refinement usually far outweigh the inspirational features. Rather than pearls of wisdom dropping from the lips of experts you tend to get very rough diamonds or even just a bucket of pay dirt. In either case it's just a beginning.

## 3.9   THE EARLY DAYS — GRAND PLANS

Many early efforts were directed at broadly-based, general tasks, such as machine translation from, say, English to Russian. Another world-wide set of projects was bent on producing mobile, perceptive robots: embryonic Frankensteinian monsters. It quickly became apparent that such broad targets were far too difficult (easy to hit but hard to kill). AI research is now closely focused onto much more specific problems, such as natural language discourse in very limited domains, or hand–eye coordination in very limited settings.

Game playing is one area that attracted early attention and proved susceptible to machine implementation. Games are a group of well-specified and constrained, but still challenging, intellectual problems. It is moreover a domain in which the performance measure can be accurately applied: a chess playing program can be accurately ranked (as accurately as humans are ranked) by its win, lose, or draw performances against ranked human chess players (or even other chess-playing programs). The current level of the best chess playing programs is that of a national champion.

## 3.10   THE SAMUEL PHENOMENON

Samuel's (1963) checker (draughts) playing program was an early landmark study in AI. This program beat the World champion and Samuel himself; and this achievement is almost as remarkable as it appears. Samuel designed a program that played the game legally, he also included mechanisms that stored and reused successful moves; the program improved its performance with experience — it learned.

The World champion was caught off-guard in the first match, but then quickly analyzed the program's basic strategies and from then on beat it easily. Although the program learned from experience, the learning was of a rudimentary and fixed nature; it did not learn new strategies of play.

The most significant achievement was that it could consistently beat its designer. Samuel has no pretensions to checker expertise; nevertheless, he did write the program and the program trounced him. Shades of the robot that refuses to obey its creator? I think so — it definitely throws doubt onto the old adage: computers can only do what you tell them to do. In a weak sense this statement is true, but it has several significant flaws when used as an assertion of the inherent limitations of AI. Samuel did not tell the computer to beat him; he told it, in a quite straightforward way, how to play legal checkers and how to improve its performance as a result of experience.

So now we also have the Samuel phenomenon in AI: with complex programs, especially if they contain learning mechanisms, it is, in practice, impossible to predict the full range of the program's possible behaviours. More succinctly, a programmer quickly loses track of exactly what he has told his program to do, or, rather, the consequences of what he has told it to do.

The existence of the Samuel phenomenon is used as a major argument in Chapter 4 for the claim that the best AI methodology is basically different from the methodology of software engineering.

"Computers are literal–minded brutes and do exactly what they are told; no more and no less." Remember the Samuel phenomenon and treat such statements with caution.

One could argue that the Samuel phenomenon is little more than a statement that Samuel is a less good computer than a computer. A computer can always compute pi more accurately than I can, even though I programmed it to do so; so what?

This is another, and less interesting, viewpoint of the Samuel phenomenon but it does not invalidate the point that I want to make, which is: when dealing with systems of the complexity of large computer programs, it is extremely difficult to get any realistic idea of "what the computer has been told to do." To be sure this information is all there with the program and the data it has processed at any point, but then all that we as humans have been told to do is, as far as we are aware, in our genes and personal life histories. That may serve as a basis for predicting the limitations of human and machine intelligence, but it has nothing to say about the limitations of computer intelligence *vis à vis* human intelligence.

### 3.11   EXPERT SYSTEMS AND KNOWLEDGE BASES

Significant successes have also been achieved within less well-structured but very specialized domains: DENDRAL, a program that analyses chemical mass spectrograms, and MYCIN, a medical diagnosis program, are just two examples. These programs, which can match and even outperform highly trained human experts, are known as expert systems.

The following example (reprinted in Barr & Feigenbaum, 1982, p. 238) is an excerpt from a session with the South American geography tutor. The student's questions and answers are preceded by ** and annotations are underlined:

What is the language of Argentina?
** Probably Spanish
Very good.
Approximately what is the area of Argentina?
        Student changes topic...
** Tell me something about Peru
Peru is a country.
It is located in South America.
The capital of Peru is Lima.
Now answer the question you didn't answer before.
        ...finally answers the question.
** The area of Argentina is 1,100,000 square miles
Approximately true, but a more exact value is 1,200,000.
The eastern bordering country of Peru is --- .
Student makes an error and is corrected...
** Catholicism
Wrong.   Catholicism is not a country but a religion.
The correct answer is: Brazil
Where is Peru?
        ...and once again changes topic.
** Is Asuncion hot?
Since Asuncion is part of Paraguay, yes.

** What is the most important difference between Peru and Paraguay?
The primary difference is: The population of Peru is larger by a factor of 7.8.

Such dialogues are definitely suggestive of intelligence (but remember the ELIZA syndrome) and a handful of expert systems have undergone field trials that appear to demonstrate that adequate or better performances are indeed reproducible.

The success of expert systems rests largely on the very restricted and specialized nature of the domains in which they operate. Intelligent behaviour within the ill-defined empirical world (as opposed to well-defined game playing and puzzle-solving situations) is founded upon vast amounts of information.

The caretaker on his nightly rounds is constantly drawing upon a huge data base of knowledge about both the world in general (anything dropped will fall downwards, rounded objects on sloping surfaces will tend to roll, etc.), and his task in particular (the usual configuration of moveable objects in each room, the location of the nearest taps for obtaining a bucket of clean water at any point on his rounds, etc.). Our unlikely expert is constantly solving tricky, ill-structured problems. For example, when to get a bucket of clean water given that it is fairly dirty now that he is close to a tap and how much more dirty it is likely to get before he is in the vicinity of the next tap. This already complex problem might well be further compounded by consideration of the possible alternative routes between the taps.

Finally as a matter of course he will perform feats of information retrieval that any AI enthusiast would give his favourite heuristic for. His duster is worn out and the storeroom contains no more. Our underrated genius might well recall having noticed, some weeks ago, a piece of rag stuffed behind a pipe. Having retrieved the information from his knowledge base he will then retrieve the object itself which will temporarily serve as a substitute for the worn out duster.

Our caretaker is, as yet, not reproducible as an expert system. His knowledge base is too vast, his information retrieval capabilities are poorly understood, and his ill-structured problem resolution heuristics are largely a mystery (and largely ill-structured as well, I suspect). Moving along from this very difficult problem domain let us examine the components of an expert system within far easier areas, areas of definite AI progress: medical diagnosis and treatment, ordering complex computer systems, and soybean disease diagnosis.

A well-known computer science trade-off is between the complexity of the algorithm and of the data structure. A given problem may be solved with a simple algorithm operating on a complex data structure or with a complex algorithm operating on a simple data structure. In AI, as usual, the problem is worse, both the algorithm and the data structure tend to hover on the threshold of human comprehension and tend to throw themselves over it whenever you don't give them both your full attention. It is then crucial to find knowledge representation schemes that can store large amounts of information, be readily modifiable, allow fast, flexible access, and can be processed without need for unduly complex algorithms. A tall order, but one that is considered to be of paramount importance in AI and constitutes a major subfield: knowledge representation.

The following trivial example illustrates a popular approach to knowledge representation in a LISPese notation (more on LISP later).

(F1    (HOBBIT BILBO) )
(F2    (UNCLEOF FRODO BILBO) )
(R1    (IFTHEN (UNCLEOF X Y) (NEPHEWOF Y X)) )
(R2    (IFTHEN (AND (UNCLEOF X Y)(HOBBIT Y)) (HOBBIT X) )

Four entries constitute this knowledge base: two facts, F1 and F2; and two rules, R1 and R2. The two facts are the given 'truths' of the system and in combination with the rules they allow us to infer further true statements. Thus if we take R1 and instantiate X as FRODO and Y as BILBO, the truth of the resultant condition (UNCLEOF FRODO BILBO), given by F2, enables us to infer the conclusion, to wit (NEPHEWOF BILBO FRODO), and so on.

Specific knowledge may be stored as facts; general knowledge may be stored as rules; and by combining the two we can infer many other facts.

Having provided an example of knowledge representation, I shall take this opportunity to briefly survey this very important subfield of AI — the area of knowledge representation.

The above example is an example of a logical representation of knowledge. This class of representation has the advantage that we can employ the well-defined semantics of logic. In addition the knowledge base is a fairly simple collection of readily understandable units.

But the fact that such knowledge bases are a more or less homogeneous collection of simple units results in an overall 'flatness', a lack of perceptible higher level structure and hence of general understanding. In addition, the well-defined nature of the basic logical operations is obtained at the cost of severe limitations on applicability in representations of the empirical world, some problematic areas are: incremental acquisition of knowledge; beliefs about truth rather than truth in some absolute sense; and the combination of general assumptions with exceptional situations that may override the normal assumption.

All of these characteristics of empirical knowledge and its use to support intelligent behaviour can be reduced to the necessity to be able to add new knowledge that may then alter the truth of some current knowledge. In logical terms this leads us into a less well-understood logical world — the domain of nonmonotonic logic.

Thus in the above example an initial belief (as opposed to an absolute axiomatic truth) that (HOBBIT BILBO) is true might have to be abandoned in the light of subsequent evidence. In general this sort of change is likely to have repercussions throughout the knowledge base; it is this context-sensitivity that, as we know, characterizes AI problems and thus undermines the utility of these simple logical representations of knowledge.

From an early, enthusiastic commitment to logical schemes based on the observation that some reasoning is logic-based, there was subsequent disenchantment and rejection due to the realization that much of the information processing necessary to support intelligent behaviour did not appear to be logic-based at all — at least not based on any simple and well-understood logic. In an appendix to an essay on knowledge representation Minsky (1981) explains why he thinks that "logical" approaches will not work. One of his points of argument is that logical axioms are "permissive" — i.e. "Each axiom added means more theorems: none can disappear."

Current interest has turned somewhat back to logical schemes in two ways: first, there are efforts to construct more powerful logics; and second, there is interest in hybrid schemes that partition representations of knowledge such that logic is used where it is appropriate and other schemes are used where logic does not seem to be appropriate — a high-level modularization of the knowledge representation problem.

An important problem with this logical type of scheme is that even if a logically valid procedure, such as deduction, is possible in principle for some application, it may not be possible in practice. The practical impossibility is a result of the fact that the logical mechanisms are unguided and then the number of search paths quickly becomes the limiting factor.

Using the above knowledge base we can deduce the truth of (HOBBIT FRODO). This involves using both F1 and F2 to allow us to draw the required inference from R2. However, it could have involved any other sequence of the knowledge-base elements — the algorithm just has to keep trying all possibilities until it succeeds (if it can succeed). This unguided, brute-force approach quickly becomes too time consuming for all but the most trivial of knowledge bases.

Consider for one moment the original knowledge base with one extra rule, R3, which says that if X is the NEPHEWOF Y then Y is the UNCLEOF X. That would appear to be a true and an innocuous piece of information to add.

```
(F1    (HOBBIT BILBO) )
(F2    (UNCLEOF FRODO BILBO) )
(R1    (IFTHEN (UNCLEOF X Y) (NEPHEWOF Y X)) )
(R2    (IFTHEN (AND (UNCLEOF X Y)(HOBBIT Y)) (HOBBIT
       X) )
(R3    (IFTHEN (NEPHEWOF Y X) (UNCLEOF X Y)) )
```

If now we want to examine the truth of (HOBBIT FRODO), we can deduce from F2 and R1 that (NEPHEWOF BILBO FRODO) is true. This is not what we want so we push on and we use say R3, then we know (UNCLEOF FRODO BILBO) is true, but this is not what we want either so we use R1, etc. It is quite possible to follow around endless loops of deductions that are not at all obvious in more complex situations — there is, in general, no guarantee that attempted proofs will terminate. (Turing and his halting problem haunt us even here.)

So even within their limited domain automatic proving mechanisms require guidance before they become viable schemes. Two general control strategies are forwards and backwards chaining. In a forwards chaining strategy we start with our knowledge base and generate implications from it hoping to chance upon the particular one that we are interested in proving.

The opposite strategy is somewhat more guided (it could hardly be less). We start with what we want to prove (e.g. (HOBBIT FRODO)) and determine what would have to be true in order to prove this goal. With the earlier knowledge base we can see that our goal will be the conclusion of R2 if we replace X by FRODO. Thus we now need to determine the truth of the condition of R2 with this replacement. We need now to prove both:

> (UNCLEOF FRODO Y) for some value of Y and (HOBBIT Y) for
> the same value of Y.

F2 and F1 give us the proofs we need when Y is replaced by BILBO. Hence we proved the original theorem by chaining backwards from it.

Other somewhat directed proof strategies are available, for example the resolution principle, but the amount of guidance is still minimal and insufficient for practical applications — much more guidance is required. The solution is to use sophisticated heuristic control strategies that can exploit both the general context of a situation, and the specifics of each individual attempted proof. This problem is then far from solved.

Having reached this point I shall briefly consider the two other major classes of knowledge representation schemes while at the same time I shall also continue with some more general problems of knowledge representation and use.

Mylopoulos and Levesque (1984) provide a concise and informative overview of knowledge representation. They characterize the other two classes of schemes as procedural and network representations.

In a procedural scheme knowledge is represented as a set of processes. One or more processes is activated by certain states and the execution of the activated process(es) transforms the current state into a new one, and so on.

Production systems are one type of procedural knowledge representation. The earlier logical knowledge base might be represented by the following productions:

> R1   IF (UNCLEOF X Y) THEN (NEPHEWOF Y X)
> R2   IF (UNCLEOF X Y) AND (HOBBIT Y) THEN (HOBBIT X)

and the current state, which is given by the facts:

> F1   (HOBBIT BILBO)
> F2   (UNCLEOF FRODO BILBO)

Notice that the facts will satisfy the condition part of both rules, thus both rules may be executed (or 'fire') in this state. If we impose a restriction that only one rule may fire for any state then a decision must be made here between these two — the conflict must be resolved. Again we need control information but this time it can be built into the set of production rules as well as imposed by external heuristic strategies.

If we assume that the set of production rules is scanned sequentially from top to bottom until the first rule that can fire is encountered, then R1 will be fired given the current facts. Control information is already implicit in the ordering of the rules. Actually rule R2 will never be fired because any state that satisfies the condition part of R2 will also satisfy the condition part of R1 and thus R1 will always be fired in preference to R2.

Building control information into the set of production rules can eliminate much of the searching that plagues logical schemes. But the introduction of these context dependencies does, of course, aggravate the problem of understanding and modifying production systems.

The general trade-off here is that between searching context-free representations and providing guidance at the cost of introducing context dependencies.

The third type of scheme represents knowledge as a collection of 'objects' and relationships between them — that is, a network representation, often called semantic networks. A semantic network representation of our knowledge base might be:

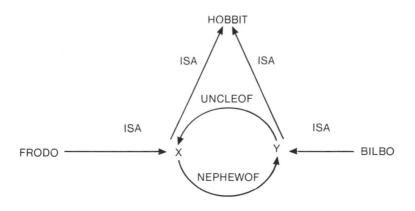

I say that the above representation "might be" a reasonable interpretation of the original logical representation because the semantic net representation does not define much (anything?). This is the major drawback of such representations; there is no well-defined formal semantics for network representations.

I think that the network that I have drawn looks like a plausible rendering of the original representation but how to interpret it in any well-defined sense is not defined.

One difference between the logical and the network representations that I have provided is that the latter is symmetrical and the former is not. I can demonstrate this lack of symmetry about the HOBBITs in the logical scheme by substituting FRODO for BILBO in F1 of the original representation, and then trying to prove (HOBBIT BILBO) — it cannot be done. F1 appears to be redundant in the semantic network; the fact that BILBO and FRODO are both HOBBITs appears to be an implication of F2, R1, and R2 in the semantic network representation.

But in the semantic network BILBO and FRODO are symmetrical with the exception of the complementary relations UNCLEOF and NEPHEWOF.

This introduction of symmetry is just one manifestation of the fact that the logical representation is a collection of context-free units whilst the semantic network is a single unit — information must be added in order to generate a cohesive whole.

In particular the logical representation specifies that the UNCLEOF relation implies NEPHEWOF but not vice versa — the semantic network includes the complementary relation, apparently. In addition the graphical representation is a considerable aid to understanding, in a general sense, the knowledge structure being represented.

But all three representational schemes, semantic nets in particular, have a tendency to induce the ELIZA syndrome in unsuspecting onlookers. You might, for example, be inclined to view my knowledge representations as somewhat male chauvinistic. Nothing could be further from the truth (or my mind)!

Surely the axiom that says UNCLEOF implies NEPHEWOF with no mention of NIECEOF is indicative of a bias in favour of the XY chromosome combination? And Bilbo and Frodo were male hobbits weren't they? No, and Yes are the answers, in that order. The relationship UNCLEOF has no necessary connection with the status of a parent's male sibling, and Bilbo is not necessarily BILBO.

There is no mention of sex in any form in my knowledge bases — in fact, there is no mention of anything semantic (apart from the formal semantics of say logic). Each of the well-defined processes described has been a syntactic activity — formal manipulations of abstract patterns that were arbitrarily labelled. It is in the reading of everyday semantic interpretations into these labels that the ELIZA syndrome strikes.

Woods (1975) addresses the general problem of what the notations and structures used in semantic networks can mean, and with the need for an explicit understanding of the intended meaning for various types of links and arcs. He also examines the representational adequacy of semantic networks for knowledge representation and finds them lacking in a number of important respects.

The problem of the unfounded persuasiveness of semantics networks is another example of the form-content problem. The form of semantic networks constitutes a difficult-to-resist temptation to the human perceptual mechanism — we invariably assume that a rich content underlies the representation and the richness of our assumptions are rarely warranted by the semantics actually implemented.

Elsewhere (Partridge, 1978a) I have previously drawn attention to the syntax–semantics (or form–content) confusion that surrounds semantic network representations. I have argued that syntax and semantics are neither absolute nor clearly separable concepts; this mixing and lack of absolute definitions are, I claim, major reasons why semantic networks invariably infect the casual observer with the ELIZA syndrome.

Hayes (1979), in a searching examination of knowledge representation, addresses this problem in terms of the "fidelity" of a formalization. "It is perilously easy to think that one's formalization has captured a concept (because one has used a convincing-sounding token to stand for it, for example), when in fact, for all the formalization knows, the token might denote something altogether more elementary."

A closely related criticism of most current knowledge bases (and yet another reason why Fig. 1.1(b) is likely to be close to reality) is that the knowledge represented does not embody a deep understanding of the domain; it is instead a collection of 'pattern → action' rules — a representation of superficial knowledge that excludes the possibility of using such knowledge to solve hard problems. The underlying principles are absent and so cannot be used to support deep reasoning.

Chandrasekaran & Mittal (1983) provide a lucid examination of this contention, which on the whole they support. But they do stress that despite the many calls for more deep knowledge there is no general agreement on the form and content of these deeper structures. In particular they illustrate that the popular belief, that 'causal' knowledge is deep knowledge, does not stand up to close scrutiny — in a nutshell: substituting 'pattern CAUSES action' for 'pattern → action' is no guarantee that deeper knowledge has been encoded.

Let us deal with one last and important question concerning representations of knowledge in general.

Suppose you are told that the computer in front of you contains an expert system — an expert on Middle-earth (i.e. you are given a context within which to draw semantic implications such as BILBO is Bilbo). Digging deeply into your own knowledge base (the one in your head) you retrieve something about little people named Hobbits, and a question for the expert system springs into mind — you type the query.

(HOBBIT HOLLY)

What is the correct response given that the expert system only has our original, ludicrously small, knowledge base to work with?

Clearly the response should be that this statement is false (Holly is a Hobbie, not a Hobbit), and the system would soon fail to deduce the truth of this query, thus it would correctly ouput:

No, Holly is not a Hobbit.

But I have glossed over an important implication here, it is that failure to prove truth implies falsity. There is nothing in the knowledge base that allows us to explicitly conclude that Holly is not a hobbit — i.e. no instance or possibility of deducing NOT (HOBBIT HOLLY).

Under the same rules the queries (WIZARD GANDALF) and (BAD-GUYS GOBLINS) would turn out to be false. And we know that they are true, at least in Middle-earth — and there is the crux of the problem. As Levesque (1984) says "the user of the knowledge base must distinguish between what is known by the knowledge base and what is true in the intended application area." Knowledge bases tend to be incomplete: i.e. they do not have all the information necessary to answer a query.

Incompleteness of knowledge bases is a property that we must be able to cope with in the ill-defined and dynamic domains of AI. A common way to deal with this incompleteness problem is to usethe so-called Closed World Assumption: the knowledge base is assumed to know everything about its world and thus if it doesn't know that something is true, then that something is false.

Unfortunately, this straightforward solution to the incompleteness problem is not very satisfactory in some AI applications; the system needs to know about what it doesn't know (as a guide to knowledge acquisition, for example) as distinct from knowing that certain things are false.

Here we see again a need for meta-knowledge arising. As usual special-purpose heuristics have been the route to dealing with this general problem. Collins, Warnock, Aiello, & Miller (1975) describe a selection of such strategies and illustrate their choices with SCHOLAR (Carbonell, 1970), the geography tutoring system that I used as an earlier example.

The beginnings of a generalized and formal approach to these problems of incomplete knowledge bases has been described by Levesque (1984). He is developing a formal language within which one can query a knowledge base as to what it knows and does not know. Thus in our earlier example the meta-level query:

Do you know that Holly is a Hobbit?

would be answered,

I do not know that Holly is a Hobbit.

(i.e. neither (HOBBIT HOLLY) nor NOT(HOBBIT HOLLY) can be proven within the current knowledge base)

I should emphasize that, although Levesque's work is a promising approach to the possibility for formalizing meta-knowledge, it is ongoing research and a number of important problems must be solved before it can become a practically useful technique.

When we add the knowledge base processing algorithms to the representation structure then we have the core of the implementation aspect of knowledge engineering (of course, it is not really possible to try to separate the algorithm from the data structures; certain aspects of the former define the latter). If we take most of the vagaries and ill-structure of everyday life out of the picture we are left with realistic and serious but potentially tractable AI problems. These problems are the grist for the expert system mill. They are also some of the best candidates for AI in software engineering, so we might be well advised to spend some more time on the practical feasibility and potential scope and limitations of a scheme for packaging general intelligence into small, self-contained, highly-limited intelligent chunks.

## 3.12   IS INTELLIGENCE NEARLY DECOMPOSABLE?

As mentioned earlier in our discussion of the importance of modular hierarchies for the management of complexity, Simon (1962) suggested that complex systems must be nearly decomposable or else they will be beyond human comprehension. Near decomposability is a property that enables a complex system to be broken down into (and thus comprehended in terms of) smaller, relatively self-contained subsystems.

How about intelligence: can we break off pieces and put them in boxes, such that each box contains a high-level, intelligent expert in some very narrow domain? Yes, a number of implemented expert systems constitute an existence proof of that, or do they?

Imagine for a moment an expert caretaker. Can this gentleman attain the dizzy heights of his chosen vocation purely on the basis of everything that there is to know about cleaning techniques? Can he know enough about cleaning techniques in isolation to do an expert job? Or would he necessarily need to understand the intended purposes of the objects, rooms, and building, as conceived by the people who use them? Should a particularly grubby object be cleaned, thrown away, or just left alone? It might be a piece of coffee-stained notepaper or a treasured personal memento belonging to the executive vice-president.

Perhaps an expert caretaker has to know a lot of things about people: their hopes, fears, ambitions, and personal idiosyncrasies. It is still an open question. What we do know is that even a very limited, low level of general intelligence is exceedingly useful in countless niches of society. In the next few years we expect to see AI successfully invade these niches. The unknown factor is the longer-term potential for incrementally upgrading specialized expertise. We just don't know the scope and limitations of highly specialized intelligence, the eventual possibilities for domain-specific expertise.

Is intelligence like a car windscreen or a hologram, objects that can be fragmented such that each small piece retains many of the properties of the whole? Or is it more like a cross between a lump of toffee and an atomic bomb? A curious hybrid that would be perhaps difficult to neatly fragment. In addition, a detached piece is liable to be lacking in critical properties of the whole — in particular, the property of intelligence.

That is to say, high level, general intelligence might be a critical muddle phenomenon: it might emerge only from a sufficiently large and inter-tangled knowledge base. Sufficiency in this respect might be orders of magnitude larger and more highly interconnected than the knowledge bases that we are striving to master today. Let's hope not. If the size and complexity of knowledge bases increase exponentially with the level of expertise exhibited by then; then we're in trouble.

Fig. 3.1 illustrates some possible relationships between the level of expertise exhibited by expert systems and the size and complexity of the necessary knowledge base. From a to c we go from the expert system builder's dream to his nightmare. Line b represents a function that is perhaps the best realistic hope: knowledge bases will steadily increase in size and complexity as the level of expertise of the system increases, but not exponentially.

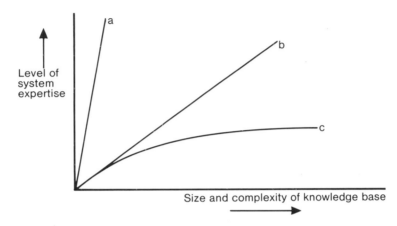

Fig. 3.1 — Some possible extrapolations of the expert systems phenomenon

In his exposition of the role of computers in basic education Papert (1980) expounds a reinterpretation of a Piaget theory; the new version is called the "society-of-mind" theory. Fundamental to this theory is the principle of the epistemological modularity of intelligence — it assumes that intelligence is compounded from the chaos and controversy of independent competing agents.

Perhaps general intelligence can be readily broken into small chunks ("mind-size bites" Papert calls them), and these chunks will still exhibit a high level of intelligence within more limited domains. We just have to find the right logical hammer. General intelligence is a species of Meccano (it certainly predates Lego). It can be constructed by bolting together a wide range of self-contained, specialized intelligence modules. It won't be that easy but let's hope that we're at least approximately correct.

Fodor (1983) in his book, *The Modularity of Mind*, has argued for the existence of "informationally encapsulated" modules in human intelligence. He argues that there is no compelling evidence for non-modularity despite the many claims to the contrary. A major thesis of the work is that input systems (such as mechanisms of visual perception) are modular in a sense that central cognitive processes (such as belief systems) are not, and further he claims that: "the limits of modularity are also likely to be the limits of what we are going to be able to understand about the mind."

From our current perspective the implications are that intelligence may, or may not, be nearly decomposable or modular. And the extent to which it is representable as a nearly decomposable structure is expected to have an important bearing on whether AI in general will be possible in the form of an understandable and thus maintainable system. Of more immediate consequence is the implication for the possibility of constructing modules that exhibit specialized, intelligent behaviour — i.e. the future of expert systems, as mentioned earlier.

### 3.13   CAN WE HAVE INTELLIGENCE WITHOUT LEARNING

Learning comes in many flavours: from being told a new fact explicitly to deducing some hitherto unrecognized abstract relationship. In terms of the system that does the learning, it may just store a new specific fact or it may integrate into its knowledge a newly discovered abstract concept. The result of learning will be an adaptation of behaviour, generally a change for the better.

Given the ill-structured nature of the empirical world and the unforeseeable perturbations that will beset any system which is attempting to behave intelligently, self-adaptation or automatic learning is highly desirable if not a necessity. Adaptive behaviour, from the plant that seeks the light to the parents who raise children, is characteristic of all living organisms. The level and sophistication of adaptive behaviour is a useful index of level of intelligence.

Consider the lowly bean randomly falling into the proverbial stony ground. Using this adaptability measure, the average bean seeking up and down for leaves and roots, and negotiating awkwardly placed pebbles has far more intelligence than any AI program yet constructed. Clearly adaptive behaviour is not the whole story. Equally clearly it is one fundamental characteristic of intelligence, and one that I shall later develop as critical with respect to the potential of commercial AI.

Every software engineer is fully aware of the following injunction: self-modifying code is to be avoided like the plague — a ground rule in the creed of their craft. So we must proceed with the utmost caution.

### 3.14   AI AND LEARNING

Does a useful AI system have to learn? The answer is, no. A number of non-adaptive, useful AI systems are extant to buttress this answer. Nevertheless it is not clear just how far this embryonic movement, the AI invasion of software engineering, can progress and yet eschew the use of self-adaptive mechanisms. And conversely, it is not clear how far the prime goals of software engineering can be met if self-adaptive mechanisms are utilized — a Catch-22 situation.

In addition, Michalski, Carbonell & Mitchell (1983), in their book called *Machine Learning*, argue that machine learning is a practical necessity. It is necessary "to ease the burden of hand-programming growing volumes of increasingly complex information," they say.

As stated earlier, there are a number of varieties of machine learning and they differ in the degree to which they can be readily controlled. At this point our task is to chart the history of their use in classical AI, and to point out the implications for practical software.

Landmarks and a few particularly illustrative studies are specifically mentioned, but for an exhaustive listing of projects the reader is referred via the bibliography to the relevant published collections. In addition, the categories of mechanisms given below are meant to provide some structure in a somewhat amorphous subfield of AI. They are just convenient hooks upon which to hang the discussion — not mutually exclusive compartments into one of which each project can be correctly stored.

Arthur Samuel's (1963) checker-playing program provides an early milestone in machine learning. As we have already described, this program achieved significant practical successes that were based upon its ability to improve its performance as a result of experience. There were many versions of the program and a number of learning strategies were tried and evaluated. Samuel employed both rote learning of board positions with their associated worth, and a scheme that attempted to select and assign relative weights to a set of the important game description features.

### 3.14.1   If it might be useful, learn it

Rote learning has always been an attractive route to the mechanization of adaptive behaviours. To begin with, it is easy to implement. Just store every new experience, and it works well given the large memories and fast, perfect retrieval typical of computer systems. It also has the important practical advantage that the resultant self-modification can be limited and localized. Hence it is a learning strategy that offers the best possibility with respect to comprehensibility and thus controllability of the overall system.

Unfortunately, the performance of a mechanism based upon blind rote learning is soon swamped by the masses of learned data that result. All available storage is eaten up at a prodigious rate and the system spends most of its time sifting through an ocean of irrelevancies looking for pertinent information: disturbingly reminiscent of the needle-in-the-haystack routine (an all-too-frequently recurring situation in AI, one that is usually overcome by a few well-engineered but highly domain-specific heuristics).

Two possibilities suggest themselves: selective storage and organization for efficient retrieval; and storage of generalized information, one general principle rather than many facts.

Our expert caretaker, when new to the job, had to learn where all of the fuse boxes were. He could memorize the facts: in room 100 it was behind the door, in room 200 it was behind the door, etc. Alternatively he could learn the general principle that the fuse box is always behind the door of the X00 room for each floor X.

There may be a space–time trade-off here between these two learning strategies. If he wants to know where the fuse box is on floor 4, he can, if his learned facts are indexed by floor number, immediately retrieve the relevant fact. But if he uses the latter strategy then actual storage space is less but more time is required to generate the necessary fact from the general principle in conjunction with the particular requirement, 4th floor.

This example also serves to introduce a perennial AI debate: the procedural–declarative controversy. Should the machinery of intelligence be represented as factual information (declarative) or as procedures for generating those facts (procedural). This question used to generate a lot of steam and finally enough light to show that the answer depends upon the context and constraints of each particular case.

To return to our caretaker: if he opted for storing the general principle about fuse box location, how did he come by it in the first place? For the rote learning scheme, the facts are given and just have to be stored. But the general principle is not given anywhere; it is in some sense implicit in the set of facts.

### 3.14.2  Learning general principles

There are two major strategies for the machine learning of such general principles: guess a general principle and then limit it according to subsequent instances of counter-examples, or make the first instance the general principle and generalize it according to the subsequent examples encountered. Both strategies have been used for machine learning in AI, and have been recently discussed in Bundy & Silver (1982). This survey is limited to the learning of rules of the form:

H1 and H2 and ... Hn → Conclusion

i.e. that a set of hypotheses (the H's) imply a certain conclusion. For example,

(a polygon) and (four sides) and (Christmas Day) → a square

is one such rule, and although not quite perfect it may be improved by each of the two major strategies, as we shall see.

#### 3.14.2.1  Over-generalization and refinement

The discrimination process, as an approach to learning requires that we first have available a general principle. This first guess may either be generated heuristically from a given instance or fact, or it may be supplied by some outside agent.

With the first approach our caretaker has to come up with a potential general principle about fuse box location when he finds the first fuse box behind the door of room 100. How is he going to do this?

He must generate a sufficiently broad principle; one that can be modified in the light of subsequent failures to find fuse boxes. It must be such that it will converge to a principle enabling him to predict adequately where fuse boxes will be.

So what is his first attempt at this principle? He finds a first fuse box: fuse boxes are found on walls. Looking around the room at the other walls which do not have fuse boxes, he refines his principle: fuse boxes are found on one wall of a room. An inspection of all other rooms on this floor leads him to the further refinement: fuse boxes are found on one wall of one room. Subsequent inspection of other rooms on other floors might well finally lead him to the general principle given earlier. That seems easy enough, and a recent study by Langley (1983) is an example of machine learning using such a scheme.

The crucial information here is knowing what are the important similarities between any two instances of finding a fusebox, and what are the important differences between instances of finding and instances of not finding fuse boxes. The similarities and differences are in fact endless, but only very few of them are relevant to the process of refining the principle. How do we know which are the important dimensions?

The caretaker's first attempt at the rule might have been: fuse boxes are found on Thursdays. A few minutes later he looks into the next room, no fuse box, ah: fuse boxes are found on Thursday afternoons at 3 o'clock, and so on. He may eventually exclude some or all of these irrelevant constraints, but will he ever find a useful general principle?

The foregoing smacks of the absurd, but remember we are going to apply these strategies in a computer, not just explain them to a fellow human being. The reason that we find these suggestions unreal is because we know that the location of fuse boxes is invariant with respect to the day of the week and the time of day; computers don't know that. We have an enormous fund of general knowledge to draw upon; no computer system yet constructed has more than a very small fraction of our general knowledge.

Returning to the earlier rule that aspires to define a square, it is obviously too general: not all four-sided polygons are squares even on Christmas Day. If we present our learning machine with a rectangle on Christmas Day and tell it that this is not a square, we have provided a non-example that the machine may use to refine its rule.

The crux of this refinement process is to notice that the attributes of the non-example presented differ from the rule's hypotheses by the fact that its sides are not all equal in length. Hence we add a further condition to the rule's hypotheses. The new rule is:

(a polygon)and(four sides)and(Christmas Day)and(all sides equal) → a square

If the machine had computed the essential difference to be a question of angles the resultant extra hypothesis might have been: (all angles not equal). This is not a disastrous mistake as further examples could be used to eliminate this wrong step (the questions of unlearning mistakes and imperfect learning in general are both considered later), but, at the same time, it is not much help.

If the machine learning algorithm had settled on the thickness of the rectangle's sides as the significant attribute, again the resultant rule would be worse rather than better. The machine must be able to select the appropriate attributes of the learning examples presented.

Typically, machine learning algorithms do not cope with the actual examples but only with abstract descriptions of these examples. Winston's (1975) famous arch-learning program, for example, was never exposed to actual arches made out of blocks, but only to descriptions of arches. And of course in a description one can omit the inappropriate attributes.

Here we see another specific example of the discontinuity between the problems faced by a system that functions in an abstract domain and one that must work with the real world as it is — abstract AI and concrete AI, they are worlds apart (a regularly recurring theme of this book, you will find). The difference that I am stressing is the difference between searching for needles in haystacks with, and without, the haystack — the latter version is difficult but the former is perilously close to impossible.

Successful machine learning requires: first, that we tell the computer exactly which dimensions of the problem are the important ones; and second, that the difference between the current approximation to the rule and each learning example (or non-example) is small (this idea of 'near misses' is discussed in the following chapter).

### 3.14.2.2  A first guess and generalization
In this, the reverse approach the system starts with a fairly specific rule and then removes restrictions in the light of subsequent examples.

Using this strategy our caretaker, on finding the first instance of a fuse box, might generate the following tentative rule: fuse boxes are found behind the blue door of room 100. When he later stumbles onto another fuse box behind the green door of room 200, he has found an example that his rule does not cover. Some modification of the rule is called for. The resultant more general rule is: fuse boxes are found behind the blue door of room 100 and behind the green door of room 200.

Clearly this strategy is going to lead to a general rule that is little more than an enumeration of the set of instances encountered. The secret here is to reduce a set of instances to a more concise general rule; we require a mechanism for inductive generalization.

The collection of specific room numbers (100, 200, etc.) should be reduced to something like 'room $x00$, where $1 \leq x \leq$ number of floors in building'. And the set of door colours should be abandoned as non-significant. Again we might ask, how did he know that door colour was a non-significant attribute of his rule? Well, he noticed that there was no regularity in the set of door colours amassed. That might be an answer, but consider how you would specify 'regularity' in general terms and algorithmically? Therein lies the problem.

Appropriate generalization of the set of room numbers is no easier a problem, but some inductive generalization algorithms have been successfully applied to certain specific problems. Quinlan (1982) surveys a few inductive generalization schemes and describes his own system in some detail. He stresses that the success of current systems is dependent upon describing the instances of the rule by appropriate attributes (i.e. room number rather than time of day for fuse box location). And he goes on to say that the much harder problem of automatically developing good attributes (called 'constructive induction') is a problem that will dominate inductive inference research in the 1980s.

Our rule that 'defines' a square is also too specific. A further example of a square on say New Year's Day could be used to motivate the necessary generalization, or could it? The modified rule might be:

(a polygon)and(four sides)and((Christmas Day)or(New Year's Day)) → a square

Again we have much the same problem (except that this time it is finite; there are only 365 different days). As an alternative to the very difficult problem of a widely applicable inductive generalization algorithm, we might use a human tutor to explicitly provide some guidance to the learning machine. There is no requirement that the machine must 'go it alone' — humans certainly don't.

Another weakness of some of these general techniques is that they rely critically on both the ordering and the choice of examples. Nevertheless, AI systems that can automatically assimilate knowledge only as a result of the ministrations of a benevolent human tutor could still be of inestimable practical value (and perhaps more readily controlled and understood just because they are externally driven).

On the other hand external tutoring puts a considerable burden on the human tutor. In fact we are beginning to see a revival of interest in more sophisticated machine learning initiated by expert systems' builders, just because this burden is becoming intolerable.

Bundy & Silver (1982) warn us that neither of these two general strategies is complete in itself (i.e. we cannot know if we have arrived at the optimal rule), we need to apply both strategies (they suggest generalization before discrimination) to be sure of arriving at the best rule.

### 3.14.3 Learning by being told

Given that AI programs tend to be both large and lacking in simple general principles, machine learning must be treated with circumspection. If learning is initiated and controlled by user interaction, then we have the best chance of maintaining control of the resultant beast. This type of scheme can also be the easiest to implement, because much of the burden remains with the human tutor.

As we shall see later, the development of an AI program is necessarily an incremental process. Learning by being told, or 'advice' taking as it is sometimes called, is a potentially very useful way of automating some aspects of this incremental development. It can thus play a lead role in system development rather than be just an inessential member of the supporting cast.

Of particular interest in this respect is the process of expert system development. An incremental process of feedback and evaluation is used to refine and extend expert system knowledge. The two essential parties are the human expert, with advice to give, and his mechanized counterpart, with advice to be woven into its current knowledge base. It is, of course, highly unlikely that these two potential communicators share a common language. So a computer expert or 'knowledge engineer' is also required as a go-between; his humanness ensures a degree of communication with the human expert, and the actual system is his baby which ensures that he can communicate with it, if anybody can.

The TEIRESIAS project (Davis & Lenat, 1982) is an attempt to shorten this chain of command and thereby allow direct human expert — computerized expert conferences (which incidentally releases the computer science expert, a scarce resource). Davis' system interfaces between a human physician and the expert medical system MYCIN.

One of the interesting aspects of TEIRESIAS is that it seizes command of the dialogue whenever possible; this all-too-human trait has several advantages even for a computer. In particular it both simplifies the natural language interface by leading the human responses into areas of very limited probability, and tries to ensure that advice is given at the level and in the sort of chunks that it can most easily digest.

Once again we must wait for time, the great leveller, to let us know if TEIRESIAS really heralds a wave of knowledge engineers on the dole, or whether the time and effort needed to tune a TEIRESIAS for each particular expert system will just increase their scarcity value.

In principle, it is true, a generalized TEIRESIAS need only be constructed once. In the last chapter I shall describe a generalization of this concept — a complete life-cycle environment — that can, I believe, play a crucial role in the further progress of AI as practical software.

### 3.14.4   Learning by introspection
This category of machine learning refers to the possibility of generating new ideas from old. That is to say, whilst cycling home after a busy night taking care of his office block the caretaker might ruminate upon his current stock of job-related knowledge — a sort of mental chewing of the cud, masticating observations, plans both successful and unsuccessful, stored facts, etc.

What is the upshot of all these mental gymnastics, you might well ask? The diverse products will be general rules, new concepts, new plans, and improved problem solving strategies — a bountiful harvest.

So let's get our AI to do some of this in its slack periods, if not in parallel while it is working flat out. And indeed there are a number of lines of AI research that have, and are still, investigating this brand of machine learning.

Over ten years ago (Partridge, 1975) this technique of machine learning was successfully employed within an adaptive FORTRAN translator. The translator contained an AI module that periodically surveyed the results of the prior parsing session and then re-organized its knowledge base. One of the tasks of this module was to remove unwanted generalization by finding the most frequently used particular instances of a general rule and promoting them to positions of higher precedence than the general rule itself.

The system learned to expect the idiosyncrasies of a given operating environment. The resulting behavioural changes were both an increase in general efficiency and an increase in quality of error correction.

Working with introspection in the opposite direction, that is, from particular instances to a general rule, is more difficult. Inductive generalization falls into this category.

A particularly interesting application of this technique is described by Michie (1983). He considers the possibility of constructing an expert system backwards because it's easier that way. An expert system can be thought of as a function from the input problem space to the expert solution space. This forward transformation is typically difficult, but sometimes the reverse transformation, the inverse function, from a given solution to the problem that would have generated it, is easily computable.

So if we can generate the space of solutions we do so, and store each one away with its easily computed problem. This bunch of solution–problem pairs is then used in the forward direction. It is an expert system.

But as you may have guessed, there's a snag. Our expert system is going to be impractically large. So Michie suggests that we loose an inductive generalization algorithm on our masses of problem–solution pairs and thereby reduce this unwieldy conglomeration to a manageable number of general rules.

An inductive algorithm identifies and extracts the significant commonalities exhibited by a set of instances (and perhaps lacking in a set of non-instances). The set of instances is then replaced by the resulting general principle.

After observing the daily milk delivery for a few weeks, the expert housewife will inductively generate the following general principle: milk is most likely to be delivered between 7:30 and 8:00 a.m. except when its raining, in which case it arrives half an hour later. This general principle is the result of a very discriminating induction process: first, it fixes on the time of delivery rather than the innumerable non-significant characteristics (e.g. the grouping of bottles on the doorstep); and second, it singles out rain as the factor that is predictive of the exceptional late deliveries, not the colour of his cap nor the snowfall on the Grampians (both of which may have a better correlation with his late deliveries).

Of course, the reason for her apt generalization is that our expert used her vast general knowledge base together with the fact that time was important to her (assuming she didn't cheat and asked him why he was late), and equally obviously our program won't have as much general knowledge although it could have appropriate goals. So once again, in the absence of mechanisms capable of identifying the significant features of sensory experience, we must specify the significant features upon which to inductively generalize.

A non-trivial learning device, human or machine, must have a complex goal structure, both immediate goals and long-term goals. It is this set of goals in conjunction with stored knowledge that singles out a very few aspects of sensory experience as significant events — events that should be given special attention in order to improve performance as a result of experience.

In the development of an expert system for soybean disease diagnosis, Michalski & Chilausky (1980) inductively derived the diagnostic rules from a collection of instances of symptoms and the diagnosed disease.

To the delight of most observers (excepting expert soybean disease taxonomists) the system using the inductively generated rules was more accurate than a system using the official rules of soybean disease taxonomy. This leads us a little aside, but field trials (excuse the pun) in AI are somewhat scarce events so we should make the most of the ones we have.

There are two points here: first, Michie's scheme is shown to be practically viable; and second, human expertise should be extracted in the form of specific examples not general rules. The moral is: take a human expert's rule with a pinch of salt (or whatever is your personal preference), but whatever you do with it don't cast it in concrete in your program without an independent evaluation.

### 3.14.5 Unlearning mistakes

Non-trivial learning in an ill-structured domain, such as the empirical world, cannot always be correct. The learning system will need the ability to unlearn the things that were incorrectly learned. This is an awkward problem for a number of reasons:

(a) The fact (more likely, suspicion) that something erroneous has been learned need not be apparent until long after the actual learning event.
(b) Even if we are sure that some learned behaviour is incorrect, correct identification of the culprit component(s) in a complex structure can be a very difficult problem — in effect, the credit assignment problem once more.
(c) Having identified the incorrectly learned feature, we must remove its adverse effects without destroying the complete structure that it might be embedded in.

Hayes-Roth, Waterman, & Lenat (1983) suggest and give examples of the use of meta-knowledge (knowledge about the domain-specific knowledge of their expert systems) for identifying incorrect rules learned from an expert. The system's meta- knowledge brings suspicious rules (such as ones in which the antecedent condition can never be satisfied) to the attention of the knowledge engineer. If the knowledge base is truely a modular collection of such rules, then removal or modification of the erroneous piece of knowledge is a relatively simple process.

This example raises two points that we should note:

(1) Modularity (a feature that I shall labour in Chapter 6) is a key aspect of manageable AI software.
(2) Meta-knowledge (a topic that I shall pursue in Chapter 7) is essential for the effective control of non-trivial machine learning.

Langley (1983) simplifies the above-listed three problems of 'unlearning' by setting up his system such that the correctness of a proposed addition will be known immediately, and it can thus be removed if it is incorrect. But, in general, we cannot expect situations with the luxury of immediate assessment.

It is instructive to examine what we know of the human solution to this unlearning problem. A first point to note is that humans are not particularly good at one-trial learning — we generally require repetition before we learn something. This is a difference between humans and machines that is often touted as part of an argument that computers can be eventually expected to surpass humans in intelligent abilities. But from our current viewpoint there may be an advantage in resistance to one-trial learning: if before we learn it, we require a certain number of repetitions of an event, then there is a chance to assess its correctness before a full commitment to learn it is made.

Studies of skill acquisition definitely suggest a two-stage learning process. In the first stage we tentatively learn a new skill, and only when this tentative learning is confirmed as correct by repeated use is the skill knowledge 'compiled' into a more efficient, but less modifiable, form. Anderson (1982) proposes such a model of skill learning: "a declarative stage in which facts about the skill domain are interpreted and a procedural stage in which domain knowledge is directly embodied in procedures for performing the skill."

The analogy with the trade-offs between interpreting and compiling computer programs is obvious and instructive.

To finish the section on machine learning, still properly under the rubric of learning by introspection, let us briefly look at an exciting development even though probably the least practical (in terms of immediate application in practical software).

### 3.14.6  Mechanized creativity

The expert housewife faced with the problem of getting her milk delivered earlier in the morning might cogitate on a variety of potential solutions: persuade the milkman to change his route; move to a house closer to the beginning of the street, etc.

But as a result of the normal social intercourse with neighbouring experts on a variety of subjects unrelated to milk delivery times, she may incidentally be informed that the milkman is induced to partake of a cup of tea every morning at a certain location. If this place of habitual refreshment is such that it encroaches upon delivery time prior to our subject's delivery then she might, with some insight, modify her delivery principle: the milk is most likely to be delivered between 7:30 and 8:00 a.m. rather than between 7:00 and 7:30 a.m. because of the refreshment stop at location X, etc.

This creative modification of the milk delivery principle may now provide a basis for a simple solution to the above-described milk delivery time problem (this is left as an exercise for the reader — exclude the possibility of putting out a contract on the tea maker at location X).

AI, as is appropriate for preliminary studies, has so far concentrated on mechanized discovery within the much more restricted and well-structured domains of mathematics and classical chemistry. The housewife's flash of minor creativity is currently too tough a nut to crack.

Human versus machine creativity is a fascinating and usually provocative subject, typically engendering copious amounts of heat and sometimes a little light. So rather than venture into this super-calorific domain, let us do little more than just observe that active investigation of the possibilities for mechanized discovery of new and unanticipated principles (as opposed to the relatively expected and foreseen results of inductive generalization) is well under way in AI.

This is important because of the general importance of machine learning, and it is perhaps dangerous because of its very nature: the results are, almost by definition, unexpected. This does not mean that they might not be extremely useful. What it might mean is that we must be apprised of each discovery and investigate its scope and limitations before we turn it loose within an application program.

So much for machine learning. Clearly there is a lot of scope for practical potential. There are definite areas of light and even a very few and limited practical applications. But in self-modifying systems, as every software engineer knows, there is also a lot of scope for disaster.

To utilize AI fully in software engineering we must trample the strictures against self-modifying code, but to do so successfully we must be fully cognizant of, and thus comprehensively guard against, the dangers. A decade and a half of admission of the software crisis has not sufficed to eliminate it, but let's not charge into a super software crisis by blindly bringing in the obvious benefits of AI without sufficient safeguards to minimize the equally obvious (although not so publicized) drawbacks.

**Bibliography for Chapter 3**

**Setting the scene**
McCorduck, P., (1979), *Machines Who Think*, Freeman: San Francisco.
— the secret history of artificial intelligence
— a fascinating study mostly straight from the scientists' mouths
— the reader might detect a certain bias toward the home territory, but that's to be expected

Boden, M.A., (1977), *Artificial Intelligence and Natural Man*, Basic Books: NY.
— a refreshingly new look from an (at the time) outside observer, based upon detailed studies of a number of important programs

Hofstadter, D. R., (1979), *Gödel, Escher, Bach: an eternal golden braid*, Basic Books: NY.
— the best AI book ever!
— a multilevel extravaganza on minds and machines (and many other things)
— thought provoking and droll investigations of all aspects of AI

Simon, H. A., (1969), *The Sciences of the Artificial*, MIT Press: Cambridge, Mass.
— a small but stimulating collection of lectures given by a pillar of the AI establishment

## The faithful
The first three works cover the U.S. establishment (MIT, Stanford, and CMU) view of AI, the fourth will give the reader a broader view and serve to introduce areas that we have not touched upon, such as brain modelling, and the fifth is the young pretender to the throne of 'standard introduction to AI'.

Raphael, B., (1976), *The Thinking Computer*, Freeman: San Francisco.
— an exposition of AIs major subfields that attempts to tread the middle ground between superficiality and technical detail

Winston, P. H., (1977, 1984 2nd edn.), *Artificial Intelligence*, Addison-Wesley: Reading, Mass.
— an introductory AI textbook
— covers the famous AI programs and their mechanisms in some detail

Nilsson, N. J., (1980), *The Principles of Artificial Intelligence*, Tioga: Palo Alto, CA.
— a detailed exposition of the technical principles of searching and structuring that have been developed in AI; such principles can be viewed as one, if not the, major contribution of AI to scientific knowledge
— but not much more than his earlier book *Problem Solving Methods in Artificial Intelligence*, McGraw-Hill: NY, 1971

Jackson, P. C., (1974), *Introduction to Artificial Intelligence*, Petrocelli: NY.
— the first (and last) attempt to cover all approaches to AI; it has a pleasing breadth but a (perhaps inevitable) lack depth

Charniak, E., & McDermott, D., (1985), *Introduction to Artificial Intelligence*, Addison-Wesley: Reading, Mass.
— probably the next standard introduction to the field
— firmly grounded in 'the old school' but moves across to fit into the 'new wave' with its attempt to use knowledge representation as the basis for a unifield theory

## The unfaithful
You ought to read some of the detractors, it compensates for the traditional oversell of the faithful.

Dreyfus, H. L., (1972), *What Computers Can't Do*, Harper & Row: NY.
— fundamentally wrong, I think, nevertheless, it is the standard work and contains a lot of good stuff but also a lot of flaws, should be tempered with Pylyshyn, Z. W. (1975) *Cognition* 3, (1), pp. 57-77.
— the second edition, 1979, was much better.

Weizenbaum, J., (1976), *Computer Power and Human Reason*, Freeman: San Francisco.
— a social argument on the lines of what AI researchers should not do
— not as clear-cut a question as Weizenbaum tries to make it, nevertheless ethical and moral questions in AI are important today and likely to become more so in the future

McDermott, D., (1976), Artificial Intelligence Meets Natural Stupidity, *SIGART Newsletter* No. 57, (April), pp. 4–9.
— a severe criticism of AI oversell and the PhD-driven research machine that accounts for most of it


**The new wave**
Since DENDRAL, the unwanted step-child of AI, has been accorded the role of guiding star, expert systems and knowledge representation are where it's all at.

Barr, A., & Feigenbaum, E. A., (1981–1982), *The Handbook of Artificial Intelligence*, Kaufmann: CA. Vols. I, II, and III (edited by Cohen, P. R. in place of Barr).
— a bid for the standard reference work in AI, and it does a good job except that it spares space for neither the biological and neurophysiological beginnings nor the on-going research that falls outside the heuristic programming approach

Davis, R., & Lenat, D. B., (1982), *Knowledge-Based Systems in Artificial Intelligence*, McGraw-Hill: NY.
— it should have been entitled "Two Knowledge-Based Systems..."
— it is divided between TEIRESIAS and AM, but there's lots on those two if that's what you want

Hayes-Roth, F., Waterman, D. A., & Lenat, D. B., (1983), *Building Expert Systems*, Addison-Wesley: Reading, Mass.
— a useful attempt to abstract from the plague of particular expert systems in order to convey general structure and principles, and describe software that is aimed at facilitating the construction of future computerized experts.

Michie, D., (1982) editor, Introductory Readings in Expert Systems, Gordon & Breach: London.
— more of a Euro-view of expert systems
— a small, but broad collection of articles aimed at introducing the technical, non-specialist to this field


**Machine learning**
Samuel, A., (1963), Some Studies in Machine Learning Using the Game of Checkers, in *Computers and Thought*, Feigenbaum, E. A., and Feldman, J. (eds), McGraw-Hill: NY, pp. 71-105.
— both rote and parameter learning, a great study years ahead of its time

— a study containing detailed empirical results: a paradigm that has unfortunately not endured
— the anthology, *Computers and Thought*, is itself rich ground for the artificial intelligence archaeologist

Nilsson, N. J., (1965), *Learning Machines*, McGraw-Hill: NY.
— a detailed mathematical treatment of machines that can be trained to classify patterns

Michalski, R. S., Carbonell, J. G., & Mitchell, T. M., (1983), *Machine Learning*, vols. I and II (1986), Kaufman: Los Altos, CA.
— up-to-date description of a number of significant projects
— contains a large bibliography on machine learning

Bundy, A., & Silver, B., (1982), A critical survey of rule learning programs, *Procs. of ECAI*, pp. 151–157.
— contains a detailed analysis and comparison of generalization and discrimination machine learning strategies

# 4

# The program development methodology of AI

If you don't know where you're going with a pile of code, it is hardly surprising that the resultant program is not a model of structured programming.

"AI is certainly in a methodological mess" (Bundy, 1983). That is a sentiment that I heartily endorse but now I plan to do something about it.

It can be argued that it is too early to try to sort out the mess: AI is too new and we don't yet have any reasonable perspective. According to Kuhn's (1962) analysis of scientific endeavours, thrashing around in an incompletely understood area is a necessary prerequisite for a scientific revolution, a paradigm shift, that will resolve the mess with the establishment of a new general paradigm. With the emergence of such a paradigm we shall be left with the tidying-up, the puzzle-solving activity of normal science.

Later in this book I shall argue that the time is becoming ripe for the establishment of a paradigm to support the research and development of AI programs as practical software; clearly I believe that such a paradigm does not yet exist.

But our task in this chapter is less ambitious: I wish first to outline and justify a minimally-contentious AI program development paradigm — again as framework of reference for subsequent discussion.

There is of course already a very rough paradigm that covers the field of AI; it is the run–debug–edit cycle, or "construct-and-test" (Newell & Simon, 1976). The above-mentioned mess is due both to the roughness of this paradigm and to the lack of accepted justification for it.

Within this chapter and the following one, I attempt to develop and refine both the AI program development paradigm and its context — its interface with the rest of computer science, in particular, with software engineering. This refinement and analysis will serve to highlight and pin down the essential points of conflict between AI and software engineering. Leaving us in the last four chapters with a set of fairly clear problems to discuss.

AI and thus the term 'AI program', covers a wide range of projects. An AI program may be a program that utilizes techniques developed in the AI domain. Heuristic search strategies are, for example, one such group of AI techniques. An AI program may be a model, at some level, of a postulated mechanism for a certain aspect of intelligent behaviour. Programs that emulate and perhaps surpass the human performance of a task that is usually considered to require intelligence are also AI programs.

I shall not venture into the murky waters of defining AI programs — it is an ill-structured concept. It is also a topical question due to the fact that it is currently both avant garde and lucrative to be in the business of AI software.

I shall approach this problem from the standpoint of those programs that must be developed using the run–debug–edit cycle to be articulated in this chapter. In other words I shall focus on those AI programs that must be incrementally developed with a machine-executable notation. I view this as a sufficiency characteristic of AI programs rather than a necessary one: some classes of AI programs can be developed largely within the conventional software engineering program development paradigm.

As discussed in Chapter 1, the inevitable increase in our understanding of this latter class of AI problems will lead to a steady expansion of the class itself. But as also argued in Chapter 1 it is difficult to see how this expansion could ever engulf all AI problems, and the residual set will contain many pressing, practical problems.

There is no generally accepted set of detailed techniques for the development of AI programs. Two extreme methodologies can be contrasted: the conventional software engineering approach to the implementation of a formalized subproblem, and the direct code-manipulation approach to obtain input–output adequacy for an ISF — the run–debug–edit cycle. I shall concentrate on, and further articulate, this latter methodology.

Consider, for example, the problem of a natural language interface to a data base. We can select a fixed and finite set of possible queries. This subset constitutes our formalized subproblem, and the process of design and implementation becomes one of generating an efficient and correct procedure for accepting the specified subset.

But if we really want a natural language interface, one approaching the sophistication of you and me, then we must move to the more dynamic paradigm. We certainly start out by selecting a subset of useful queries, but then we explore their operational adequacy knowing full well that the necessary relaxation and imposition of restrictions might eventually take us anywhere. Notice also that the restrictions will not necessarily be rigid limitations on either the size or structure of acceptable queries if machine learning is a possibility. For we humans clearly have in-built limitations with respect to the set of queries that we can handle, but our limitations are neither simple superficial ones (such as a limit on the number of adjectives of say, colour), nor are they rigidly fixed except at the deeper levels involving speed and memory size.

I shall argue that incremental, code-modification is the fundamental paradigm of AI, not because of any failure to appreciate the hard-won lessons of software engineering, but because it is the best way to tackle a rather different class of problems. This incremental development paradigm, often denigrated as speculative code hacking, can be justified as performance-driven evolution of a machine-executable, tentative problem specification.

As an example of an AI problem consider the high-level design of Fig. 4.1. This chart (it is a non-terminating control loop, complicated by the

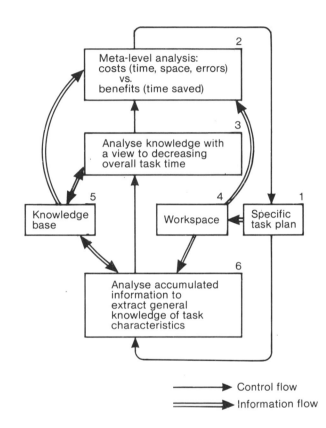

Fig. 4.1 — A high-level design for a cognitive industrial robot

addition of some information-flow paths) specifies the operating procedures for a cognitive industrial robot; that is, an industrial robot that repeatedly performs some prespecified task (box 1: an example task is the pick-up-and-place task described in Fig. 2.3), and in addition it collects performance information, adapts to its particular task configuration, and generally attempts to improve its performance.

The control loop specifies that it performs some task and then analyses its performance, repeatedly. Each time the task is executed information is collected in the workspace (information flow to box 4 from box 1); this information will be the times taken to execute subtasks, details of environmental fixturing, etc.

This information is then analysed by the function specified in box 6; it extracts general knowledge about the execution of the task, in this particular operating environment. This function involves the machine learning discussed in the previous chapter and thus we have the question of what in general are the appropriate attributes of task execution to collect in the workspace? Part of the answer to this question is provided by the goals of the complete system: it is aiming to improve task execution efficiency. Thus timing data for each subtask would seem to be critical, but over and above that it is not at all obvious what the appropriate attributes are. In general I can suggest that the time and place (within the environment) of appearance of goal objects for the component subtasks would probably also be important.

Thus if some goal object tends to appear at some fixed location then the robot will find it more quickly if it exploits this consistency than if it searches blindly for it each time. The goal of the function in box 6 is to extract the consistent and hence predictable features common to each execution of the task. This generalized knowledge is stored in the knowledge base (information flow from box 6 to box 5).

A second analysis function (box 3) 'reasons' about the robot's knowledge with a view to increasing the task efficiency by exploiting the 'perceived' environmental consistencies. This function uses the stored knowledge but it is also expected to rearrange or generate useful knowledge itself, hence the two-way information flow between boxes 5 and 3.

A final function (box 2) analyses the situation at a meta-level to compare the costs and benefits of the basic learning and reasoning. The results of this analysis are used to balance actually getting on with the task against the overhead of collecting and processing information in an attempt to further improve task efficiency.

This problem is an AI problem primarily because of the nature of the functions specified in boxes 2, 3, and 6. There is no correct way to implement these functions, the best that we can hope to do is to devise and develop heuristics that will give us an adequate implementation.

An adequate implementation will be applicable to some range of typical industrial robotics tasks. In addition, it will improve its efficiency in executing those tasks by exploiting the environmental consistencies that are manifest in each unique application environment.

Fig. 4.2 depicts an application of the cognitive industrial robot to the pick-up-and-place task described in Chapter 2 and illustrated in Fig. 2.3.

The impact of the AI functions is in subtasks 1.1.3.1, 1.1.3.2, and 1.4; that is in the pattern recognition subtasks and in the (added) subtask of moving the robot hand to some start position in preparation for the next execution of the task. I should make it clear that there is no necessity in the application of the AI to these particular subtasks; it is just one possible application of AI to this problem — I could instead (or as well) have chosen

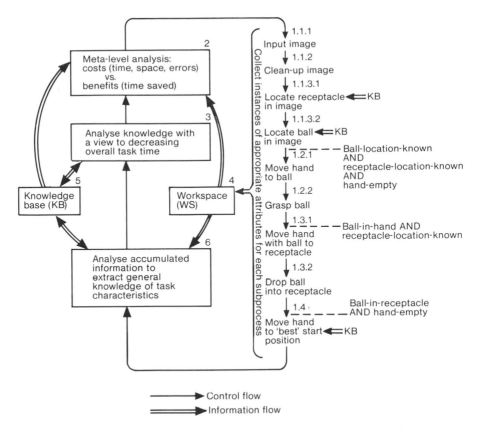

Fig. 4.2 — The cognitive industrial robot and pick-up-and-place task

to try improving efficiency by using the knowledge base to restructure the component subtasks.

The use of AI that I have in mind is that knowledge of particular environmental consistencies (e.g. the ball invariably appears at some particular location) can be automatically acquired, and then combined with knowledge of the task plan, in order to produce more efficient task execution for that particular application environment. And if the constancies change even within a particular application environment (e.g. the ball begins to appear somewhere else, or just begins to appear in seemingly arbitrarily chosen locations), then the robot will adapt to this new situation.

The information flow from the knowledge base (e.g. the ball tends to appear at position X,Y) is used predictively by the pattern recognition algorithm to increase recognition efficiency (search and analysis is replaced by prediction and confirmation). The AI of the system results in context-directed or top-down pattern recognition.

I can envisage the application of AI to subtask 1.4 as again an example of the use of a prediction (of where within the environment the ball will appear); in this case the prediction is being used to move the hand to an appropriate pick-up position rather than to some arbitrary start position.

I have explicitly placed this example in the domain of industrial robots rather than say household robots. I have done this because I believe it to be an interesting and useful practical application of AI that is somewhat closer to being practical software than the household version is.

The basic reason for the difference is one of necessary complexity: the household robot will have to deal with tasks that are more difficult by several orders of magnitude. In contrast, the cognitive industrial robot can fill a real and useful need in environments that are highly constrained. This makes adaptive top-down pattern recognition, for example, a likely possibility in the near future.


## 4.1  THE RUN–DEBUG–EDIT CYCLE

The computer can be used as a tool for investigating and thus developing partially specified problems. Specifications can be tentatively completed in different ways, programmed, and then run on a computer to see what happens. The behaviour observed is then used to assess the components tentatively added. In this application the computer is a substitute for a pencil and paper. Not just a convenient alternative but a necessary one in the domain of large and complex problems that AI typically addresses. The size and complexity of the putative specification is such as to require the use of a computer for investigative purposes.

The computer is a unique tool for investigating and developing problem specifications. Formal notations and techniques for analysing the implications of formal constructions were available and in use long before the advent of computers. In principle, computers and high-level programming languages bring with them nothing very new and startling. But in practice the amount of highly-reliable, logical (in the sense of simple rule governed) analysis that computers make easily available means that formal constructions of a new order of complexity may be explored and tested. A difference in quantity has resulted in a difference in kind.

Elsewhere (Partridge, 1981, and Partridge, Johnston, & Lopez, 1984) I have argued for this point. And although the scope and limitations of this new class of tool are still very much a subject for debate, I do not think the claim that the computer is a unique practical tool is a contentious statement.

Weizenbaum (1976) states that, "Tools shape man's imaginative reconstruction of reality." Computers and high-level programming languages are the tools that have provided the basis for AI as a practical reality.

Even though a new tool may fire our imagination, it must be used wisely if our imaginings are to become a reality. The clarion call for caution comes, as it so often does, from Dijkstra (1976), "we must realize that each flexibility, each generality of our tools requires a discipline for its exploitation." To a large extent this book is aimed at demonstrating the need for discipline in AI and describing the features of the necessary discipline. But it should be noted that it is not the discipline of conventional software engineering that I will advocate; it is a different discipline, one that reflects the differences between AI and conventional software engineering.

A rule of software engineering is that modifications are introduced at the highest possible level of design, and then the modified design is refined and reimplemented; speculative code modification (i.e. hacking ) is a recipe for disaster. How then can we justify code modification as a basic component of the methodology of AI?

The answer lies in the fundamental difference betweeen conventional software engineering problems and AI problems. Fixed, formal specification does not, in practice, readily apply to AI problems. And although some might argue that a fixed specification is a nonsense in practical software engineering as well, it should be noted that a specification that is changed in well-defined, discrete steps (the software engineering arrangement) is not the same as an intrinsically ill-defined and dynamic problem description. Compare snapshots of say, a car emerging from a distant fog with a film of changing cloud formations; in both cases we must deal with describing changes, but nevertheless the two situations are fundamentally different.

In AI a necessarily incomplete description of performance within a range of environments is the type of problem specification available — an incompletely specified function, as I described in Chapter 1. Given this characterization of AI problems, the controlled modification of a machine executable version followed by observation of performance and thus reappraisal of the current version is the best technique available. This is known as the run–debug–edit cycle. Fig. 4.3 is schematic overview of the general paradigm.

Not all uses of the run–debug–edit technique are code hacking. I shall argue for a disciplined use of this technique that is particularly suited to the ill-structured problems of AI. I shall also make the case that one of the major drawbacks of this technique — the incomprehensiblity of machine-executable notations — is not inherent in the technique but is, to a large extent, a reflection of the current state of the art of programming language design. It is due to the programming language inadequacy gap — the PLIG.

The PLIG is the difference between state of the art programming languages and problem specification languages; it is the difference with respect to the general clutter of implementation considerations and hence comprehensibility. It is not a well-defined concept, but it is an important one nonetheless. Balzer, Cheatham, & Green (1983), for example, lament the existence of this lacuna; its presence seriously undermines their "new paradigm" for software technology (I discuss their suggestions in Chapter 7).

The immediate significance of the PLIG for us is that it seriously weakens the utility of the run–debug–edit paradigm for AI program development; it makes program development too much like code hacking. We can't see the specification for the implementation details.

We must work through the distractions of the implementation language in order to manipulate the underlying specification. There is a general problem of lack of closeness between form and content that I shall examine

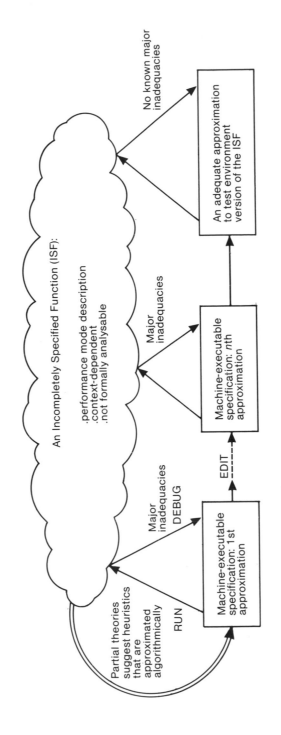

Fig. 4.3 — The AI-program development process

later in this chapter. In fact, the PLIG provides a minimum distance between the form and content levels of Fig. 4.5.

The optimistic view of the PLIG recognizes that the size of this gap is just a reflection of the state of the art in programming language design, and thus there is every hope that it can be closed — perhaps completely. The advent of high-level programming languages (contrasted with machine codes and assembly languages) drastically reduced this gap — perhaps the next generation of programming languages will take another big bite out of it?

Extra-high-level programming languages have not proved to be easy to find — at least, not ones with any general applicability. I can identify several different and somewhat successful attempts to move in the direction of such extra-high-level languages. One route is via a separation, within the language, of the significant and non-significant aspects of a specification. Ada is an example of such a language and I shall examine the potential of this strategy for AI software development on several occasions later in the book.

The language Prolog exemplifies a different type of attempt to factor out implementation detail; the general strategy is to separate declarative structure and control structure, and this strategy is also examined later. Kowalski (1984), for example, offers the prospect of a new software methodology based on this idea. His "new technology is characterized by the fact that it allows knowledge to be represented explicitly... . It disentangles what the computer knows from how the computer uses it." He claims to use Prolog as an executable specification language that allows us to short-circuit "the conventional software development life cycle, completing it without leaving the executable systems analysis stage."

One of the problems associated with 'pure' specification languages that are machine executable is that neglect of implementation detail means losing fine control of what is happening (the problem is the same as that of approximating heuristics, discussed earlier). Keen assembly language programmers are always quick to point out this disadvantage of the traditional high-level programming languages. On balance, the loss of fine control and machine efficiency that using, say, Pascal involves is more than compensated for by the advantages of being able to disregard most machine-level details. Current high-level programming languages may represent some optimal position within this trade-off.

But whether we will do much better in closing the PLIG in future remains to be seen. At the moment we must deal with it as best we can, Fig. 4.4 illustrates the current situation. In Chapter 5 I take a long look at a scheme for traversing this gap.

## 4.2  INCOMPLETELY SPECIFIED FUNCTIONS

As we have already discussed in Chapter 1 (Section 1.5), many AI problems can be characterized in a functional manner: the problem is described in terms of associations of certain classes of inputs with certain classes of outputs. But both classes tend to be infinite and only loosely circumscribable. It is typically easy to provide examples of elements that are either

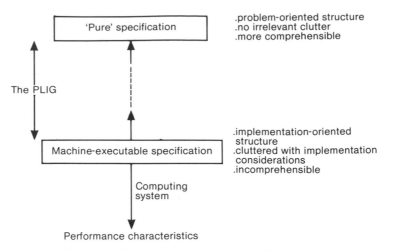

Fig. 4.4 — The programming language inadequacy gap

clearly in some class, or clearly not in a given class. But it is also usually easy to find elements that are both in and not in the class dependent upon the context involved.

For example, consider once again an intelligent, natural-language interface to a banking system. We might attempt to deal with the class of requests for the balances of accounts. This class of inputs will contain such requests as:

"What is the balance of my account?"
"How much is in my account?"
"Can you tell me exactly how much money is in my account?" etc.

Neglecting the loosely-coupled context sensitivity here (e.g. the person making the request must have an account), the associated output is a response that states the amount of money in the appropriate account.

But is the following request in the above described class of inputs?

"How much is in that other account?"

In the context of a dialogue in which two accounts have been discussed the reference "that other account" may be readily resolved to indicate an appropriate account. Then the request is in the class of inputs that we are currently considering.

But in the absence of such a preceding dialogue this request may be nonsense and therefore it falls into a rather different class of input.

We have called this type of incomplete and only loosely-describable function an incompletely specified function (ISF). Certain input–output relationships are necessary, the necessity of further classes of such relationships is dependent upon context, and the necessity of a final class of relationships is unknown. Thus we know some things that an implementation of an ISF should definitely do and not do; we also know some other things that it should do one way under one set of circumstances and do differently under others; and for some possible situations the expected behaviour of our implementation is unknown because either there are no guidelines or we just have not thought of certain possibilities.

In Chapter 1 I named these three components of an ISF: the well-defined component, the context-sensitive component, and the unforeseen component, respectively. In the first chapter I also looked at degree of context sensitivity as a method of discriminating AI that can currently be practical software, and AI that has not yet been transformed into practical software. I considered two classes of context sensitivity — loosely-coupled and tightly-coupled — and identified the former class with AI that has immediate potential in practical software, while the latter class was considered to be descriptive of AI problems that must await advances in both methodology and basic research before it can become practical software.

This rough, binary division of a complex, multi-dimensional phenomenon, context sensitivity, although extremely crude, does nevertheless provide some useful structure as described above. A second useful application of this two-way division of context sensitivity provides another viewpoint on the first two components of an ISF.

What I have called the well-defined component can be viewed as the context-free or only loosely context-coupled component. This component is relatively well-defined only because the context sensitivity involved is either minimal or fairly simple and thus relatively well-defined. Thus theorem proving is a loosely-coupled context sensitive problem: it can be largely viewed as a context-free problem (i.e. it is just the abstract proof rules), but there are also some context-sensitive aspects (e.g. the use of content, the meaning of the symbols, to assist in making intelligent choices within the intractably large space of purely logical possibilities — sometimes called problem domain heuristics). Human expertise in say, medical diagnosis may also prove to be a loosely-coupled context-sensitive problem. Certainly, there is a large loosely-coupled component: the basic expertise that so many expert systems aspire to capture. But there is also at least one prominent tightly-coupled context-sensitive component: the capability of explaining complex decisions. And this aspect of expert systems is one of the major stumbling blocks in expert system development, as you might expect if my analysis is correct. Human expertise then, as an ISF, appears to have a significant well-defined component (the mechanics of diagnosis, or whatever), and a non-trivial context-sensitive component (the ability to explain its behaviour) whose actual significance within the overall ISF is yet to be determined.

As a further example of this point consider once again the natural-language interface to a banking system. The class of requests referring to the balance of an account is an example of a set of relationships within the well-defined component of the ISF. But there are some loose context-couplings here. One such coupling is that between the actual account referenced and the person making the request; before the balance is output the system should be reasonably assured that the request comes from a person who has

a right to the balance requested. The context sensitivity involved in processing this class of requests is fairly simple and well-defined, and thus readily
implementable within the proposed natural-language interface.

The context-sensitive component of the ISF is the set of tightly-coupled,
context-sensitive relationships. The nature of complex context sensitivity
means that the elements of this component are relatively ill-defined. This
tightly-coupled context sensitivity arises whenever an appropriate response
is dependent on complex and ill-defined contextual features such as a
sophisticated understanding of some preceding dialogue, or a common
understanding of the typical human goals, objectives, and expectations with
respect to a banking system.

We are not able to specify comprehensively, in a well-defined manner,
such complex context-sensitive relationships. We have little idea of the
relationship between the level of intelligence implementable in such an
interface, and the degree to which the system must be able to deal with these
context dependencies.

The analytically-intractable complexity and inherent ill-structure of such
problems both strongly suggest an evolutionary or incremental approach to
the development of an adequate implementation. The software engineering
concept of a correct implementation of a rigorously specified problem just
does not apply here.

Of course, the steady increase in our knowledge of typical AI problems
coupled with the development of more powerful formal analytical techniques can be expected to support more thorough formal analyses of AI
problems, but, as I have argued earlier, a significant ill-structured kernel will
always remain, at least in practice.

This type of problem, sometimes known as a 'wicked' or an ill-structured
problem is in no sense mysterious. The incompleteness or ill-structure can
be viewed as a result of the in-principle–in-practice dichotomy. From this
viewpoint all the necessary information is available to determine say, what I
mean by some utterance — perhaps it is all just in my head. But there is little
hope of actually being able to examine and evaluate that evidence. For all
practical purposes such meaning is an ISF, although some might claim that it
is well-defined in principle. The range and domain of a typical AI function
are both infinite, and the function itself is complex and far from being
context-free such functions are highly context-dependent. My characterization of AI problems as ISFs presupposes a certain degree of loosely-coupled
context sensitivity in intelligence (or near decomposability, or modularity
you will remember from Chapter 3). I am assuming that general intelligence
(the only sort known) can be broken down into a collection of ISFs. The
contextual interrelationships that such a fractionation violates will then be
found in the context-sensitive components of the resultant ISFs. These links
must be sundered by approximation if we are going to implement each ISF
independent of its context — again, a move that is dictated by practical
necessity. In practice, we thus aim to implement a function that deals
adequately with a maximum number of the most common and the most
important cases. And to maintain an intelligent level of performance

through both time and space the implementation must be capable of tuning itself or of being tuned to continue to deal adequately with the essential dynamics of the AI problem. The complex context-sensitivity discussed above usually involves the empirical world; this phenomenon is constantly changing. An AI implementation must keep abreast of the relevant changes or become an unintelligent anachronism — this implies an adaptive implementation. The degree of adaptivity necessary will depend upon the degree to which the empirical world impinges upon each particular AI problem; and this, of course, is just another approach to the division of AI problems with respect to tightly- and loosely-coupled context sensitivity. Thus medical diagnosis, it seems, can be treated largely as an abstract problem independent of the current state of the empirical world; explanation, on the other hand, cannot.

In principle, the problem of playing chess is solved by a well-specified, optimal function. In practice, we strive for an adequate approximation to this function. Furthermore, it is usually hard to find reliable metrics for adequacy. Program behaviour within the application environment is typically the best guide to adequacy. Notice that an ISF is a performance mode specification; it is a description in terms of desired behaviours. So the adequacy of an implementation is most naturally gauged by observation of its behaviour.

To illustrate these points we can consider the problem of natural language communication. Most people have adequately approximated this ISF, some more adequately than others. All computerized approximations so far have fallen a long way short of adequacy in terms of depth, breadth, and flexibility: computerized natural language interfaces tend to be superficial, restricted in scope, and applicable only to a fixed, prespecified set of possibilities.

To begin with there is no formal specification of the natural language communication problem. More than that, there is no adequate formal specification of the set of grammatical utterances that is English, despite many years of work. In fact it is tempting to believe that an adequate formal specification of English is not possible even in practice were it not for the de facto example in almost every human being.

An AI problem might be to implement an intelligent, natural-language interface for a complex system. An adequate implementation will allow the people who need to use the system to be able to do so as easily as possible and with a minimum of knowledge about the details of the particular implementation of the system.

An initial ISF will include sets of questions and responses that the interface must support. It will also include examples where the question-response relationship varies dependent upon, say, the expertise of the user; and this variability is itself likely to be an incompletely-specified subfunction. The designers will also be aware that certain important characteristics of the function will have been totally omitted because nobody has realized either their existence or their importance.

A more specific example of an ISF is the function described in box 6 of

Fig. 4.2. In general this function must accept sets of data values for the attributes of particular instances of task execution and combine them with current general knowledge to generate better generalizations. So a sequence of repetitions of a task will generate a set of locations for each target object. Each set of location values is then combined with the existing location prediction for the same target object with a view to generating a better prediction to be exploited in future executions of the task.

In more detail we know that sets of subtask timings should result in some 'average' time to complete each subtask. We don't know exactly what this 'averaging' function should be (straightforward numerical average could be a first approximation), but this aspect of our ISF appears to be largely context-free. Time efficiency is the major goal and average subtask times would seem to be important irrespective of the overall task being optimized.

We also know that this function should generate from an input set of timings and locations some 'average' or constancy measure for the environmental objects critical to task completion. Such constancies contribute to environmental consistency that once discovered can be exploited to speed future task execution. But what these objects are, and what constancies are important, are highly task- (and task-plan-) dependent — this is part of the context-sensitive aspect of this ISF.

For the pick-up-and-place task time and place of appearance of the ball are important possible constancies. How best to search for such constancies, in general, is another problem whose solution will be the goal of the incremental development process.

Inappropriate inputs to this function are not hard to find — how about the football results? But unforeseen input remains as elusive as ever.

I have not argued that ISFs are rigorously partitionable into three components. I have only tried to establish that even an ill-defined and loose decomposition of such ill-structured problems is possible and that it will provide an appropriate, albeit shaky, framework upon which to build a discussion in an area that is otherwise totally nebulous.

As stated before there are good and bad versions of the run–debug–edit technique. Speculative code hacking or just hacking is at the bad end of the range and controlled modification occurs at the good end. This then leads us onto the questions: Where does the initial specification come from? What is controlled modification? And how does it differ from hacking? Before dealing with these questions let us make some observations that pertain to the specification-modification versus implementation-modification controversy.

## 4.3 SPECIFICATIONS AND IMPLEMENTATIONS

A charge often levelled against AI program development techniques is that modification and development should occur at the level of problem specification, not at the level of implementation. The good reason for this is that the specification is the more fundamental description; it is not biased to any particular implementation and it is also uncluttered with particular implementation details.

Unfortunately the distinction between the terms specification and implementation is ill-defined: a specification can often be respecified in a more abstract notation and an implementation can often be implemented in more detail using a more concrete language.

For example, the process of sorting a list of numbers into ascending order can be specified at a high level in terms of a transformation from an arbitrarily ordered list to one in which each element is not less than the preceding one.

A more specific specification might determine a particular class of sorting algorithm such as a bubble sort.

The general bubble-sort algorithm can be refined to one of many possible alternative detailed designs.

The detailed design may be implemented in some high-level programming language.

The high level programming language may itself be implemented in terms of some machine code that in turn is implemented in a particular hardware.

There are several points to note from this example. First there is a series of successively more specific specifications or successively more abstract implementations. A series from abstract data types to concrete data structures provides another ready example from the field of computer science.

Secondly, the term implementation rather than specification is usually applied to machine-executable notations. There is no intrinsic difference between these two concepts, they are just a reflection of the current level of machine-executable languages.

Thirdly, we might note that a specification-implementation sequence need not necessarily be a series that exhibits a continuous increase or decrease in level of abstraction (even apart from the fact that "level of abstraction" is another ill-structured concept). FORTRAN can be implemented or specified in LISP, and LISP in FORTRAN. Swartout & Balzer (1982), arguing for "the inevitable intertwining of specification and implementation", point out that the conventional partitioning into specification and implementation "is entirely arbitrary." I shall examine their work on a new software development paradigm in Chapters 6 and 7, for it contains a number of points of correspondence with the view that I shall advocate.

But given that specifications and implementations typically fall into a spectrum of descriptions differing in degree of abstraction, the preferred strategy is to develop a design at the highest level of abstraction. But given also, the need to generate and examine the full consequences of a complex design, mechanical manipulation of our description is highly desirable, if not a practical necessity. The best practical strategy is then to develop the design at the highest level of machine-executable description: that is, in terms of a high-level programming language. Much of the development of very high-level AI languages can be viewed as an effort to produce higher level (than the more general-purpose high-level languages) machine-executable, problem-description languages.

Thus the criticism of code modification techniques as opposed to abstract specification modification is to some extent a comment on the current state of the art of high level programming language development. The difference between the level of a machine-executable specification language that is effectively free of implementation clutter and current high-level programming languages, I have called the programming language inadequacy gap. Within computer science substantial effort is being put into the design and implementation of high level specification languages, which will in effect reduce this gap (see Ross (1977) for a general overview, and Boehm (1984) for more recent work).

Machine-executable specifications — that is, programs — are typically non-transparent objects. We have some assurance of completeness, and some firm knowledge of the implications of our specification just because it does run on a computer and thus exhibits certain behaviours.

But programs as objects to support human comprehension and hence understanding of the specification leave much to be desired. This is especially true for the programs generated by the run–debug–edit paradigm. The structured programming movement grew as a response to the need for human comprehension of programs. It works very well when we have an RFS to implement, but the incremental development of an ISF seriously hampers any attempt to produce a structured program. Hence AI programs tend to be particularly lacking in transparency, a serious problem when the program embodies the problem specification (this is the problem that we address in the following chapter).

Programs tend to be opaque for two rather different reasons:

(1)  The underlying virtual computer (a combination of the actual hardware and the software supporting the chosen programming language) swamps the specification with irrelevant clutter.
(2)  Computers permit the exploration of specifications to a greater logical depth and complexity than has hitherto been possible.

The first type of clutter that detracts from program transparency is largely a problem with the currently available programming languages. We can expect improvements in this respect as our expertise in programming language design develops.

Apart from the obvious development of higher-level languages, I expect improvements in the syntactic and semantic support for abstraction techniques within programming languages. And this will become a major route to the separation of implementation clutter from the specification. This latter idea is pursued with an example in Chapter 6.

The second type of clutter is an unavoidable consequence of the power of the computer as a tool for the investigation and development of complex specifications. A complex object is, almost by definition, not a readily comprehensible object.

Arbib (1972) suggests that AI theories should be constructed in the form of a machine (by "machine" he means formalism, not necessarily a programming language) in order to be able to test the workability of theories of the requisite logical depth. Although he is in agreement with my argument of the potential for detailed complexity in AI problem specifications, Arbib does not appear to support the above-described view that machine-executable formalisms are a unique class of formalism with respect to the testability of problem specifications or theories.

Arbib focuses on the statement that, "If you understand something, you can 'build' a machine to imitate it." Although I subscribe to this view, a change in emphasis is required to support my arguments on the role of machine-executable specifications in AI. My point is not just that if you can understand something, you can program it, but that programming may be prior to a full understanding. Stronger than that: I claim that programming can always facilitate understanding and can carry understanding further than would otherwise be achieved.

I view the run–debug–edit cycle as the use of a machine-executable specification in order to develop understanding of an ISF and thereby generate an adequate approximation to it.

An abstract specification is typically not available. An adequate implementation contains a de facto specification as we shall see in the following chapter, but the AI task is to generate this adequate de facto specification by means of successive performance evaluations.

There is also a further point concerning the loss of detail as we move to higher-level, more abstract, specifications. Loss of detail, despite the fact that it generally facilitates understanding, is a loss of information.

In AI we are attempting to implement an approximation to an ISF, not an abstract specification. Analysis and modification at some specific level of fine detail may be required. The simplicity and consequent conceptual clarity provided by abstraction is nearly always beneficial, but not if it omits necessary detail.

Code-modification then can be viewed as development of a machine-executable specification. But first we must obtain the initial specification-implementation.

## 4.4  GENERATING AN INITIAL SPECIFICATION-IMPLEMENTATION

A major subproblem in the development of adequate AI implementations is the generation of a not-too-inadequate initial, machine-executable, specification. We are faced with a problem similar to the requirements engineering task described in Chapter 2.

Certainly some requirements analysis can and should be undertaken in an AI project. There is always some conventional software engineering in an AI project; it should be fully developed to assist in the management and control of the AI aspects (a general strategy that we will return to in Chapter 6). But in AI intangible human needs are part of the essence of the whole problem not a feature that can potentially be isolated and factored out by a process such as requirements analysis. Even in principle it is difficult to envisage the possibility of complete requirements analysis for AI problems.

The software engineer not only has the principle at hand, he also has practical techniques that have been shown to be effective.

A second and related point of contrast concerns the fact that requirements analysis aims at defining the boundaries of a software engineering problem. Clearly an explicit, complete, and rigorous statement of the scope and limitations of the problem to be implemented is a valuable, perhaps invaluable, aspect of the RFS. Consider the problems of comprehensive testing if various aspects of the problem have ill-defined boundaries — such is the nature of AI problems.

A major problem in AI research is: what is the scope and limitations of a given AI program? We know some things that the program does adequately, and we know a much larger set of things that it does inadequately, but we don't know where the intervening boundaries are. In a research environment this is a nuisance; in a practical application environment it is intolerable. Scope and limitations are thus another obstacle to the development and marketing of AI software.

Warnings to prospective AI software buyers are already surfacing, 'caveat emptor' is the rule of purchase, it will be especially important for the buyer of AI software. AI requirements engineering differs from its software engineering analogue in that we do not expect to generate an initial specification that is totally adequate. If we do produce an initial, adequate specification then the implementation can be accomplished using the conventional software engineering methodology of Chapter 2. But this is unlikely for two reasons: first, adequacy is primarily a performance mode measure so the adequacy of a non-executable specification would be difficult to gauge; second, the detailed complexity and ill-structure of typical AI problems is such that an adequate first approximation is a very unlikely event.

The crucial difference between requirements engineering within these two domains is that in software engineering a formalized statement of requirements is the basis for the rigorous specification — the standard by which an implementation is judged. In AI the fundamental basis for judgements of implementation adequacy tends to be a performance description that is only loosely circumscribable. The initial specification of an ISF is not intended to be an end in itself; it is a first approximation that is to be subjected to the run–debug–edit cycle in order to eventually develop an adequate approximation.

The intended uses of an initial specification in AI and in software engineering are different; it should not be surprising that the means to achieve these specifications are also different. In software engineering the emphasis is on attaining a provably complete and consistent specification to implement. In AI the emphasis is on flexibility and immediate behavioural testability. We must be able to evaluate the performance of our initial approximation and it must also be readily modifiable.

It is true that "design for change" is also a useful principle in software engineering. At the formal end of the software engineering spectrum it is a principle of lesser importance; it is a handy quality to have in the program but one that is very subsidiary to the qualities of correctness and of comprehensibility. At the other end of this spectrum ease of modifiability of a program has gained considerable importance primarily because we fully expect to have to modify the requirements and the RFS.

Despite this approach of the modifiability of conventional software to the level of importance that the run–debug–edit paradigm accords designing for change, I still maintain that there is a critical difference in emphasis: it is one of the two most important qualities of an AI specification-implementation; it is at best still a secondary quality of conventional software.

An extension of this principle, which results in a difference in kind, is given by Brooks (1975), "plan to throw one [version of the system] away … you will anyway." Such a strategy smacks of a reversion to, or an absence of progress from, the "Wright brothers' technique" (Naur & Randell, 1969): "build a whole airplane, push it off a cliff, if it crashes start again." The only way to gather enough detailed information to design and implement complex software is to build and attempt to run a throwaway version.

Later in this chapter I shall consider how the run–debug–edit paradigm seeks to moderate the Wright brothers' technique to yield a more efficient process. In software engineering we find the idea of rapid prototyping being explored to perform much the same role. We shall deal with these convergent ideas in Chapter 7. But, again, although there is an undoubted similarity between the idea of rapid prototyping in software engineering and the run–debug–edit cycle in AI, there are also significant differences. The AI methodology must support a very fluid problem description whilst software engineers are prepared to explore a relatively small number of relatively well-defined perturbations to their problem specification. Neverthless, a significant similarity exists and it should be exploited in the development of the run–debug–edit paradigm.

For the moment I wish to point out that use of the unadulterated Wright brothers' technique provides us with another characterization of the difference between what AI has largely been, and what it aspires to become. The history of AI is a chronicle of throwaway systems, and this situation is defensible in a research environment (although the amount of useful knowledge gained thereby is a subject of much debate in AI).

But in the world of practical software we must eventually build systems that will satisfy actual user needs over a reasonable period of time. So the transition for AI can be seen as a switch from throwaway to usable systems.

### 4.4.1  The desired characteristics of an initial approximation
The two major desiderata of an initial implementation-specification are:

(a)  The first approximation must be complete at some level of detail. The system must both be executable and be capable of exhibiting behaviours to support adequacy judgements. An unevaluatable, partial implementation is not much use.
(b)  The system must be readily modifiable. This requirement implies a

number of others: comprehensibility, modularity, and in general all the prerequisites of maintainable software.

Getting a good initial approximation off the drawing board and into the computer is the crucial first step into the run–debug–edit cycle.

### 4.4.1.1  *It should be complete*

The completeness requirement appears to be in direct conflict with the basic idea of approximating an inherently incomplete ISF. This conflict is resolved when we consider the phrase "at some level of detail" modifying the completeness stipulation.

We can always construct a complete approximation at some level of detail — in general, the higher the level (i.e. the less detail) the easier it is.

For example, a complete approximation to a natural-language interface (for any system) is a program that answers every input with:

"I am sorry, I do not understand."

Although this is in some sense a complete approximation — it covers every possible input — it is a dismal failure with respect to its potential for evaluation and subsequent modification. So the goal for the completeness criterion is, complete at a level of detail sufficient to enable us to make adequacy judgements that will guide subsequent modification.

Another view of this criterion and one that is worth emphasizing is that this initial approximation must be sufficiently close to the ISF. In one sense any object is an approximation of any other object. If they bear no apparent resemblance to each other then the approximation is a particularly poor one, but it is an approximation nonetheless.

Thus the above high-level approximation to any natural-language interface is also an approximation to a chess-playing program!

In general, the closer the approximation the more easily we can apply the run–debug–edit paradigm. A minor perturbation is easier to correct than a gross mismatch — the degrees of freedom for potential corrections are fewer in the former case.

Numerous examples of this principle can be found especially in research on machine learning. Thus Langley's SAGE system (Langley, 1983) can discover a better solution to a range of problems provided it already has a solution and thus can immediately determine when a possible improvement diverges from the known solution path and is thus not an improvement.

The 'near-miss' is a much-used concept in machine learning. The machine derives a better approximation to some concept as a result of having two almost identical representations to compare; it is the small, well-defined difference that focuses the machine learning onto that aspect of its current representation that needs to be altered. You may remember the discussion (in Chapter 3) of the problem of focusing machine learning: if the system lacks general knowledge it tends also to lack the ability to distinguish the trivial from the crucial aspects of a learning situation. The near-miss idea provides the necessary direction for the learning algorithms.

Thus Winston's (1975) arch-learning program was fed near-miss examples of arches (i.e. examples of non-arches) in order to direct the program to learn the essential aspects of an arch (e.g. it should have a hole through it), and neglect the non-essential aspects (e.g. the colour of the materials used).

In their perceptive survey of a number of rule learning projects, Bundy & Silver (1982) describe several attempts to deal with "far-misses" (i.e. more than one 'difference' between the compared representations). Rather than use contextual knowledge to distinguish between the significant and non-significant differences, or to exploit the global information that a combination of differences might contain, the learning algorithms took the brute force approach of trying all possible combinations. This technique can be made to work in the highly constrained environments that these systems function in, but it cannot be expected to be successful in the almost unconstrained situation of modifying approximations to an ISF. Thus the more aspects of our first approximation that fall close to the near-miss zone around our ISF, the more chance we have of closing in smoothly on an adequate approximation.

But however close and complete the initial approximation is, the AI program developer is going to have to deal with many 'misses' that are so far wide of the mark that current machine learning algorithms would fail to spot any similarity between the two representations. In these regions — the far depths of description space — there is, unfortunately, no substitute for inspiration, luck, and above all, perseverance.

So we need a closeness of approximation, we should also consider a second dimension of closeness: closeness between form and content. The important decision that this similarity feature gives rise to is: how best to *represent* our approximations to the ISF? This is not just a question of what language shall we code it in, but also, in what way to code it into some language — how do we structure our approximation to facilitate modification within the run–debug–edit cycle? (This question is perhaps more properly part of the following subsection but it is also tied to the idea of closeness of approximation so I will deal with it here.)

Lenat & Brown (1983) describe an instance of this aspect of similarity in a revealing paper that addresses the problem of why the AM program appeared to discover interesting mathematical principles while a more abstract version, EURISKO, had little success.

The crux of the problem is that of the 'distance' between a given representation (the form), and what it is representing (the content). AM had a closeness between form and content that Eurisko lacked. Structural changes in AM result in 'similar' semantic changes, such was not the case with Eurisko.

The objects of interest in the AM program were maths concepts that were each represented in LISP by a very few lines of code. The charging of one syntactic unit of the LISP code tended to result in a meaningful semantic change in the function represented. By way of contrast, EURISKO was concerned with heuristics that were each represented by several pages of LISP code. Furthermore, they were represented in such a way that syntactic changes in the LISP representation did not usually amount to any change in a semantic unit other than the introduction of an error. The somewhat fortuitous similarity between LISP code and the maths concepts was lost when the heuristics were coded in the same manner. The desired semantic changes in the heuristics required the coincident change of a disparate collection of syntactic units.

Another example of this phenonemon, one that can be readily appreciated by most programmers, is seen in the use of high-level programming languages instead of machine codes. Any given algorithm can be represented in a high-level language, say Pascal, or in a machine code. On the vast majority of occasions the high-level language alternative will be the easier to debug. From our current viewpoint, there is a closeness of form and content in the high-level language version that the machine code version lacks. In particular, we might note that, apart from the machine-dependent clutter, machine codes tend to scatter the underlying semantic concepts, such as printing out the value of a variable, in a number of different syntactic constructs. The structure and arrangement of the machine code representation is likely to relate more closely to the associated hardware than to the algorithm coded.

An important example from computer science of where form and content mesh almost to perfection can be found in the use of the Backus--Naur Form (BNF notation) for defining the context-free syntax of programming languages. The content (i.e. the allowable structures) of the definition can be expressed clearly and directly in BNF with very little extra clutter (just the very few meta symbols).

MacLennan (1983) is, I believe, making this point when he writes that the BNF notation "combined the advantages of both examples and a formal specification since the formulas above look like example expressions, while at the same time precisely describing ... expressions."

He precedes this statement with a precise definition of a syntax for numeric literals, but he provides the same definition (i.e. same content) in two different representation languages (forms) — English and BNF. The English definition is large, complex, and unintelligible; the BNF definition is quite the opposite in all three respects — this difference is a result of differences in distance between form and content.

A final example that illustrates this point by contrast is the field of cryptography. We can view the devising of secret codes to be an attempt to maximize the distance between form and content. In a well-encrypted message the superficial form of the message should provide a minimum of clues as to the content.

The significance of this 'closeness' between form and content for our current purposes is that desired semantic changes will 'suggest' the necessary syntactic modifications. We wish to incrementally improve the underlying approximation but we must do it via the chosen representation. Fig. 4.5 is a schematic illustration emphasizing the role of these two distance metrics within the run–debug–edit cycle.

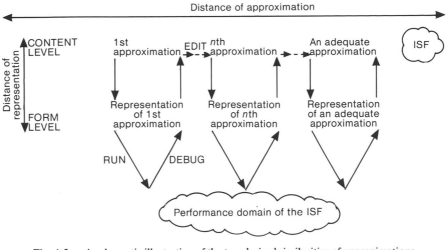

Fig. 4.5 — A schematic illustration of the two desired similarities of approximations to an ISF

As an aside, we see in this phenomenon a resurrection of a problem that was instrumental in the extinction of the simulated evolution approach to AI (see Fogel, Owens, & Walsh, 1966, for the first and last survey of this novel approach).

In the context of research on solving somewhat well-defined puzzles, Korf (1980) addresses the problem of changing the representation of a problem in order to make it easier to solve. With respect to the current discussion I can say that the representational change that facilitates problem solving is one that results in a closeness of the content of the puzzle and its form with regards to the problem-solving strategy applied. This paper is also of interest because the author provides a meta-language for specifying representations. In addition, he suggests two dimensions of representation space that characterize changes of representation. The dimensions are "information structure" and "information quantity", corresponding to tranformations along the structure and quantity dimensions, respectively (but beware of the term "information"; it is not the usual ill-defined concept, it is the one from Information Theory — Partridge (1981a) is one of the many discussions of the misinterpretations of this formal quantity).

The run–debug–edit cycle is the crux of a paradigm for machine-assisted human learning; we learn about an ISF through the implications of successive approximations and aim to eventually discover an adequate approximation. Humans are currently far better than machines at analysing problems and devising solutions, nevertheless, the better approximation we have the easier it is to improve it.

As described in Chapter 3 within the discussion of machine learning, the credit assignment problem is a fundamental difficulty — i.e. what feature of the current approximation gets the credit (or better, blame) for some perceived inadequacy? This problem is closely related to the quality-of-approximation problem discussed above. We have got to get reasonably close to the target ISF in order to identify and correct individual behavioural inadequacies.

A final point concerning the completeness criterion for initial specification-implementations is that they should generate an output for every input — they should completely cover the function. It is of course not necessary (or possible) to prove that the initial approximation does completely cover the target ISF, but it is a guideline to bear in mind.

The principle behind this injunction is that, truth emerges more readily from error than from confusion. An inadequate response to some input is far better than no response.

Elsewhere (Partridge, 1976 and 1978) I have argued for fulfilling this part of the completeness requirement by constructing the system with an 'active bias'. This active bias ensures that the system will always generate an at least inadequate response in the context of incomplete and missing information — in the worst case it should generate output even if it has no information towork with (although "no information" is not usually a practical possibility), that is, it should guess.

Given this implementation strategy we can view the run–debug–edit cycle as a means of adding information to the system to restrain the active guessing mechanism such that it produces successively more adequate outputs. I use the word 'guess' signify the result of heuristic reasoning based upon incomplete information.We can view intelligence as an informed guessing mechanism. Pure guessing is quicker but reasoning based on a maximum of information is likely to be more accurate. Guessing may be more or less informed dependent upon the amount of information used to generate a guess. Intelligent behaviour may be the result of appropriately balancing guessing (for reasons of both speed and necessity), and information processing to restrain the guessing; and thereby a system might achieve adequacy with respect to ISFs.

The XSEL system, a computer sales person's assistant, is described in these terms by McDermott (1982) "Currently XSEL has a few rules that enable it to avoid obviously poor choices; it will need a significant amount of additional knowledge before its choices will be consistently adequate."

Hayes-Roth, Waterman, & Lenat (1983) outline three generic situations where guessing, or plausible reasoning, is important.

(1) Incomplete knowledge, a characteristic of AI problems, implies guessing to bridge the gaps.
(2) If a search space is quite dense in adequate solutions,efficiency considerations suggest that we 'grab' one such solution with a guess and continue from there.
(3) In situations of systematic convergence on solutions (e.g. top-down

refinement), it may be appropriate, and more efficient, to guess ahead even when solutions are rare.

I can divide these three "generic situations" into two categories:

(a) Guessing as a matter of necessity because required information is missing: this is a common situation in real-world problem solving, we (almost) never have all of the relevant information available — nevertheless decisions must be made. (Note the connection with tightly-coupled context sensitivity.)
(b) Guessing as a matter of 'efficiency' because although all of the required information is available, it would take too long to process it exhaustively: this is also a common situation in AI problems, search spaces are often very large or infinite — as search spaces approach the latter possibility, so guessing for efficiency purposes becomes guessing as a practical necessity. Chess is a good example of the efficiency consideration becoming practical necessity. In principle, all of the information necessary to select the next best move is available in a game of chess; in practice, we must do some guessing (informed guessing for sure, but guessing nonetheless), and the guessing is buried in the heuristics we use.

In summary, I would prefer to refer to the following three generic situations in which guessing mechanisms would be used:

(i) guessing as a necessity because not enough information;
(ii) guessing as a necessity because too much information; and
(iii) guessing as simply an efficiency expedient.

And as with all heuristic devices we must face the problem of identifying and recovering from wrong guesses.


### 4.4.1.2  *It should be modifiable*
The other major desideratum of the initial specification-implementation is modifiability. I have already considered potential modifiability in terms of two types of similarity. I shall now examine more specific guidelines for achieving modifiability. To be readily modifiable a system should possess two further qualities: it should be comprehensible and it should be modular. Both of these qualities are discussed fully later. The comprehensibility of AI implementations is the general topic addressed in the following chapter, and the uses and benefits of modularity in AI programs are discussed in Chapter 6, Section 6.2.1.1.

I consider that a disciplined strategy for the edit step in the AI program development paradigm, which I call controlled modification, is crucial to the overall success of this methodology. Controlled modification is introduced in the next major section and elaborated upon in the next chapter.

Hitherto designing for change has not, I believe, been sufficiently emphasised in AI. A dominant AI strategy has been to devise and explore micro or toy worlds. Winograd's (1972) blocks world is an important example of this approach to AI.

This is a legitimate way to cut down the complexity of an ISF to more manageable proportions. But all too often the micro-world becomes an end in itself with little regard for the original ISF as a number of critics have noted (see for example, McDermott, 1976, and Wilks, 1976). The main thrust of the criticism is that what were originally just initial, arbitrary, limitations are exploited to the extent that they become an essential feature of the problem specification. Thus the micro-world implementations lose flexibility and cannot be extended to more closely approximate the original ISF. Design and implement for change have been ignored.

A specific example of this pitfall can be found in the five-year project funded by the United States Advanced Research Project Agency (ARPA) to demonstrate the feasibility of programming a computer 'to understand' connected speech. The project terminated in 1976 with a report "that the specifications ... were met" (Medress, 1978). We have yet to see any development out of this project that even approaches a practical application of connected speech understanding — that is strange if the practical feasibility was so convincingly demonstrated with working systems in 1976.

An important reason for the lack of significant subsequent progress in connected speech understanding is that the specifications were taken as an end in themselves — and an end they proved largely to be. Individual programs were constructed to meet the specifications (in itself a challenging task), and by so doing they effectively eliminated all possibility for improving these systems much beyond the specifications.

Not that one should have expected these programs to have been developed and extended in the subsequent years, they were only constructed to demonstrate feasibility. But one could reasonably have expected the underlying mechanisms and computational techniques to have been extended and become manifest in some subsequent speech understanding programs, if these techniques had been designed with future potential in mind rather than the 1976 deadline and specifications.

This area of AI is not dead, but it has certainly shrunk drastically rather than blossomed since 1976. I am not claiming that the ARPA project was an unmitigated failure, quite the contrary, an enormous amount was learnt about AI system development. The point I am making is: if you target specific but arbitrary limitations as ends in themselves then you tend to sacrifice future potential, and the ARPA project is an example of this phenomenon — the specifications were met yet subsequent development of the major problem has been disappointing, to say the least. (This saga is reported in a somewhat more optimistic light in Barr & Feigenbaum, 1981; the adverse effects of the pressure to meet specifications are hinted at by Newell, 1977, at an AI conference in which several other people made the charge explicitly from the floor although their comments did not get into the published proceedings.)

What we witness here is an example of Fisher's Fundamental Theorem, which as Weinberg (1971) translates it into the current context is: the better adapted a system is to a particular environment, the less adaptable it is to new environments. We can produce a showy version of the current approximation (and thus exploit the ELIZA syndrome), but only at the cost of limiting the scope for further development of that approximation.

It may be that self-adaptive AI must either undermine this theorem or walk a carefully balanced path between adapting closely to the current situation and preserving adaptive potential for the future.

Sacerdoti (1982) suggests that this phenomenon, in the specific form of high performance but specialized programs versus moderate performance more generalized alternatives, may be a significant problem in the marketing of AI software. Restricted and highly specific non-AI programs may always be able to out-compete, in a limited but highly visible sense, the more general alternatives offered by AI software. We can, perhaps, take some comfort in the observation that most AI people would welcome the problems that marketing generalized AI software would bring, if only because these problems would have been preceded by the successful construction of the generalized AI software itself.

Winston (1977), in his influential AI text, has tried to justify the micro-world approach to AI by offering the analogy that, "limited domains of discourse are the E. coli of language research". The critical dimension along which this analogy fails concerns the fact that E. coli is an existing, real-world system that molecular biologists must deal with as best they can; limited domains of discourse, on the other hand, are artifacts that can be restructured or created at will to facilitate the application of any particular theory. In the second edition (Winston, 1984) the explicit claim has been omitted, but still E. coli research in molecular biology is adduced in support of the use of artificial micro-worlds in AI — the fact that one type of limited domain is a product of the imagination and the other is not, does not seem to be an important difference for Winston.

An extended criticism of the micro-world approach to AI, and a comparison with the general methodology described in this chapter can be found in Partridge (1978).

There is a growing realization in conventional software engineering (see for example Giddings, 1984, and "domain dependent" software) that a fundamental feature of such software is that it also grows and changes (or that it should). This being the case, the static SPIV paradigm is being seriously questioned as to its appropriateness as a standard to be achieved (see for example, Balzer, Cheatham, & Green, 1983, and for a different perspective De Millo, Lipton, & Perlis, 1979).

Hence 'design for change' is gaining importance in more conventional software, although it is mostly viewed in terms of 'design for reuse'. An important manifestation of this movement is the effort to construct libraries of reusable modules. This has not been a great success except for mathematical software (which, significantly, is context-free). A major problem has been that each reuse is slightly different and it has not been easy to construct library modules that will function appropriately in a variety of different contexts.

Programming language designers are responding to this problem via abstraction mechanisms: a library module specifies an abstract function only and the required specific details are instantiated afresh with every reuse of the module. The language Ada (Barnes, 1983) offers this and a number of other mechanisms to support the development of libraries of reuseable modules.

Here we see mechanisms of abstraction and instantiation as a rather different approach to the problem of 'designing for change'.

Parnas (1979) states that in conventional software engineering one is designing not a single program, but a family of programs, and hence he considers a special case of design for change: the design of software to be extensible and easily contracted so as to be readily modifiable to fit any particular application within the family of possibilities.

This is clearly a more limited situation than that we are likely to be faced with in AI, but Parnas' methods for the design of flexible software may be useful nevertheless.

He describes four steps towards more flexible software, but he prefaces his descriptions with "one of the clearest morals ... about 'design for change'": it is that one must anticipate changes before one begins the design. The difference in the practical applicability of this moral in software engineering and in AI illuminates the difference in 'design for change' methods within these two fields: in software engineering one is expected to foresee the changes (and as Parnas says that is part of requirements definition), in AI such foresight is, in general, not possible.

To elaborate on this point of difference: the predictability of changes in software engineering does not refer to a clairvoyant ability to foresee precisely future changes in the problem (who can predict changes in the tax laws?). It refers to the constraints (generated during requirements analysis and used by the system designer) on what types of future changes can be accommodated within the system designed. Changes that do happen to fall outside the 'predicted' (and designed-for) set also fall beyond the pale of the system designer's responsibility; the system designer cannot be held accountable for unanticipated changes, the problem is no longer the one prescribed, or better, the one circumscribed by the requirements analysis.

So, for example, with respect to a system for income tax computation, a well-designed system should have sufficient flexibility to be able to readily accommodate changes in the tax rates, changes in the thresholds for the various rates, etc. But it might not be readily modifiable to encompass a radical revision of the tax laws. This latter change will have created a new problem, the resultant income tax computation problem is no longer the one that the system was designed for — it is a different software engineering problem.Notice that all of these changes are discrete: there is a relatively well-defined step from what the tax laws were previously to what they are as a result of the changes. A software engineering problem can be discretely changeable within the limits specified in the requirements statement; outside of those limits it is a different problem. AI problems are decidedly more protean: a cloud is still a cloud whatever its shape, and English is still English whatever the grammatical contruction or, indeed, bizarre usage of words (this is an overstatement, but not by very much). As Humpty Dumpty was quick to point out to Alice when she questioned his usage of words: "When I use a word, it means just what I choose it to mean — neither more nor less" — that is what I call unpredictable! In a natural language understanding system the meaning of utterances is not so much in the actual words and grammatical contruction used as in who is using them and for what purpose. This is not a problem that design for change in conventional software engineering even begins to approach, but it is one that must be tackled if we are ever to realize the full potential of AI.

There is a difference here between the tax law problem and natural language understanding in that the former is, or should be, a well-defined, abstract problem whilst the latter is an inherently ill-defined, real-world problem. I shall return to this important distinction — abstract versus concrete — later; it is not the major point of distinction here. The crucial difference that I want to bring out at this point is one *of purview*. The software engineer's range of responsibility is prescribed. Whether a certain prescription (RFS) prescribes what the user wanted is a different question, the point is that there is a fundamental assumption that it is possible (and desirable) to formally circumscribe the problem. In AI the problems tend more to exist in the empirical world. Any attempt to produce an adequate implementation can rely on no well-defined boundaries to limit, a priori, the necessary exploration of possibilities.

I have already described, in essence, most of Parnas' methods that would seem to be applicable to AI, except for his "uses" relation. Systematic application of the "uses" relation results in a "uses" hierarchy in which each level offers a testable and usable subset of the system — clearly another route to flexibility as a result of modularity. But the "uses" relation is not the "invokes" relation although there is substantial overlap between the two. Parnas formulates the "uses" relation as "requires the presence of a correct version of".

Thus a program A may "use" B even though it never invokes it; for example, a program may "use" an interrupt handling routine even though it never calls it. The "uses" relation may be particularly useful in AI programs which often tend to deviate from the straightforward, sequential call-and-return control structures.

In passing I might note that one of the currently most successful design-for-change strategies in AI is the tabular representation of knowledge. This can be viewed as an AI development of the well-known software engineering route to flexible systems: table-driven mechanisms, using for example, decision tables, or parsing tables. And the ready modifiability of such mechanisms derives from that ubiquitous 'goodthing' — modularity (more on the potential beneficence of modularity anon).

There are often two rather different applications of modularity in table-driven mechanisms: first, a procedural–declarative separation of information — a control module operates on the declarative modules, the table; and second, the relative independence of each table entry. The ease of modifiability is then based on the property that pieces of declarative information (individual table entries) can be added or deleted in a relatively context-free manner.

Unfortunately this is an idealized scheme: actual knowledge bases are always complicated by a certain degree of control information in the relationships between the rules. Hence entries cannot be added and deleted in a truly context-free manner, and thus we have the problems associated with incrementally extending knowledge bases (a small survey of knowledge representation schemes is given in Chapter 3).

Having spent some time on the desired characteristics of an initial approximation and some of the wider implications for the methodology in general, it is time to consider the sources of information from which to construct the initial approximation.


### 4.4.2   The sources of an initial approximation

The potential sources of information for developing an initial specification-implementation are also similar within AI and software engineering, but again the emphasis on these sources is different. The potential information sources are: theories that pertain to the problem domain; protocols from humans performing this and related tasks; introspective analysis by, and quizzing of, "experts" in the field; the expectations of potential users of the finished implementation.

The difference in emphasis can be illustrated with the last information source listed above. In software engineering potential system users can more likely specify what they want, check their expectations against the RFS, and expect to get it implemented as defined. In the AI domain potential users are likely to be specifying only part of what they want, often in terms of generalities. The subsequent development is expected to reveal both inconsistencies in the major desiderata and the scope and limitations of implied subsidiary options. Together these two sets of features are developed until they constitute an adequate implementation. As mentioned earlier, although the similarity between software engineering and AI is persuasive, there is a fundamental difference in purview.

In software engineering, requirements analysis is prior to specification as well as implementation, and at each stage the user should be able to determine quite precisely what he will be getting. In AI the user must try to assess adequacy for his purpose probably without ever knowing exactly what the scope and limitations of the system are.

In software engineering there is the opportunity, which should be exploited to the full, of capturing, independent of any particular persons, a complete and rigorous specification of the problem. That is not to say that human wishes can be ignored, on the contrary that must be taken into account. But this contrasts sharply with typical AI problems wherein certain humans are the only known embodiments of adequate implementations.

In recent years the problem of extracting the requisite information from these organic exemplars of adequate implementations (i.e. humans) has come to the fore and is known as the transfer of expertise problem or knowledge acquisition process.

The scenario usually involves prolonged discussion between the human domain expert and a computer science expert or knowledge engineer as he or she has come to be known. As we discussed in Chapter 3 the problem of extracting accurate and implementable information from a human expert is difficult. It may be just that the problem is relatively new and ill-understood. Certainly progress is being made.

Hayes-Roth, Waterman, & Lenat (1983) offer a number of specific strategies gleaned from the relatively short history of expert systems' construction. They suggest, for example, that a small but interesting subproblem may be identified and used to focus the knowledge-acquisition process.

In an attempt to circumvent the need for a knowledge engineer in the knowledge-acquisition bottleneck much research is currently being directed at developing tools to automate his or her role. The proposed tools vary from TEIRESIAS, which guides the domain expert in updating the MYCIN expert system, to AM and EURISKO, which attempt to synthesize new knowledge from old (both systems are fully described in Davis & Lenat, 1982, and neither are marketable software, but they may be pointers for the future).

An intermediate approach to automating the acquisition of domain-expert knowledge is that advocated by Michie (1982). Michie presents the following tabularization of a domain expert's repertoire of skills.

**Table 4.1** — Two views of an expert's repertoire of skills

|  | Power to recognize examples of key concepts | Power to describe these | Power to identify key primitives | Power to generate good tutorial examples |
|---|---|---|---|---|
| As seen by the expert | Good | Excellent | Excellent | Good |
| As seen by the analyst | Excellent | Very poor | Moderate | Excellent |

Reproduced with permission from *Introductory Readings in Expert Systems,* D. Michie (ed.), Gordon & Breach: NY, 1982.

For Michie the domain expert's strengths and weaknesses suggest that we stop badgering our expert to describe his skills and instead ask him to supply key primitives and tutorial examples. The knowledge engineer then sits down with the program containing this basic information and trains it.

In another, rather different, approach to this transfer of expertise problem (Schvaneveldt *et al.*, 1985), the view is taken that current weak methods (i.e. interviews and protocol analysis), apart from being tedious and time consuming, are inadequate for eliciting tacit knowledge and may, in fact, lead to inaccuracy in the knowledge base. In the proposed scheme the experts are asked to judge the relatedness of concepts in their domain of expertise, concepts such as "airspeed" and "barrel roll" for fighter pilots. The computer system then derives the appropriate cognitive structures automatically; derivation techniques based on multidimensional scaling and link-weighted networks have been explored.

In this section, I have concentrated on expert system research; there are two reasons for this:

(i) The current burst of interest in expert systems has resulted in a relative wealth of practical expertise with respect to them.
(ii) Expert systems are only a portion of AI, but it appears that knowledge bases will be important in all AI, and expert systems are knowledge based.


## 4.5  CONTROLLED CODE MODIFICATION

Editing is the important step in the run–debug–edit cycle; the quality of the editing largely determines whether a program subsides into uncontrollable chaos or progresses to ever more adequate behaviours. The temptation to go for quick potential fixes in the code must be resisted in favour of designing and then implementing modifications.

Controlled modification and underlying abstract representations are discussed fully in the following chapter. In this and the following section I only introduce these concepts in order to complete the description of the AI program development paradigm.

Code modification should be systematic and based upon the abstract representations that underlie a given inadequate implementation. We have to work with the machine-executable description but we use the underlying specification and less abstract intermediate representations (a possible design sequence) as the basis for guiding implementation development. In terms of the desired similarity between form and content described with examples in Section 4.4.1.1, we want to get through the superficial form to work with the content, the closer that these two correspond, the easier the necessary penetration will be.

The obvious example for the computer scientist is in the use of high-level programming languages as an alternative to machine code. The form or structure of high-level language statements, such as WRITE(X), reflect their content or meaning. The form of machine code tends to reflect the machine architecture and to obscure the meaning of the algorithm — the form does not closely correspond to that aspect of content that is the programmer's main concern, i.e. the underlying algorithm.

Behavioural inadequacies of an implementation are analysed in terms of the underlying specifications; and design modifications to remove these inadequacies are formulated; the implementation is re-refined to reflect these changes; and the new implementation is executed, and its resultant performance is assessed.

There are several points to notice here. Firstly, the continual need to translate from implementation to underlying abstract representations and back again is partly due to the level of machine-executable descriptions currently available. It is also due to the need to test the implementation at one level of detail and the advantages of analysing the implementation at a less detailed (and therefore less cluttered) level.

Secondly, once we have a first implementation that functions within (a model of) the application environment, the development process is driven by removal of performance inadequacies.

Thirdly, the problem of developing an adequate AI program has much in common with the maintenance of undocumented software discussed in Chapter 2. This similarity suggests an answer to the questions, what are the underlying abstractions and how do we get hold of them?

## 4.6   THE UNDERLYING ABSTRACTIONS

The underlying abstractions (including a de facto specification) are similar to the design abstracted from an undocumented program to guide software maintenance. And a similar process of abstraction is used to obtain them. Nevertheless there are important differences in both what is abstracted and the process of abstraction. The next chapter is devoted to explaining and illustrating my ideas relating to abstraction. For the moment I need to introduce the ideas and to skim over the range of possibilities in order to complete this chapter. A full illustration of each of the points touched upon in this section is given in the next chapter.

For maintenance purposes a software engineer aims to abstract a description whose prime characteristic is perceptual clarity; it should be a key to the conceptualization of the program as a whole. Across the board omission of detail usually leads to the desired goal. Similarly, for the implementor of an AI problem, abstraction is a route to conceptualization of the program; but it must also lead to a comprehensible description of the problem as specified by the current implementation and be focused upon the dynamic AI modules — that is, it should be concentrated on the modules most likely to be edited. The significance of various aspects of the underlying problem description are likely to differ, and the degree of significant detail is likewise expected to vary. Neither use of the term 'significance' applies in an absolute sense; what is significant depends upon both the implementor's general conception of the task and the particular analysis contemplated. Is the implementor exploring a particular theory, or just trying to get a particular output? Do we require an abstraction that omits a uniform level of detail, or one that preserves detail with respect to some aspect of the program and ruthlessly condenses it elsewhere? Answers to these sorts of questions determine the best abstraction process to apply. For the software maintenance engineer the appropriate abstraction process will produce descriptions containing a uniform level of detail that will serve as maintenance support documentation over the long term for all types and aspects of enquiry.

AI program abstractions to support controlled modification are likely to be non-uniform with respect to the level of detail retained (an example is given in Section 5.2.1.1). The process of abstraction will be applied most heavily in those areas of the implementation that are deemed to be least significant.

As we do not have a comprehensive specification for our AI problem, the descriptions abstracted are the de facto specification and design for which the program is an implementation. That is to say, it is also possible (and exceedingly useful) to abstract a possible specification (note: not *the* specification) and design sequence from a working program.

Abstraction as an aid to conceptualization is an important technique both for the development and adequacy assessment of AI programs, and for the continued maintenance of AI software. I shall therefore look more closely at this technique in the following chapter.

Having introduced the idea of the edit step as controlled modification based upon abstract representations of the program, we now need to consider the possible motivations for editing.

## 4.7   PERFORMANCE EVALUATION

The function of the run step in our paradigm is to evaluate a given implementation on the basis of its behaviour. An ISF is a behavioural characterization of the target problem. Evaluation is then assessment of how well the behaviour of a particular implementation matches up to that described by the ISF.

ISFs being what they are, complex and ill-structured, make performance evaluation a difficult task. But editing and thus development of the current approximation depend on it, so it is a task that must be well done.

In software engineering the formal specification is the yardstick by which the correctness of an implementation is judged. The demonstration of an error is the motivation for modifying an implementation. But the subsequent diagnosis of the problem and the prescription for correcting the design is a non-trivial task that can stretch human problem solving abilities to the limit.

For the AI problem implementor the measure of program adequacy is based upon an ISF. It is also true that errors can be detected and rectified in the same way as in software engineering; for a program characteristic that is not consistent with a known feature of the target function is an error. But peculiar to an AI implementation is the additional problem of the adequacy of the program's behaviour in the incompletely known, or unknown, areas of the target function.

The driving force behind a modification is the removal of a behavioural inadequacy of the program. When such an inadequacy is identified, analysis of the underlying specification is undertaken, and a modified specification is produced and tested. The analysis and modification procedure is at least as difficult as the software engineering debugging and maintenance procedures: the credit assignment problem still obtains, and generation of a modification is a non-trivial, creative act.

In fact the AI implementor probably faces a more difficult task, for he is dealing with questions of adequacy and inadequacy rather than correctness and incorrectness.

The goal of overall adequacy is attained by removal of inadequacy. If an AI implementation is no longer inadequate then it has achieved its goal — an adequate approximation to an incompletely specified function — in the strongest sense one could demand.

In the context of architectural design, Alexander (1964) appears to have been an early advocate of achieving adequacy in ill-structured domains by means of eliminating inadequacies — although he termed it the absence of misfit. Thus our implementation of an ISF is an adequate approximation if there are no glaring inadequacies in its behaviour.

Software engineers also toyed with this idea at the very same meeting that served to launch the term 'software crisis' (Naur & Randell, 1969). A preoccupation with developing the formal end of the spectrum of software engineering methodologies may account for the failure of this technique to land a leading role in the software scene.

De Millo, Lipton, & Perlis (1979) have argued fairly convincingly that the possibility of ever formally verifying real-world programs (as opposed to well-defined abstract functions) is vanishingly small, and even if verification were possible it would not contribute very much to the development of production software. Hence "verifiability must not be allowed to overshadow reliability. Scientists should not confuse mathematical models with reality."

These authors expose what I believe to be a critical discontinuity in computer science in general, and in AI in particular: the world of abstract problems does not transform smoothly into the world of concrete problems — i.e. problems in the empirical world. It is true that certain features carry over but it is equally true that methods that are successful in one domain will not necessarily be appropriate in the other — program development methodologies are an example of non-transferable methods.

Later architectural designers have shown that Alexander's linear scheme is too simplistic. For example, what is and what is not a major solution inadequacy can be strongly influenced by societal and personal bias. In expert systems' research we do at least have a domain expert who is presumably good at making such judgements.

But what about a natural-language interface? Who is the domain expert? None of us? All of us? Behavioural inadequacy judgements, as one would expect, cannot generally be based upon a simple, context-free procedure.

Nevertheless, identifying major inadequacies does seem to be a simpler process than estimating relative adequacy. As Alexander's successors assert, performance evaluation may still be "an argumentative process between those concerned" (Bazjanac, 1974), but for us the arguments are severely constrained by the general context of the current approximation (explicit, detailed, and comprehensive) and the particular behaviours in question.

The problem in the run-and-debug component of the AI program development paradigm is not so much finding the bug — that is there as well — but one of deciding if there is a bug and what it is. Clearly this is an escalation of the problems described in Chapter 2 for conventional software engineering.

One software engineering technique that may help to further constrain and simplify the ill-structured subproblem of identifying major behavioural inadequacies is top-down design and testing. System inadequacies can be exposed in steps of successively more detail. Behavioural information can be utilized to modify gross features of the system structure before we make a commitment to an implementation of the relatively finer ISF features.

Unfortunately any attempt to apply the run–debug–edit cycle to an ISF in a top-down manner must give precedence to the completeness criterion described earlier — again we do not have all the freedoms of the software engineer.

Nevertheless it is a good strategy to bear in mind and exploit insofar as is possible in order to impose some structure on the performance evaluation problem in AI.

Hayes-Roth, Waterman, & Lenat (1983) state that "development of the prototype system is an extremely important step in the expert system construction process." They also state that the prototype is used to test the adequacy of the basic underlying ideas and that some of the code may be salvaged for later versions.

This is clearly consistent with the idea of top-down implementation and testing. Dependent upon how much of the implementation is thrown away and how much goes into the next version, we have more of a high-level implementation for refinement and less of a throwaway prototype or vice versa.


### 4.7.1 Testing
So far we have only considered how to treat the behaviours of an approximation to our ISF, and how, in general, to structure performance evaluation. We now need to consider how to select test cases in order to expose performance inadequacies.

The first point to note is that we cannot expect to have a complete and rigorous statement of the scope and limitations of our problem — far from it. Thus the construction of a set of test data, although it should follow the guidelines of software engineering (see Section 2.4.1), will inevitably be a pale shadow of the more well-structured analogue.

Hayes-Roth, Waterman, & Lenat (1983) attempt to outline a testing strategy for expert systems. They also discuss formal versus informal testing and note that acceptance testing for expert systems is a complex problem but one that has been dealt with for a long time — in assessing the competence of human practitioners. But that does not mean it has been solved, only that we have a lot of prior experience to draw on. They also present some evidence that "formal evaluation can be seriously misleading — even when methodologically sound in its statistical design."

A general strategy is suggested by the nature of ISFs — ISFs are usually founded upon intangible needs in the empirical world. Thus the natural-language problems are founded on our needs to communicate. Medical diagnosis problems are founded on our needs to do something about disease and bodily malfunction, etc.

The general testing strategy is then to expose our implemented approximation to that environment from which the need arose.

The ultimate test for an adequate approximation is that it displays no major inadequacies within its intended application environment. This is also true of conventional software; the difference is that comprehensive testing of conventional software is possible before exposure to the user environment. Comprehensive bench testing of AI software is hardly a possibility.

An instructive example of the complexity and ill-structure associated with implementing AI problems can be found in the report of Gaschnig (1982) on the development of the expert system, PROSPECTOR. He gives details of performance evaluation and specific examples of performance inadequacies that suggest further refinements of the system.

To the software engineer the surprising aspect of the testing reported by Gaschnig is that the implementation was tested with the data that formed the basis of the design! In software engineering this is no test, certainly not a test of general accuracy or adequacy. Gaschnig, himself, states these limitations of the testing he presents, but he claims that they "have proved useful in the ongoing model refinement process."

The point is not that AI program developers don't understand the fundamentals of testing, but that AI implementations are so complex and based on incomplete specifications that such a first level of testing is required. We must first determine that the heuristics as implemented do indeed collectively function in the intended manner, if so, we have overcome the first major hurdle and can push on and further refine the implementation.

Weizenbaum (1976) captures something of the feel of this type of performance evaluation with an apt simile. He says, "computer modeling provides a quick feedback that can have a truly therapeutic effect precisely because of its immediacy. Computer modeling is thus somewhat like Polaroid photography: it is hard to maintain a belief that one has taken a great photograph when the counterexample is in one's hands."

A final point on adequacy judgements is that the decisions may not be so critical for sophisticated self-adaptive systems. If we can just get the system to some threshold level of adequacy it might well be able to take over from there. This is clearly a speculative observation but it is, I would claim, very much along the line that AI must take.

## 4.8   SPECIFICATION DEVELOPMENT

An adequate AI implementation embodies a completely specified function. This function is an adequate approximation to the incompletely specified function that originally served as the means of characterizing the problem. This initial specification probably no longer holds, because the process of AI problem implementation is very much a process of specification development.

The original incompletely specified function is not incomplete as a matter of choice but as a matter of practical necessity. The process of computer implementation (each implementation embodies a formal specification) refines and develops the incompletely specified function, even perhaps to the point of eliminating all incompleteness. More likely, the domain of known input–output relationships will be extended; the domain of context-dependent relationships refined and better understood; and within the domain of unknown relationships particular elements may be singled out as warranting a decisive ruling from an empirical, theoretical, or even ad hoc basis.

Generation of the full implications of an approximation to an incompletely specified function can often lead to a more completely specified version of the function. This is because specification of some aspects of the function will indirectly specify further functional characteristics but these further implications may be the outcome of a complex network of interactions. Such implications of a specification can be reliably explored only with the aid of a machine executable notation. The sheer size and complexity of a tentative specification necessitates the use of a mechanized means of exploring its full implications.

Pessimists might argue that programs which have probed any reasonable depth into AI turn out to be catastrophes looking for somewhere to happen. Some might even claim that these programs don't do much looking, the catastrophes just keep happening. The PhD candidate whose dissertation is at the mercy of the program's behaviour spends an inordinate amount of time trying to coax and cajole his unmanageable creation into behaving long enough to get the requisite few examples of intelligent behaviour out of it — such is not the stuff of practical software. Our task then is to adapt this incremental paradigm such that programs of practical software quality are forthcoming.

# 5

# AI into practical software

An important question in relation to an AI
program is: How does it do it?

## 5.1 WHAT'S THE PROBLEM?

In software engineering we don't start coding until we have both a full
specification of the problem and a series of designs differing in level of detail.
The initial specification is definitive. If a mismatch between implementation
and specification is detected, then the implementation is incorrect. If the
specification needs to be altered we must redesign and reimplement the new
specification.

In AI we start wherever we can and hope to emerge with a behaviourally
adequate program. In the previous chapter I have articulated the developmental paradigm of AI in some detail; enough fine structure has been added
to change the 'hope' of the preceding sentence into a much more positive
feeling.

We must now tackle the subsequent question of what, if anything, do we
need to do in order to make the I–O-adequate programs so produced
function as practically useful software? If we develop a behaviourally
adequate program, what have we got? Roughly stated, we have a pile of
code, usually a large and intricate one, that exhibits no major behavioural
inadequacies in so far as it has been tested.

This last limitation would seem to be the same as that which must be
applied to all practical software: it is only free from known error, at best. But
with conventional software although the testing of all possibilities is not
practically feasible, the scope and limitations of potential tests is well-
defined. So strategies for comprehensive testing on the basis of only a small
subset of all possible tests can be devised. There are typically no such
constraints within which we can comprehensively test the adequacy of an AI
program. An incompletely specified function does, of course, embody some
constraints but the set of constraints is orders of magnitude looser than that

associated with the formalized specification of a conventional software engineering problem.

Testing and maintenance have not hitherto been major AI problems only because AI has been an almost exclusively research area and AI programs have been experiments. But if we intend to push on with our AI programs into the harsher world of applications software, we will require all of the usual desiderata of practical software:

(1) perceptual clarity;
(2) robustness;
(3) reliability;
(4) maintainability.

At a meta-level we would also like to see an accumulation of AI competence (from specific algorithms and data structures to abstract principles), independent of any particular implementation or even implementation domain, such that each new AI application does not have to be incrementally developed from the ground up. This problem is on a different level and to some extent forms the basis for achieving the above-listed desiderata of practical software. Success in contructing robust, reliable, etc. AI software will be due in part to the achievement of a situation where each new venture can draw on a collection of tried and tested techniques — minimization of necessary creativity is likely to maximize practical utility.

In the current chapter I thus consider this problem of accumulating general expertise in addition to several other problems (including the technique of controlled modification introduced in the preceding chapter). The general problem is that of an AI program as a pile of code and its relationship to some underlying representation. We need to access underlying, abstract, representations as a basis both for controlled modification within the incremental development paradigm, and for the post-adequacy stage — the application as practical software.

An adequate program has demonstrated that an adequate approximation to the ISF is practically feasible. It is a detailed specification of how the ISF can be adequately approximated. The program developer will have at least a rough plan of what this approximation does.

Unfortunately the 'how' is dispersed and interred in masses of ISF-irrelevant idiosyncrasies of both the programming language and its implementation. Similarly the plan of what the approximation does may be little more than wishful thinking after a long series of iterations through the run–debug–edit cycle.

Before there is any hope of applying an AI program as a practical software system, there are a number of preliminaries that will have to be observed.

The nature of the AI program development paradigm and the dynamic nature of AI programming languages are such that, despite the use of controlled modification, the resultant program is unlikely to possess a transparent structure. In traditional software engineering one of the major goals of the program development methodology is perceptual clarity of code. It is also a goal in AI program development, but it is a goal that is both secondary to the generation of an adequate approximation, and difficult to achieve given the often low level and incremental nature of the run–debug–edit cycle.

Thus both the 'how' and the 'what' of an AI program are likely to be subjects for debate, even for the program designer himself. But a firm grasp of these two properties of a program is an essential prerequisite of practical software. It is a necessary first step irrespective of whether we wish to utilize the AI program as is, or whether we intend to restructure and recode the underlying algorithm to some extent.

Other reasons for requiring cognizance of these two keys to program understanding are:

(1) as a basis for controlled modification of a program during the run–debug–edit cycle described in the previous chapter;
(2) as a basis for effectively communicating the general principles that the program embodies.

Let us now examine, one by one, these reasons for wanting to access abstract representations embodied by an AI program. In the earlier terminology of form and content, we wish to access various aspects of the content of the program uncluttered by the impedimenta of a machine-executable form. We need abstract representations disencumbered to enhance cognitive efficiency when dealing with the complexities of AI programs.

## 5.2 THE UNDERSTANDINGS OF AN AI PROGRAM

### 5.2.1 A basis for controlled modification

We are developing an adequate approximation by iterating around the run–debug–edit cycle in, hopefully, ever-decreasing circles — as measured by the number of major inadequacies perceived. A crucial link in this circular chain, the one that determines whether indeed convergence on adequacy is likely, is the edit step: having identified a major performance inadequacy we must analyse the cause, find its origin, and then design a modification that will eliminate the inadequacy without introducing any new inadequacies.

All this was discussed in the previous chapter. Now the task is to examine in more detail a strategy to support controlled modification and with it the hope of steering to convergence, as opposed to haphazard hacking, a procedure that will converge only by pure chance.

Computer programmers tend to be optimists; they have to be to survive in a relationship with a partner (the computer) whose fast, uncompromising logic tends to immediately reduce one's best and hard-won efforts at communication to a catalogue of errors. AI programmers are, perhaps, even more optimistic than most; can that be the rationale for the prevalence of haphazard code hacking as the chosen route to adequate AI programs?

The AI program development paradigm is also seductive in that it encourages the pursuit of undisciplined program development strategies.

The AI program developer is not forced to analyse inadequacies thoroughly before designing a modification; the opportunity is always there to just modify the code on a largely speculative basis, and then run it and see what happens — especially as the cost of mistakes is low in an interactive environment with a neatly embedded error monitor and editor.

Analysis of the cause of a performance inadequacy and design of an appropriate modification both require comprehension of the program at several levels. There is a need to look carefully at the details local to the inadequate code and at the relationship of the problematic module as a whole *vis-à-vis* the other modules with which it interacts.

Every time around the run–debug–edit cycle the AI program developer faces much the same problem as the software engineer who is required to modify an undocumented program. Both persons need to generate effective documentation from the code, documentation in the sense of multi-level representations that will facilitate understanding of the program code. Although the eventual modification must be in terms of the idiosyncrasies of a particular programming language, inadequacy analysis and subsequent redesign should be based upon the highest possible level of abstract representation. Controlled modification exploits the conventional wisdom of practical software engineering: changes should be made at the highest possible level of design and then refined back down to the level of program code.

The AI programmer does not have the luxury of a multi-level design; he must abstract one from the code. One mitigating circumstance is, of course, that each time around the run–debug–edit cycle the abstracted 'design' from the previous iteration will be available.

There appear to be two major strategies for abstracting representations to support controlled modification:

(a) Abstract and maintain a virtually complete 'design' throughout the process of program development.
(b) On each iteration of the run–debug–edit cycle abstract as much of the 'design' as is necessary to support analysis and redesign of the inadequacy found.

Strategy (a) requires a large initial effort but a minimum of additional effort in the subsequent program development sequence. Strategy (b) results in a spreading of the abstraction effort throughout the program development sequence. Given a long development sequence involving a wide range of inadequacies the differences between these two strategies will disappear.

Fig. 5.1 is a schematic illustration that focuses on the process of controlled modification; several points should be noted. First, the EDIT step is not code hacking; it is primarily a process of analysis followed by synthesis at some appropriate level (or levels) of abstract representation.

Second, to document a program as a basis for debugging, something more than the program code is required. The program developer also needs to apply his knowledge of the goals and objectives of the program.

Third, the degree to which both analysis and modification are based

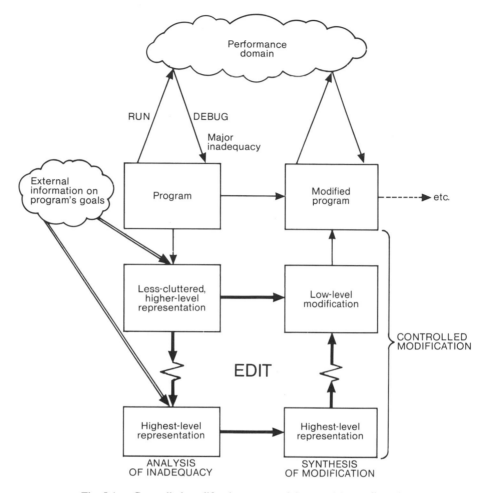

Fig. 5.1 — Controlled modification as part of the run–debug–edit cycle

upon high-level, abstract representations of the program is dependent upon the nature of the particular inadequacy detected.

At each occurrence of the edit step a number of sub-steps need to be executed. We need to generate some uncluttered abstract representations that will provide us with a coherent and comprehensible picture of what is going on in the program with respect to the suspected source of the inadequacy. In order to generate such abstract representations we will require (apart from the code itself) a substantial injection of external information, in particular, the goals and design considerations that led to the code that we have at hand.

Having abstracted representations that have reduced the complexity of the problem to manageable levels by ignoring or generalizing the non-significant features of the program, we must analyse the perceived inadequacy and then synthesize a solution. The modified abstract representation must then be expanded to yield an executable program once more.

A question that naturally arises here is: how do we know which aspects of the underlying structure to abstract in order to facilitate analysis of a particular behavioural inadequacy? A good question, but unfortunately no definitive answer naturally arises in its wake.

Locating errors and generating appropriate modifications are both 'five-star' creative processes. With respect to localizing the symptoms of a perceived inadequacy and thus focusing an abstract representation correctly, the best advice is to modularize your system exhaustively in the hope of localizing your troubles (the splendours of modularization as a complexity management strategy are discussed in the following chapter). The hope is that all your inadequacies will be limited!

A further useful device for locating the sources of an inadequacy would be the mind of Sherlock Holmes, and the way to get it seems to be by practice, perseverance, and luck — not necessarily in that order.

### 5.2.1.1   A representation to support controlled modification: an example

A program was developed to explore physiologically-based mechanisms and their ability to support basic learning behaviours; it was fundamentally an infinite loop structure. We modelled an organism that received an input from its environment, processed the input through a neuron-like network, generated responses (an orienting response, movement within its environment, and expectation of next input stimulus), received another input, and so on. Fig. 5.2 illustrates the basic structure of the program and is the type of representation that can be abstracted to assist a maintenance engineer to gain a general familiarity with the program (as described later in Section 5.2.4). The important loop structure is specified in node 1.5; nodes 1.1 to 1.4 specify the initial setup only.

For the purpose of incrementally developing the program we found that the type of representation illustrated in Fig. 5.3 was by far the most helpful for both analysing the source of inadequacies, and designing subsequent modifications.

The representation in Fig. 5.3 captures and blends very high level structure with very low level structure whilst focusing on the most troublesome area — the processing of an input stimulus within the network. At the highest level this representation captures the input–process–response loop (essentially the equivalent of node 1.5.1.4 in the loop specified at node 1.5 in Fig. 5.2); the basic structure in the diagram is this loop. The circles divided into two sections and the other rounded objects divided into three sections represent fine implementation details: internal nodes in the 'neural' network were implemented as three component objects; input and output nodes were two component objects. In an abstract sense each internal node contains only an activity value, but three fields were used in the implementation: one, to hold this current activity; a second to hold the previous activity value; and a third to facilitate sequential simulation of a conceptually parallel process of transfer of activity around the network. The $I$s and $E$s represent input activity and expectation activity respectively, whilst the subscripts refer to the number of times around the basic loop.

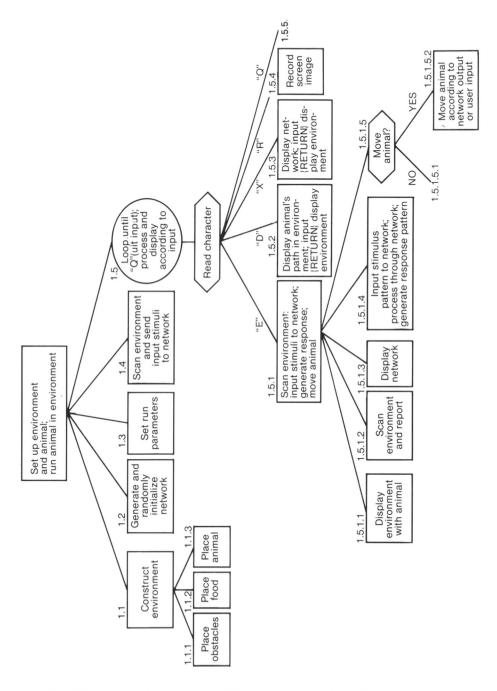

Fig. 5.2 — A structure diagram of the program for exploring basic learning behaviours

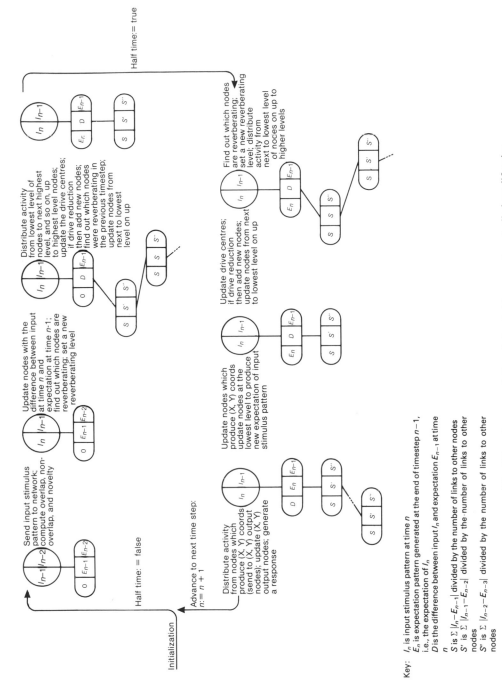

Fig. 5.3 — A representation abstracted to support controlled modification

The principles that we were exploring concerned the relationships among strategies for processing and distributing "activity" in the network, and the relationship between these strategies as a whole and the behaviour of the system. The foci of our incremental development were the network nodes hence we have detailed schematic representations of the nodes in Fig. 5.3. On traversing the loop of Fig. 5.3 in a clockwise direction from the "initialization" point on the left side, we encounter successive 'snapshots' of the network through the course of the basic cycle of: input stimulus; process stimulus; generate response.

Between each pair of node diagrams is a summary of the algorithms that are executed at that point in the loop. This multi-level blend of representations seems to focus on the problematic details of the program but displays them each within their own general contexts.

Notice that this representation to support controlled modification is derived from several disjoint parts of the overall program (nodes 1.5.1.4 and 1.5 of Fig. 5.2): namely the ill-defined AI segment and the significant aspect of its context — the loop. The bulk of the system (the rest of Fig. 5.2) is a well-defined testbed for the AI subsystem. This strategy of AI-after-software engineering is developed and explained in the following chapter.

The purpose of including these two rather complex figures in this example is not to overwhelm the reader with detail, but to provide actual examples of useful underlying representations. And further than this I wish to contrast two different representations from the same program in order to illustrate my contention that different types of abstractions best support different activities within the overall process of developing AI software.

There is thus no need (and no expectation) that the reader will fully comprehend the details of the two figures. The expectation is rather that he or she will appreciate the general differences between these two figures, and will understand how they reflect the differences in the understanding necessary to support controlled modification as opposed to the general comprehension of the program.

### 5.2.2  A basis for effective communication of AI programs

It is sometimes necessary for the program developer to communicate to other persons both what a given AI program does, and how it does it. It may be necessary to transmit a basis for understanding the program during the development cycle (for the purpose of obtaining developmental assistence) as well as to communicate a 'finished' product. Although it should be obvious from earlier discussion that there is no well-defined line between the absence and presence of a major performance inadequacy, hence AI products are never really 'finished'.

The difference between this communication problem and that of the previous section is that we are not communicating to the designer himself (the person most familiar with how and what the program ought to be doing); we are instead charged with the task of communicating the program to someone who may have been totally outside the development process.

The obvious solution to this problem is: wrap up the code nicely, perhaps sprinkle it with a few extra comments, and give it to any interested party. Unfortunately this neat technique is an utter failure for a number of reasons:

(i) AI programs tend to be both large and complex, and lacking the "structured" organization that well-designed software should exhibit.

(ii) AI languages coupled with dynamic modification strategies must lack perceptual clarity when compared with the static, disciplined languages of conventional software.

(iii) The goals and objectives of the program are nowhere in the code (although they could be in the comments).

Self-documenting code is a contentious quantity in conventional software engineering. In AI software all basis for contention is eliminated: realistically self-documenting AI software is probably rarer than unicorns in Hyde Park.

What we require once again are some abstract representations generated by omitting program detail and blending in the developer's knowledge of the program's goals and objectives.

As on several earlier occasions what we need in AI is similar to a process that is commonly used in practical software engineering; after the fact generation of documentation is a well-known process. Apart from some tidying-up and rounding-off, the documentation, the basis for communicating a traditional software engineering product, will always be available alongside the program code; in fact most of this documentation should be available prior to the program code.

Unfortunately, the AI program development paradigm does not exhibit this very handy characteristic. Clearly an AI program developer must have some goals and objectives with respect to program design prior to any implementation. And although these design strategies will also be refined as the incremental process of program development proceeds, they are likely to be too crude and incomplete (and perhaps inaccurate) to serve as more than a rudimentary basis for effective communication of the 'what' and the 'how' of the program.

From our preceding discussion of controlled modification it will be apparent that a disciplined and comprehensive use of this technique should make a significant difference both to the level of refinement and to the extensiveness of the design schemata extant when the program's behaviour is judged to be adequate. I say "should" rather than something more positive because, as we shall later discuss, it is not at all certain that the underlying representations that best support one operation on the program (e.g. controlled modification) are the same as those that best support a different operation (e.g. communication of the general principles).

Why do we need to communicate the 'how' and 'what' of AI programs? The answer is that we would like the introduction of AI into practical software to be, as far as possible, a cumulative enterprise; we do not want to keep reinventing the same wheels to support each new application of AI.

Charniak, Riesbeck, & McDermott (1980) have attempted to bring together the "practice" aspect of the "small core of accepted theory and practice" in AI. They describe and provide examples from a comprehensive library of programming tools. They present a set of tools that will simulate an AI-conducive computer on top of a LISP system. Then the AI programmer can concentrate on the higher-level aspects of the problem without the constant distraction of having to reinvent the necessary software base. This is indeed an attempt to exploit an accumulation of expertise but it is also necessary to accumulate more implementation-independent knowledge.

The level of knowledge that it will be useful to abstract from an I–O-adequate program and contribute to this corpus of AI expertise will vary enormously. It will be useful to accumulate a whole range of structures, from particular algorithms in particular languages, through abstract algorithms and data structures, to very general domain independent principles.

Knowledge bases are an example, perhaps the most successful one, of such a transfer of knowledge from particular AI research projects into the domain of practical software. Even this specific example has multi-level representations.

At one level a knowledge base is a, not very precisely defined, abstract data structure. At a more detailed level, production rules are one particular implementation strategy which if adopted still leave many degrees of detailed implementation freedom from which to select a specific implementation.

Cerri (1984) discusses the social potential of AI and the possibilities for limited resource communities to get access to the potential benefits. He claims "that AI requires a new type of know-how," and that "the traditional computer scientist does not have *in principle* an adequate education for the AI tasks". He further states that "results in AI have not yet been *cumulative*" and he believes that this lack of cumulative results is inherent in AI. I think that the outlook is brighter than this even on the basis of our current, rather limited, accumulations of AI knowledge.

### 5.2.2.1 *Principles from programs: an example*

Concern for AI as a surfeit of programs and a dearth of justified principles has long provoked calls for abstracting or extracting underlying principles from AI programs, as can be found in Wielinga (1978) and Pylyshyn (1978) for example.

The problem is that no one has described how it should be done. A second problem is how to justify that the abstraction is in some sense valid, and is not just wishful thinking.

The problem of exactly what principles to abstract is to some extent constrained by the I–O-adequate program in that the program's behaviour is interpreted by means of a semantic mapping. That is to say, the formal computational objects input and output are typically mapped into another domain to obtain the desired meaning.

Within the example to be used, a model of basic learning behaviours, an input array of integers is interpreted as an input stimulus pattern, and an output integer is interpreted as the orienting response (OR) measured by say, Galvanic Skin Response; an OR is usually interpreted as indicative of a significant stimulus and as a precursor of learning processes.

Clearly there are still many degrees of freedom for abstracting principles that relate to these input and output interpretations. There is in fact a circularity here, the abstraction of principles that relate the input and output interpretations can provide some of the justification for these initial, input and output interpretations. Awareness of this difficulty should help us avoid it.

A program is a pile of code, it does not contain any principles in isolation. A human theorizer applies an interpretation in order to make the claim that the program has some interesting behaviour. He can then apply further interpretations to abstract underlying principles.

Each of these interpretations, or semantic mappings, must be justified, they cannot be proven. To support the abstraction of principles we need to make the necessary justifications explicit. The major point to be made is that the principles abstracted are not necessarily correct, in some sense, but they are explicitly justified and hence we have a firm basis for discussion and criticism. When a theorizer abstracts a principle from a program it is a personal and unprovable claim; it is also largely unchallengeable on any systematic basis. Such is the state of most AI principles. Abstraction of a principle from a program is only a partial fulfilment of the goal of accumulating a body of program-independent AI knowledge.

Anyone can abstract any principle from any program, almost. We change the names of variables (if done consistently we have the same program), we neglect structure that we don't want, and we preserve or develop structure that supports the principle that we are aiming at.

Add to this the fact that most AI programs are very large and complex, and that comprehensible principles are short and simple. There are two justification problems here:

(1) How do you justify the abstraction of a principle that is, probably, in a different language than the program, and is many orders of magnitude smaller and simpler?
(2) How do you justify an abstraction that does bear an obvious structural similarity to the code from which it was derived and is thus only slightly smaller and simpler?

We will deal with the problem (2) here and then progress to problem (1) in Section 5.4 because it is a general problem associated with all aspects of understanding AI programs.

Problem (1) is not peculiar to AI, it must be faced whenever models are used to justify a theory. It is the problem of justifying a semantic mapping from the objects of the model to the objects of the principle, and this includes a justification of why some aspects of the model are non-significant with respect to the abstracted principle.

The justification for this semantic mapping typically derives from a combination of the larger theoretical context and from a correspondence between empirical data and the model's behaviour. No new contribution is claimed here except to say that the major components of this semantic mapping should be made explicit — again as a basis for discussion.

The behavioural adequacy of the example program has been demonstrated in Johnston, Partridge, and Lopez (1983) and Fig. 5.4 provides a

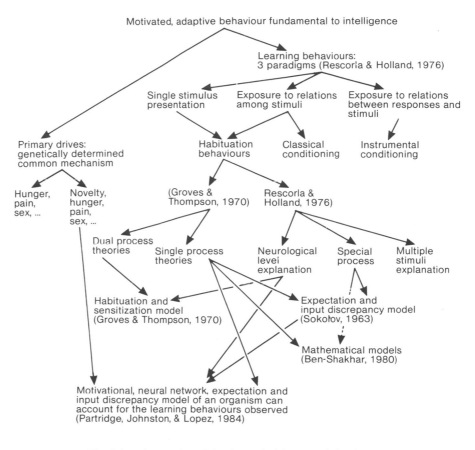

Fig. 5.4 — A summary of the theoretical framework for the program that explores basic learning behaviours

summary of the larger theoretical context of the program.

At a more detailed level the program statement:

$$ORESP:=round(((NOVELTY+0.1)*MAGNITUDE)*4)$$

is abstracted to the principle that,

> Orienting response is $f$(novelty of input stimulus, magnitude of input stimulus and expected stimulus)

The relevance of this principle to AI is that it postulates a mechanism to account for the human ability to pay attention to (i.e. orient to) only 'significant' events. You may recall the discussion about deciding upon the significant features of an event as a problem in machine learning. Human beings are the only sophisticated learning devices that we know of, thus mechanisms that humans appear to use are a major source of inspiration for heuristics to support machine learning.

Schank (1982) has written a complete book on "expectation failure" as a high-level mechanism that accounts for cognitive behaviour and, in particular, high-level learning behaviour. I believe that expectation-failure-controlled processing may be a generic strategy operating at many levels within the system that produces intelligent human behaviour (see Partridge, 1985).

I am currently applying this principle and several others that derive from the same program to the problem of a cognitive industrial robot (briefly described in Chapter 4); the robot proceeds 'mechanically' with its task whilst sensory input conforms to its expectations but if an unexpected or novel event occurs (sensory input and expectation do not match) then the robot 'orients' to the discrepancy detected (it enters a problem solving and learning mode).

The justification for the above principle is based upon:

(a) the above-cited justifications for interpreting program output as the orienting response;
(b) the Sokolov (1963) theory of novelty of input stimulus coupled with the behavioural adequacy of the program; and
(c) empirical data that shows a direct relationship between the intensity of the input stimulus or a missing but expected input stimulus, and the magnitude of the orienting response.

In order to evaluate such justifications we might need to determine exactly how the values of the variables NOVELTY and MAGNITUDE are computed; or better than that, we could examine the abstracted principle for the novelty computation and its justification, and so on. We might also want to examine both the basis for Sokolov's theory, and the empirical data referred to in (c).

This example raises two points. First, justifications cannot be expected to be complete or proven. They are the bones of an argument and by being explicitly given they provide a firm basis for discussion of their validity and hence the validity of the principles abstracted.

Second, the use of suggestive names in a program clearly facilitates perception of the correspondences between the code and abstractions derived from it. But the use of overly-suggestive names is a pernicious AI trend that McDermott (1976) drew attention to some years ago. Again empirical data and theoretical context is an explicit attempt to justify the suggestive naming of objects both within the program and within the principles abstracted. This attempt to explicitly justify important relations (between formal objects in the model and concepts within the domain of the principles abstracted) should help to achieve a balance between helpful and meaningful names, and overly-suggestive, misleading names.

It is these two classes of justification that give credibility to the above principle concerning the orienting response as opposed to the interpretation implied by the computationally equivalent program statement:

$$ORESP:=round(((TIME\_OF\_DAY+0.1)*HUMIDITY)*4)$$

from which we can abstract the following principle:

The orienting response is $f$(time of day, humidity).

Such an abstraction is not invalid; it is just more or less credible. The credibility of this principle must also be based upon the dual grounds of wider theoretical criticism and empirical scrutiny of the executing program. There is no requirement of a one-to-one correspondence between programs and principles; the relationship is one-to-many in both directions (two significantly different programs may be advanced as independent bases for different formulations of the same principle; we then have competing formulations of the principle to evaluate.)

The foregoing is not an attempt to justify the abstracted principle concerning the orienting response. It is an example intended both to demonstrate the abstraction of a principle, and to stress the requirement of accompanying justifications — a requirement that is different in nature and, far less contentious if we are abstracting, say, maintenance documentation. A more complete treatment of this example can be found in Partridge, Johnston, & Lopez (1984).

### 5.2.3 A basis for redesign and reimplementation

Closely related to the above-discussed, long-term, benefits of abstracting techniques and principles from particular programs, is the immediate practical problem of converting a typical AI program into an 'equivalent' structure that is widely acceptable in typical application environments.

This problem could be largely a teething problem associated with the newness of AI in practical software. It should certainly become less of a problem as AI hardware, AI languages, and program development environments (these crucial aspects of AI program development and maintenance are discussed in the next chapter) become more commonplace within potential application environments. This is not to say that this problem will ever vanish or even decrease significantly in the near future.

Charniak, Riesbeck, & McDermott (1980) have approached one part of this problem from the stance of "changing the surface structure [of LISP] with the judicious use of well-designed macros". As a particular example, they develop loop macros to replace the recursive mechanism of LISP — a problem that we will return to below.

In the following chapter we consider the problems that AI techniques and principles will engender in practical software regardless of the implementation environments (hardware–software combinations) employed. Herein let us consider the more immediate (but less fundamental) problem of the implementation environments typically used for AI program development and their mismatch with the majority of application environments.

The incompatibility in question can be seen to stem from the differences between the AI and the software engineering program development paradigms; these differences have naturally led to two significantly different classes of implementation environments. In particular, the AI programming languages, exemplified by LISP, are radically different from the languages favoured for the construction of reliable and robust, comprehensible software. And in more recent years AI has received a substantial boost from specialized AI hardware: particularly the LISP machines and their high-powered program development environments (discussed in the following chapter).

Artificial Intelligence Corporation, who claim the first successful commercialization of AI technology with their natural-language data base query system Intellect, specifically recognized this potential problem and solved it by abandoning LISP as the language of choice; they implemented Intellect in PL/I for IBM machines (Eisenberg & Hill, 1984).

One trend that suggests that this problem is going to get worse before it gets better is the development of software tools for constructing, in particular, expert systems. A number of these tools are developed both on and for the AI implementation environments thus binding AI program development even more tightly to these highly specialized environments.

An example is VERAC Corporation's development of an environment, OPS5E, to run on the Symbolics 3600 LISP machine and facilitate the construction of expert systems using the OPS5 language.

Sacerdoti (1982), speaking from the Machine Intelligence Corporation's experience in marketing vision systems, says: "There are a number of barriers standing between development of a successful laboratory prototype and producing a marketable product." He goes on to suggest that the primary barrier is the lack of a machine-intelligence infrastructure in the marketplace.

I would not cast this aspect of the problem in this primary role, for I view it as a relatively minor problem, and certainly subsidiary to the substantial technological barriers that stand between laboratory prototypes and commercial software. But perhaps by "laboratory prototype" Sacerdoti means an AI problem that has been 'solved' in a technological sense, even to the extent of exhibiting all the desiderata of practical software — to me that seems to include a lot more than the term "prototype" should connote. One possible explanation may be that Sacerdoti is primarily concerned with vision projects, and vision is one AI area in which significant, useful, and reliable context-free algorithms have been developed.

One easy solution to this marketing problem is that potential users of AI software will buy LISP machines and train their software maintenance staff to cope with LISP and its relatives. This is possible, but given the inertia within the potential applications domains (witness the continued stranglehold of FORTRAN and COBOL despite the fact that they are outdated relics of a bygone age) we have to wonder how likely it is — as Sacerdoti says, "Introduction of new technology must be evolutionary, not revolutionary."

A notable exception to this tendency to resist change has been the Digital

Equipment Corporation (DEC). According to McDermott (1982), DEC set up and trained a group of 12 people specifically for the maintenance and continued development of the R1 expert system.

A second route to solution of this problem is to abstract the underlying algorithm at some level and then refine and implement it again within a target application environment. So yet again we have a need to abstract an underlying representation from a specific implementation.

A further need to redesign and reimplement AI programs in order to obtain practical software concerns the lack of transparency that is typical of the products of the run–debug–edit cycle. It is not that the competent AI program developer is unaware of the importance of comprehensible code; it is just that several other requirements are of more immediate importance and the development process itself contains little direct incentive for developing transparent programs. By way of contrast the software engineering paradigm is primarily geared to encourage the construction of readily comprehensible programs. This methodological difference is a reflection of the fact that research environments have been the home of AI and practical applications environments have nurtured the software engineering paradigm.

Competent and extensive use of the controlled modification techniques can aid the building of transparency into AI programs. But the ultimate complexity and ill-structure of the problems being tackled is probably bound to have an adverse affect on program transparency. If you never know quite where you are going with a pile of code, it is not at all surprising that the end result is not a model of structured programming when you finally get there. Sandewall (1978) suggests that we need a discipline that he terms "structured growth"; I also believe in this need. Controlled modification is one component of such a discipline and several other contributive strategies are discussed in the following chapter.

Another important reason why the AI program developer might have difficulty in producing clearly structured code concerns self- modifiability in AI systems. In the next chapter I make the case that the full potential of AI in practical software necessarily involves sophisticated adaptivity or self-modifiability. Such a capability puts a layer of indirectness between the program developer and the code (or data structures) being generated by a running, self-modifying program. Clearly the task of designing self-modifying (i.e. learning) mechanisms which themselves will always generate transparent structures just adds another aspect of complexity to the heap.

In Michie's description of the automatic induction of expert system rules (described in Chapter 3) the inscrutability of the results of machine learning is already a problem. Michie (1982) points to the necessity for machine learning as the scope of expert systems increases but the structures automatically generated, although they perform very well, "proved to be opaque to the eye of the domain expert". Michie sees this general problem as one problem that will grow in importance and he recommends a man/machine approach, which he names "structured induction", to the automatic induction problem.

Comprehensibility, which is founded on transparency of code, is the fundamental requirement of practical software, especially for AI software as we shall see in the following chapter. One route to comprehensible code from an adequate but perceptually opaque program is through redesign and reimplementation. Hence we first require the abstract design that underlies the inscrutable code.

### 5.2.4   A basis for the maintenance of AI software

Programs that do well in cosy research labs under the expert ministrations of dedicated and highly competent researchers are likely to be rated less highly in an application environment where the levels of human indifference and incompetence will be considerably higher; the program will be expected to continue to perform adequately under relatively minimal human supervision.

One major headache of all practical software applications is maintenance: someone other than the designer has to keep the program performing adequately in the face of unavoidable but unforeseen environmental situations. For AI software this problem is qualitatively worse (discussed in detail in the following chapter), part of this escalation of the problem is due to the AI development paradigm — it delivers a pile of adequately performing code that is not necessarily accompanied by a significant amount of documentation.

So the AI software maintenance engineer is faced with much the same problem as the non-AI software engineer when presented with a program whose documentation has disappeared (not a very rare event)? No, for the AI software maintenance engineer the problem is likely to be much worse (assuming the same level of competence in the design of both classes of program). Nevertheless, the initial problem is the same type of problem in both situations: maintenance must be supported by documentation generated from the code. Yet again we see a need to abstract underlying representations from an AI program.

Another, and better, way to view this problem is: a major component of the process of transforming a product of the AI program development paradigm into practical software is the abstraction of program documentation. This is clearly a superior approach, for much of the desirable information to support program maintenance is not in the program; the maintenance engineer must do the best job he can, the program developer would presumably be capable of generating more comprehensive documentation.

Before moving on to a discussion of the process of abstraction and the types of representation that may be abstracted from program, let us consider an interesting parallel between the AI and the software engineering program development paradigms.

First, there is an obvious reverse correspondence between these two paradigms: in software engineering we have design followed by coding, in AI we have coding followed by documentation (including abstraction of a design).

Second, a useful software engineering rule is that coding and design are done by different people. If the design is complete and unambiguous someone other than the designer himself should be able to implement it.

The implication seems to be that someone other than the AI program developer should generate the documentation. Earlier I stated that the AI program developer would generate better documentation than would an outsider, the maintenance engineer.

The hint of contradiction here can be resolved easily. The AI program developer is capable of generating better post-coding documentation because of the wealth of program-specific knowledge uniquely available to him by virtue of being the program developer. But there is also a danger that such documentation will be based upon what the developer thinks that the program is doing rather than upon what and how the program actually does what it does; the developer's incorrect assumptions may be inadvertently transmitted into the documentation. So what's the answer?

Clearly we require a mixed strategy in which we both fully exploit the developer's unique knowledge of the program, and also use an outsider to check for the general validity of the documented claims as to how and what the program does. Later we consider the possibility of maintaining the program development knowledge within the system as a basis for the system to generate its own documentation.

The ease with which such checks can be made is dependent upon the structure abstracted. It is, for example, relatively easy to check for the validity of a structural abstraction intended to facilitate conceptualization of the implementation details and thus support program maintenance. A much more difficult question is the validity of an abstracted principle; a structure intended as a contribution to the sum of AI knowledge and for future use to guide the development of subsequent AI implementations. We touched on this subject earlier (Section 5.2.2.1), and elsewhere (Partridge, 1984) I have presented a scheme for providing an explicit basis for discussion of the intricate and unprovable justifications that should support the abstraction of general principles.

The above discussion of checks and justifications for abstracted representations raises the so far implicit point that a variety of rather different objects can be abstracted from a given program. The type of object abstracted depends upon the purpose to which it is to be put. Likewise the details of the abstraction process depend upon the type of object to be abstracted.

Let us now take a closer look at the general methodology of abstraction.

## 5.3   THE PROCESS OF ABSTRACTION

The AI program development paradigm yields primarily a pile of code that performs adequately within some ill-structured problem domain. The program developer most likely has the best idea of exactly what the program will do, and how it does it. But as we have argued earlier even his knowledge will probably need to be checked.

If this AI program is to be released into the empirical world then there are many more people who will need to understand it. This understanding will vary from fairly low-level, implementation-structure details for the program maintenance engineer to high-level scope and limitations for actual users of the program.

Understanding of a large, intricate, and finely detailed object fundamentally derives from succinct, abstract descriptions that are biased toward a particular type of understanding. The process of abstraction produces a more concise and perspicuous representation of the program by omitting the least significant detail, and substituting succinct generalization for collections of specific details.

With the necessity for decisions on the relative significance of components of the program code and on the perceptual clarity of the structure abstracted, the process of abstraction is an art. Thus there is no single correct abstraction or series of abstractions associated with a given program. There may be good and bad series, and ones that are more appropriate for one specific area of interest than another. Nevertheless, it is expected that, as with the well-known and somewhat complementary technique of stepwise refinement, guidelines can be developed to direct the process of abstraction.

A further type of abstraction step is to translate (and perhaps even expand at the notational level) from the source notation into a notation that more readily supports whatever type of understanding that the abstraction process is intended to foster. For example, to reimplement a LISP AI program in FORTRAN it might well be appropriate to first abstract (and probably expand) the algorithm into, say, pseudo-Pascal.

### 5.3.1   Goals of an abstraction step

Large structured objects tend to be opaque whilst small structured objects can be perceptually transparent. A major goal of an abstraction process is to transform objects in the former class into objects in the latter.

A second goal is to preserve or promote important substructures during this transformation. In an AI program the important or significant structure varies according to the purpose of the understanding required. The significant structure might be some underlying theory as opposed to idiosyncrasies of the chosen programming language.

Whilst succinctness is certainly no guarantee of comprehensibility, it is, nevertheless, a major guideline. Other components of perceptual transparency may be divided into:

(1)  simplicity of structure for human comprehension; and
(2)  appropriateness of notation for particular target audiences.

For guidelines within the first category we expect to lean heavily on the lessons learnt by the structured program design movement (as, for example, in Weinberg, 1971, and in Gries, 1981). A prime goal in program design is perceptual clarity, this is also a prime goal for an abstraction process.

A specific example of the use of an abstraction step to enhance human comprehension of AI programs can be found in the use of the technique of recursion. Recursion is a mechanism, favoured in AI programming languages, for implementing repetitive processes in an algorithm (an alternative to loop constructs). Recursive implementations can be extremely elegant and simple to design, implement, and test. But the perceptual clarity of recursive code appears to be a result of special training and as such ready comprehension of recursive structures is not a capability that most people enjoy.

Miller (1966) has probed the average human ability to comprehend grammatical but recursive sentence structures; he concludes that humans are very poor at dealing with recursive processes. Whilst this is not quite the same thing as lack of ability to comprehend recursively specified algorithms, it is suggestive of the view that we did not evolve extensive power for dealing with recursion in general. So we might well want to abstract explicit loop structures from a recursively specified algorithm in order to facilitate communication of the abstract algorithm to an appropriate audience.

In Section 6.2.2.1 this strategy is used, in reverse, in order to facilitate communication of a LISP implementation of a recursive function.

For the second feature of perceptual clarity — appropriateness of notation — we don't even have any guidelines. The appropriateness of a notation would seem to depend on one's training, and, in the absence of training, natural language is probably the most appropriate notation.

A useful general guideline might be to strive for an analogic representation of the information: that is, one in which there is a closeness between the notation employed and the abstract concept it represents. Form should reflect function; a fundamental principle to support the comprehensibility of programs.

Lenat & Brown (1983) make this point about analogic representation with respect to the interpretations that we place on AI programs (the AM program in particular). I summarize this notational question in point 3 of Section 5.4.1.


## 5.4   STEPWISE ABSTRACTION

We have now established that there are a number of different reasons why we might need to extract some essential, underlying component from a pile of code — our AI program. The process of extraction is abstraction but there are several reasons why one abstraction step is not enough.

(a) There is a wide gulf between a large AI program and a succinct, readily comprehensible abstraction. This gulf must be bridged by a sequence of abstractions both to obtain the sufficiently succinct abstraction in the first place, and to provide an audit trail as a basis for justifying the final abstraction itself.

(b) Communication of complex structures is best achieved by means of a sequence of different level representations. First the general structure is comprehended from the relatively uncluttered, high-level abstractions. Then comprehension of detailed structures and their specific interrelationships is obtained by reference to intermediate-level abstractions under the guidance of the general knowledge already assimilated.

Hence the basis for communicating an understanding of the AI program will, in general, be a sequence of successively less detailed abstractions. This sequence is obtained from a series of abstraction steps — a process of stepwise abstraction.

In each step several component substructures are (usually) condensed into a less structured, generalized component structure. This process of successive abstraction terminates when a complete abstraction has reached a level of conciseness and simplicity that makes it readily comprehensible to the target audience.

Every abstraction step implies some design decisions. It is important that these decisions be made explicit, and that the designer be aware of the underlying criteria and of the existence of alternative abstraction sequences.

A guideline in the process of stepwise abstraction should be the principle to coalesce detail as much as possible, to simplify by subsuming entangled structures under a structureless (or more simply structured) generalization, and to defer those decisions that contain the most significant details as long as possible. This will result in abstractions that combine a maximum of the important aspects of the program with a minimum of clutter and hence a maximum of clarity.

This is perhaps the place to point out that the goals of stepwise abstraction may also be significantly different from those of stepwise refinement (or even more closely analogous, the goals for developing program documentation from an undocumented program). The differences hinge upon the interpretations of the phrase 'significant structure'. Within the earlier sections on the needs for different types of understanding, theoretically significant structure (to be preserved across an abstraction step) may, or may not, be structure that is significant for the maintenance of the program.

A schematic description of how the program works (e.g. Fig. 5.2) is often most appropriate for the general maintenance of a program, whilst the principle abstracted (in Section 5.4.2) to support understanding of the problem domain (machine learning in the presence of uncertainty) is clearly not such a description. The former type of description is implementation oriented whilst the latter is oriented towards the problem domain — both types of description may be abstracted from a given program.

There is also an important difference in emphasis: the aim of program documentation is to communicate the structure of the program, the aim of theory abstraction is to communicate an underlying theory. These two objects, program structure and underlying principles or theory, may be critically different in a number of respects. For example, structure that is important with respect to maintaining a program may be theoretically non-significant. In which case this structure would be preserved and highlighted throughout good documentation and yet be omitted at the first level of theory abstraction. Program structure is intrinsic to the program whilst the underlying theory derives from the external semantic mappings imposed by the theorizer, and its significant structure may or may not accord well with various aspects of program structure.

A good documentor abstracts the inherent structure of a program; a theorizer abstracts a personal argument for the program as an implementation of general principles. Furthermore, the quality of the argument, the sequence of abstractions, rests upon both the behaviour of the program and the credibility of the semantic mapping from formal notation to phenomenon under study. By way of contrast, the quality of program documentation is judged by the degree to which it facilitates understanding and hence manipulation of the program largely as a formal object.

### 5.4.1 Goals of stepwise abstraction

The general goal of the stepwise abstraction process is to generate from an intricate formal object (an AI program) an inter-linked sequence of complementary representations of the original object. The goal sequence is characterized by successive increases in comprehensibility (from original object to final abstraction) and similar increases in detail and accuracy in the reverse direction. Fig. 5.5 is a schematic summary of this process (and a develop-

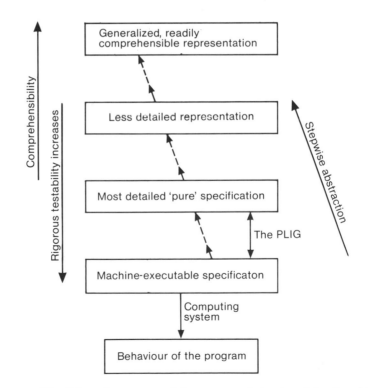

Fig. 5.5 — A summary of the process of stepwise abstraction (after Partridge, Johnston, & Lopez, 1984)

ment of Figure 4.4). The sequence of complementary representations provides the basis for communicating some aspect of the original program. Three main uses of this basis structure are envisaged:

(i) A carefully selected and structured composite including all of the original structure should facilitate general comprehension of the original structure. As with commented code for program comprehension a careful balance must be maintained between the advantages of multiple, differing level, representations and the disadvantages of clutter.

(ii) Some selected level of representation may best support a given class of enquiry. Typical user enquiries, for example, concerning the mechanisms of a program may be most usefully answered by a representation that is less precisely accurate than the program code or low-level abstractions, but perhaps a good deal more comprehensible.

(iii) The complete basis structure will enable top-down comprehension of any or all of the fine structure of the original program. In addition, the full sequence will support expert criticism and discussion at all levels from detailed specifics to that of abstract structures and their interactions. Thus, in AI for example, one can more usefully query the abstract concepts in a purportedly underlying theory when the implementation of each concept in the model is explicitly available at various levels of abstraction.

I shall summarize the description of stepwise abstraction with five points based upon the points that Wirth (1971) used to summarize stepwise refinement in his classic paper.

(1) The effective communication of an AI program is based upon a sequence of abstraction steps. Typically in each step a number of substructures are condensed into a single, simple structure (often a structureless node). But on occasion, translation from an obscure to a less obscure notation may also be involved.

(2) The degree of conciseness and modularity of the abstract representation obtained in this way will determine the ease or difficulty with which the program can be understood and facilitate changes in the abstraction process so that the representation obtained can be understood in different ways for different purposes.

(3) During the process of stepwise abstraction, a notation which is natural to the program at hand should be used as long as possible. The direction in which the notation develops during the process of abstraction is determined by the language most suitable within a particular target audience and for the type of understanding desired. This language should therefore allow us to express as naturally and as clearly as possible the structures which emerge during the design of the effectively communicable representations. At the same time, it must give guidance in the abstraction process by exhibiting each abstract representation in terms of basic features and structuring principles which are natural to the target audience.

(4) Each abstraction implies a number of design decisions based upon a set of design criteria. Among these criteria are succinctness, clarity and the preservation of significant features of the program.

(5) The design of an effectively communicable sequence of representations from an AI program is not a trivial process. It is a major problem area in our efforts to transform the products of the run–debug–edit paradigm into practical software. It will remain a problem area until guidelines for the varieties of stepwise abstraction are refined and honed to the extent that they currently are for stepwise refinement, or until AI problem solutions can be specified in more readily comprehensible machine-executable notations, free from the customary non-significant clutter (or until self explanation becomes practically viable, see Section 6.2.2.3).

Stepwise abstraction of program documentation to support conventional maintenance (AI software maintenance will involve some unconventional features, see Section 6.2.2.2) is a fairly well-accepted, although not well-defined, process. Therefore I have chosen to illustrate stepwise abstraction with the more contentious and ill-understood goal of abstracting underlying principles. The example demonstrates that stepwise abstraction is, in general, a feasible route to such principles; it is not intended to be the last word on how principles should be abstracted in detail — that is still very much an alive, wriggling, and slippery research topic.

### 5.4.2  A learning principle from a program: an example of stepwise abstraction

As an example of the above arguments a basic learning principle was abstracted from a program; a program which exhibited a wide range of basic learning behaviours.

The principle abstracted was:

> Humans are genetically predisposed to learn only significant events.

A question that might then arise is: what is meant by the term "significant"? By recourse to lower levels the question can be answered. Within the next more detailed level of abstraction it will be found that "significant" was derived from:

> ...primary drive reducing.

This might give rise to two questions: what are the primary drives and how are they reduced? Within the next level down we find some of the answers.

> ...$f$(food when hungry, pain when sensitive, novel events when bored)...

The above abstraction shows that the model employed three primary drives and that the significance of an event is claimed to be some function of all three individual drives. Inspection of the program code will reveal that the function employed was addition. This is the point where the levels of abstraction pass from theoretically significant detail (in the above abstraction) to convenient implementation only (the use of addition in the program listing). But the point in the abstraction sequence at which this transition occurs is a decision of the human theorizer and one that he must be prepared to justify.

But the results presented were based upon reduction of only one primary drive and so the drive interaction function did not have any effect on the program's behaviour. Novelty drive was the primary drive under investigation so for the results presented the term "significant" in the highest level abstraction of the theory was, in effect, derived from:

> ...novel events when bored...

A number of questions might arise from this statement. How is the novelty of an event measured? How is "bored" computed? What, if any, is the relationship between novel events and boredom?

Reference to the next level of detail will reveal that the novelty of an event is the discrepancy between the input stimulus pattern received by the animal and the pattern that it expected to perceive.

> novelty is $f$(input-expectation discrepancy)

There are many ways to compute such a discrepancy, the next level of detail shows that the function used was computed with measures of both the qualitative and quantitative differences between the two patterns.

> novelty is $f$(quantitative difference, qualitative difference)

Clearly this statement could be traced down through further levels of detail to determine how each of these differences was computed and exactly what function was used to combine them. Instead we will return to examine more detail for the broader questions of novelty, boredom and their interrelationship.

The above given abstraction, viz.

> novel events when bored

was derived from:

> boredom is increased by expected stimuli and decreased by novel
> stimuli, and significance is the lesser of, novelty or boredom level

which was abstracted from:

> boredom level increased by $f(\text{novelty}^{-1})$;
> IF novelty of input stimulus < boredom level
>     THEN significance is $f$(novelty) and
>         boredom level is reduced by $f$(novelty)
>     ELSE significance is $f$(boredom level) and
>         boredom level is a minimum;

This last abstraction gives more detail as to the computation of significance as a function of the novelty value of an event and the boredom level of the animal.

Notice that the last abstraction is no longer stated in English. The language is pseudo-Pascal, a semi-formal language intermediate between English and the language of the program, Pascal. Within computer science a host of such formal and semi-formal problem specification languages and program design languages have been developed as an aid to program development. With a change of emphasis these languages serve admirably for the representation of successive abstractions.

The final level of detail is the Pascal program code itself, and it is as follows:

```
boredomlevel := boredomlevel + stimulusexpectedness;
IF novelty < boredomlevel
    THEN
        BEGIN
            significance := novelty;
            boredomlevel := boredomlevel − novelty
        END
    ELSE
        BEGIN
            significance := boredomlevel;
            boredomlevel := 0
        END
```

So the above section of program code is the implementation of the concept "significant" within the principle abstracted.

The fundamental justification for this principle and a small collection of others is that the behaviour of the program is consistently interpretable in terms of a wide range of data on basic learning behaviours.

The principle has been applied to the development of a cognitive industrial robot (Burleson, Partridge, & Lopez, 1985 provides details, and Fig. 4.2 is an overview of this implementation) in which machine learning is controlled by the 'significance' of each event: for the robot, significance is defined in terms of its current task goals and in terms of the general expectedness or novelty of each event.

I shall make it quite clear at this point that I am not saying that principles can be the output of the AI program development process.

"But you just abstracted a principle from a program (or at least pretended to)," you might claim. Well so I did, but I also knew more or less where I was going when I did the stepwise abstraction originally.

The interest, in the incremental development of AI programs with respect to the accumulation of program-independent principles, lies in the above use of the phrase "more or less". The principles are not the input to the AI program development process, neither are they the output. We input a more or less rough and incompletely understood set of principles and we expect to gain, when the cycling is over, a less rough and a more completely understood set.

When abstracting a principle you know roughly where you are going and by going there via a sequence of explicit steps you expect to clarify a number of ill-understood concepts. In addition the act of abstracting the largely expected principles involves justification at each step, and thus you learn about the credibility of the principles with respect to the particular program. The sequence of abstractions and the associated justifications are not a proof of the correctness of a principle, they are the primary information upon which discussion of the credibility of the principle can be based — they are a basis for refutation. Potential refutability is an essential quality for any enterprise that purports to be scientific; AI has been sadly lacking in this respect (see, for example, McCarthy, 1984). Bases for rational discussion, comment, and criticism of much AI work do not exist; stepwise abstraction of principles is just one such basis.

In an interesting debate in the pages of the *AISB Quarterly*, Ohlsson and Bundy dealt with just this problem. At one point Ohlsson (1983) suggested a principle about machine learning as a tentative law of AI. And Bundy's (1984) subsequent analysis of this principle claimed to expose it as superficial and misleading. The very fact that a product of AI can be analysed and subjected to criticism is an advance I would claim (and so did Ohlsson, 1984).

And of particular relevance to my argument for the justification of principles (instead of just presenting the principle itself), is that at several points Bundy's analysis bogs down just because the meaning of seemingly straightforward terms in the principle is open to several different interpretations. This is exactly the time when we need the precursor lower-level abstractions to clarify the basis for some term in the principle — as I did with the term 'significance' in the earlier example.

Principles in AI are a move in the right direction, but they are barely a beginning without some supporting derivation. In terms of the Bundy–Ohlsson debate, I am suggesting that we need to abstract both behavioural descriptions (which Ohlsson favours), the highest level versions of the principle, and mechanistic descriptions (which Bundy is more partial to), the lower level abstractions. It is a lot of work but it seems that nothing much less will suffice.

Stepwise abstraction is not just program documentation — the sort of ad hoc thing every software maintenance person does when confronted with an ailing but undocumented program; this is just one aspect of stepwise abstraction.

I am arguing that the nature of AI programs, AI languages, and the run–debug–edit paradigm are such that stepwise abstraction must be elevated to the status of a principal component in the overall strategy for diverting the full potential of AI into practical software. It must be developed as a general methodology (in the same way as stepwise refinement) within which acknowledged variants are delineated. The set of variant processes supports abstraction of the different types of representation required to facilitate the various uses of the code as described in section 5.2.

There is more to extract from a body than the bones; you may be interested in the particular circulatory system; you may want support for a general physiological principle of the nervous system; you may want to rebuild the same thing in leather-look vinyl. Similarly, there is more in an AI program than an abstract algorithm — although an inter-linked series of successively more detailed versions of this algorithm may be the key infrastructure.

AI into practical software is initially a communication problem: what is the underlying algorithm?; what is its scope and limitations?; what general principles does this program implement?; where is the code that implements a specific feature?; what does a specific piece of code contribute to overall behaviour? Subsequent to the communication problem — once we have an appropriate understanding of the AI program — we must then consider the problems of integrating the likely characteristics of AI programs (ill-defined scope and limitations, self-modifiability, etc.) into a framework that exhibits the fundamental requirements of practical software (reliability, maintainability, etc.). This is the subject of the next chapter.

## 5.5   WHY CAN'T A PROGRAM BE SELF-DOCUMENTING?

Abstracting underlying representations from large and complex programs is a procedure with much the same lack of appeal as the conventional software maintenance process, I suspect. To someone with an interest in AI the question, 'Why can't the program do it itself?', is not at all odd.

Why can we not devise an algorithm that will abstract underlying representations from other algorithms? There are two parts to the answer.

First, abstracting underlying representations is, in general, an AI problem. So we need AI software to help us construct AI software — an awkward situation (although not impossible), and one that will become a familiar refrain in the next two chapters. Disciplined algorithm development is one approach to this problem. One that can make automatic abstraction algorithms a lot more feasible given our current state of knowledge. Section 6.2.2.3 in the following chapter contains an example of this approach.

The second part of the answer is that the program, which is just a pile of code, does not contain sufficient information to, say, abstract an underlying principle, or the design sequence. Where is this information? Well the human designer(s) considered it and developed it on the way to generating the final algorithm. But then it was most likely thrown away, or encoded in program documentation that would be extremely difficult for a machine to decipher.

I will suggest in the final chapters that the computer system might mediate the design and development process, and store in a convenient form any information that it might need as soon as this information is available. We're right back to a prerequisite need for sophisticated AI again!

In the context of expert systems, Hayes-Roth, Waterman, & Lenat (1983) point to the potential for "dynamic documentation." They envisage that "the program has available to it, explicitly, a model of its organization, overall design, detailed algorithms and knowledge representations, typical behaviors, and more." I am a good deal less sanguine than these authors about the temporal proximity of such capabilities.

Nevertheless I believe that this is the way of the future for commercial AI, but first we must do what we can with our current levels of expertise — a selection of strategies that offer more immediate help are considered in the next chapter.

# 6

## AI and software engineering: an uneasy alliance?

It takes AI to make AI.

Software engineering has repeatedly demonstrated the benefits of computers in all aspects of our lives. But the other side of this coin shows an impoverishment of the quality of life due to the mass production aspects of many computer applications: we are all treated in exactly the same way and must respond according to a fixed pattern in order to interact successfully with these pedantic systems.

In recent years AI has begun to show a promise both for dealing effectively with the ill-defined aspects of human society (e.g. natural language) and in particular for interacting with people as individuals.

Hence AI in software engineering holds a promise of societal enrichment through cheap (relative to human specialists), personalized and sophisticated applications in all aspects of our lives.

So much for the credit side of the ledger. On the debit side, we have software engineering and its problems with verification and correctness. We also have AI with its additional problems of ill-definition and dynamic structure. In brief, we have all the ingredients for a super software crisis. But if we can develop a discipline of AI-system development, and if we add to this more support from the computer itself, then there is every hope that the resultant amalgam will promote societal enrichment rather than chaos or disaster.

The intent of this chapter is to describe and illustrate strategies and techniques — some more components for a discipline of AI-system development — to ensure that the AI-software engineering marriage is one that will endure and progress from strength to strength. Let us try to avoid an over-hasty and ill-considered union that results in immediate divorce and mutual hostility for years afterwards.

## 6.1   PROBLEMS WITH THE MARRIAGE

Successful AI software will have to exhibit the major desiderata of applications software in general; the characteristics we seek are reliability and maintainability. In addition, in its role of substituting for intelligent human activities, there is also a requirement of comprehensibility for the system users: domain experts such as physicians, chemists, housewives, and caretakers. Comprehensibility of a different kind will be necessary for computer science experts — the system maintenance engineers.

The necessity for, and a method of obtaining, the various 'understandings' of an AI program have been discussed at length in the previous chapter. In this chapter we will look at the extra problems of comprehension introduced by the dynamic complexity of AI software, and at ways in which the AI software itself can foster the necessary understanding of its behaviour.

Let us consider each of these requirements in the context of AI software, bearing in mind the special peculiarities of AI problems and the resultant methodological discordance between AI and classical software engineering.

Eisenberg & Hill (1984), describing Artificial Intelligence Corporation's natural language data base query system called Intellect, list three problems that had to be solved to make this technology commercially viable. The problems listed were: robustness with respect to minor user mistakes in typing and grammar; the mismatch between the AI environment and the user environment (a problem discussed earlier in Section 5.2.3); and the cost of "customizing" each system to a new data base. Generalized versions of the first and third problems are dealt with in Sections 6.1.1 and 6.1.5 respectively. For the Intellect system the problems were solved by limiting its application to small, prespecified, static environments. The full potential of AI software can only be realized when such limitations are no longer necessary.

### 6.1.1 Reliability: it stays up and running

The system has to stay up, running, and performing adequately despite the "slings and arrows of outrageous fortune." In a well-designed software engineering environment fortune is kept in check and not permitted to be as outrageous as it is prone to be when given a free rein.

The interface between a classical software system and the real world is well-defined. If oddities are permitted then the software is designed to be ready, waiting, and prepared to deal with them; they are an integral feature of the interface specification.

If an occasional sling or arrow does bring the system to its knees then the interface controls are at fault; the demands on the system are outside its specification (assuming it was correctly designed). Without wishing to suggest that unforeseen environmental perturbations are not a real problem in software engineering, I do maintain that the problem is qualitatively worse in AI system development. As with many important AI problems, they can be found in embryonic form in practical software engineering;

although they may be absent from the idealized, verified software schemas which are not yet attainable in practice.

If a classical inventory control program crashes because a clerk enters one too many varieties of a given commodity then the blame can be accurately placed by reference to the system specifications. If this eventuality was included in the system specifications then the system designers are to blame. Otherwise the user is to blame for not controlling the software environment sufficiently closely.

The conventional role of a stock control program, keeping tags on the amount of stock on hand etc., is a well-defined procedure that is subject to a straightforward correctness judgement.

If the program says that you have only 10 packets of cornflakes in stock then you can go and count them to decide quickly if it is correct or not. If it is not correct you can check the logic of the cornflake-count computation. If that logic is correct then packets of cornflakes are either entering or, more likely, leaving the store through channels other than those that the program monitors. All in all, with regards to the non-AI program, you have quite straightforward and readily decidable questions to answer. But the AI version is a horse of a different colour.

Let's take a similar look at an AI inventory control program. Suppose that this program contains a heuristic and adaptive module (the essential AI of the system) for ordering stock. Although the store manager may be able to specify precisely when a fresh batch of each particular item should be ordered (i.e. when only so many of a particular item are left in stock), the amount to order is most accurately characterized by an incompletely specified function; it is an AI problem.

Good stock ordering has to take into account the interaction of conflicting interests. For example, the more ordered at one time the cheaper it will be but the more storage space it will take up. Such conflicts add complexity to the ordering function but the trade-offs are fairly well-defined.

By way of contrast consider how to decide the rate at which an item is likely to sell. It is true that a baseline measurement can be computed from earlier selling records but no future selling period is ever going to be quite like any past one.

High quality ordering requires that one-time, ill-structured, contingencies be taken into account. For example, a virulent press campaign against some product might definitely signal, to an astute stock manager, a fall off in sales for that product. But what will it do for related products? The answer depends on both the exact relationship between the two products and a knowledge of likely customer reaction to the specific events.

A related product that possesses a property that the customers perceive to be the same as the property that led to the downfall of the out-of-favour product, will also be a prime candidate for a dive in sales. But a related product that substitutes for the vilified product without possessing the denounced property may possibly undergo a sharp rise in sales.

Adequate decisions on the above and the many similar problems in the stock ordering function require an up to date and broadly based knowledge of current affairs, the weather, customer psychology, etc. — clearly an AI problem.

If the system chokes in the midst of a decision based on a particularly odd and awkward conglomerate of information, then pinning the blame (if indeed there is any blame) could be a very tricky problem. In practice this aspect of reliability, also called robustness, is a continuum shading across from software engineering to AI; if it is a grey area in software engineering it is of a much more of a sinister black tone in AI.

Furthermore, not only is stock ordering an incompletely specified function, but evaluation of any approximation to it, which is less than disastrous, will be very difficult. Does the program manage the stock as well as an expert stock manager does? A multi-dimensional comparison over a prolonged period is the only route to an adequacy judgement. Any particular example of over- or under-stocking may not be significant. The heuristically driven stock ordering module can be expected to perform adequately only on the average. A particular failure with some item may be more a function of an unforeseeable perturbation in the empirical world (e.g. a very warm winter in place of the forecasted very cold one) than an inadequacy of some heuristic — a human stock expert may have made the same or a worse mistake.

The problems of evaluating a particular AI system leads us on to the second facet of reliability.

### 6.1.2  Reliability: it gives the right answers
In software engineering terms we require *accuracy* of behaviour, in AI this must be watered down to *adequacy* of behaviour. This aspect of reliability is a more obvious AI problem than the robustness question discussed above.

Not only do we have the problem that the system may generate inadequate behaviour; additionally we face the task of distinguishing inadequate and adequate behaviours. Typically the demarcation criteria are complex, ill-understood, and context-dependent as the above example of an AI stock ordering system illustrated.

We have characterized AI system construction as the development of an adequate approximation to an incompletely specified function. Even though system development tends to clarify and thus remove some ill-structure, it would be rare to eliminate it all. Since development seldom terminates with a completely specified function, use of a system that is deemed adequate will always involve some degree of system development. A final fixed system is a somewhat unusual occurrence in software engineering; it will be a much rarer event for AI systems.

There are two major levels of viewpoint here, and we need to distinguish between them. A learning system, by virtue of its self-modification ability, is not fixed with respect to system details — it is constantly learning and thus changing some details of its structure.

But if the same system is a 'perfect' learning system (the result of which is that the result of the learning is never a degradation of general performance) it will appear, to the user, to be a fixed system. (It is true that the user might realize that the system is in fact constantly changing to maintain its performance in a changing world, but as far as performance adequacy is concerned, the system is a fixed and finished piece of software.)

We have a contradiction: the above-described AI software will be a final, fixed system, and my earlier claim that this situation will not in practice occur in AI. The resolution is found in the phrase 'perfect learning system': a 'perfect learning system' is probably impossible in principle due to the unpredictability of the empirical world. In practice, a system that remotely approaches perfect learning, in a complex environment, is a very long way off.

Perfect learning would cause a lot of my concerns for AI software to vanish (this viewpoint is illustrated graphically in Fig. 7.2). Imperfect learning will do just the opposite; it will quite easily scale-up the software crisis to what I have termed a super software crisis, if we are not very careful. But imperfect learning is, I will argue, a practical necessity for the advancement of AI in commercial software.

So for the foreseeable future AI software will not be a final, fixed system from either level of view.

### 6.1.3  Maintainability

Maintenance of conventional software involves system modification to both eliminate newly discovered errors, and enable the system to meet specification changes; this is another problem that the inclusion of AI modules can only aggravate. The continual development of incompletely specified functions is characteristic of AI systems. This process, in an applied system, can be viewed as maintenance to meet a change in the de facto specifications.

The house-cleaning robot, once on the job in a range of different domiciles, might be observed to do an inadequate job of emptying a certain style of ashtray. Maintenance is required to eliminate this performance inadequacy.

Back in the factory, system designers pore over the abstracted de facto specification of the robot as sold. A fix is devised, tested on a local specimen, found to work, and thus distributed to all of the lucky owners of the Expert Housecleaner (EH). All owners of EHs reboot their mechanical home helps with the modified software, and the troublesome ashtrays yield to technology. But someone forgot about the deluxe model, EHT, (Expert Housecleaner, Trainable). Soon the owners of EHTs are calling in to report bizarre and unfortunate happenings which remind the maintenance crew of their oversight. The EHT models have been steadily learning and thus modifying their own software. A special fix will be required for them. Worse than that, much worse: each EHT has modified its own software to provide a superior service within the idiosyncrasies of a particular house. Every EHT has different software!

The above horror story is only fiction, I hope, but it does serve to underline the possibilities for the escalation of maintenance headaches when self-adaptive AI software hits the market. Once again, although a pale shadow of this problem occurs in conventional software engineering with many different versions of a complex software system, the difference in degree associated with self-modifying AI software is sufficient to make the AI software problem different in kind.

### 6.1.4 Understandability

As the previous chapter should have made abundantly clear, understandability is a very desirable feature of all computer programs; it is a basic prerequisite that supports debugging and maintenance in general. In AI software it may well take on a further dimension.

If the human user, expert or not, disagrees with the output of an AI expert system, there are several possibilities: one of them is wrong, they're both wrong, or it's an open question that must go to arbitration. In any event it becomes important that the AI system can explain the method behind its seeming madness.

To resolve this conflict the human faction must be able to understand the reasoning that generated the contentious result. The human party is most likely to be neither interested nor capable of wading through acres of parenthesized lists (or whatever) to gain an understanding of the program's foibles. The program must explain itself.

The power of self-explanation has long been recognized as an essential feature of AI systems. The use of dependency records and a jargon-to-English translation module can provide a self-explanation capability that is sufficient for most practical purposes. An example of this type of explanation capability is given later, in Section 6.2.2.3.

But AI systems have been limited to research laboratories in which Anglicized logic is an appropriate medium of communication. Suitable explanations for Mr. General Public are likely to be a lot harder to produce.

The proud owner of an EHT will be quite within her rights to expect an explanation of the cat being shut in the bureau drawer. Before the surgeon starts to cut she needs an explanation of the computer's diagnosis especially if it does not exactly accord with her own decision.

For AI software the ability to explain itself is essential. This capacity for self-explanation is not usually found in conventional software (although it could, of course, considerably enhance such software). It is thus another requirement when AI invades software engineering.

### 6.1.5 Trainability: the system adapts to the user's peculiarities

Effective AI software must deal with the grey areas of the incompletely specified function for which it is an approximation. I am referring to all of those areas within the problem domain where the adequate output for a given input is context-dependent.

In particular let us consider the situations when the major contextual variable is the human user. An adequate implementation must adapt to the preferences of each user.

A good computer-aided instruction (CAI) package for teaching any skill will have to respond according to the expertise of each particular user. This expertise is a complex, multi-dimensional quantity: it involves levels of skill specific knowledge, related skills knowledge, level of general education, age, skill acquisition abilities, etc.

The sophisticated expert just brushing up on a previously learned skill will be bored and irritated by repetitive, low-level responses. Conversely the novice seeking to learn a new skill for the first time will be baffled, disappointed, and 'turned off' CAI for life by the level and speed of tutoring that the lapsed expert required.

Such personalized software can to some extent be produced by selection from a predefined range of possibilities: one set of parameter values for the expert, and a different set for the novice. But anyone who has used such fixed-menu CAI systems knows that they do not come close to being adequate personalized tutors. Each range of possibilities is a continuum, there are many such continua, and they interact: attempts at simplistic, discrete simulation do not succeed.

The difference is the same as the gulf that separates human language from animal or computer languages: an open-ended and rich continuum of possibilities as against fixed, discrete ranges. The combinatorial possibilities of the latter structure are sometimes impressive but they do not compare with the wealth of expressions derivable from the former scheme.

Current CAI research has moved decisively into the AI domain (it is then Intelligent CAI, ICAI), utilizing sophisticated adaptive mechanisms, in an effort to produce software packages that are responsive to people as individuals. ICAI projects such as GUIDON (Clancey, 1979), which aims at teaching medical diagnosis, dynamically learns to build a model of each user in an attempt to capture enough personal information to support an effective individualized response pattern. Some successes have been reported, but they tend to suffer from fragility, a malaise endemic in AI. They also need extensive hand-crafting to deal with particular problems, thereby reducing general applicability outside the research environment.

Bramer (1982), in a survey and critical review of expert systems research, states that automatic acquisition of new information is a problem area within current expert system development. He concludes, "If a computerized system is to be useful in changing circumstances and different locations, it may be necessary to give attention to such contextual factors." Herein I maintain it is not a question of "may be necessary" but one of "will be necessary".

With regard to the need for context sensitivity in expert systems and the current state of affairs, Hayes-Roth, Waterman, & Lenat (1983), make the following point: "Explanations by human experts, in general, are tailored to their audiences. The details of reasoning as related to another expert in the same domain will be different from those related to a layman. This will require a kind of intelligent behaviour not apparent in the explanation facilities of current expert systems."

Good AI software will have to be sensitive to each user's strengths, weaknesses, and preferred style of interaction. Such sensitivity can be realized only by means of sophisticated adaptive mechanisms: the system must be trainable. The degree to which it trains itself or is externally tutored is another question. Machine learning and the pros and cons of the various strategies for practical software were discussed in Chapter 3.

The point to be made here is that effective AI software will be dynamic. Continually modified (especially self-modified) code and data structures have nothing positive to contribute to the software crisis; they can only exacerbate an already very difficult problem.

Personalized software will be a potent force in the battle for a more humanitarian world. Self-adaptation is the only viable route to the ubiquity of such software. Self-modifying systems are, quite rightly, an anathema to software engineers; this crucial antithesis must be confronted and resolved.


## 6.2   COUNSELLING ADVICE

The benefits of AI in software engineering are clear, but the problems are also clear and there are many of them. What can we expect to do to lessen the drawbacks that AI threatens to bring along with it? Do we have to face a super software crisis? Is that the price of intelligent computers? Alas, it might be. Intelligent human assistants clearly have their drawbacks as well as their advantages, sometimes unquestioning obedience is just what's required.

Perhaps we face a major bifurcation in computer applications: the obedient slave and the intelligent assistant. Probably we do, and AI in software engineering is largely a development of the latter role.

To some extent, Minsky's ACM Turing Lecture on "Form and Content" (Minsky, 1970) presages this two-way development of Computer Science. He voices a concern that a preoccupation with formalism will impede development in ill-understood areas — areas in which we have a lot of specific knowledge (i.e. content) but little in the way of abstract principles (i.e. form). AI is such a content-rich but form-poor area (this point should not be confused with the form–content discussion in Chapter 4).

Since Minsky's warning the formal science of software engineering (as opposed to the practical science of software engineering) has moved progressively towards a concentration on form, and Dijkstra's Turing Lecture (Dijkstra, 1972) was a driving force behind this movement. Attempts to generate rigorous specifications and to prove that algorithms are correct is, of course, vital work in our efforts to gain control over computer software — but it has not been a resounding success in large-scale practical software. If we now add AI to our goals for practical software then we definitely shift the balance of our enterprise way over from the form to the content end of the scale.

This does not mean that we should abandon our search for useful abstractions, far from it, but we should recognize that for AI software all indications are that content is currently the key. Instead of attempting to bend AI programming into a SPIV-like paradigm as in formal software development we should acknowledge the basic validity of the run–debug–

edit cycle and develop a discipline for its best use. I detect something of this change of emphasis in the program support environments described in Chapter 7, especially the one described by Winograd (1979).

The following discussions on strategies for averting a super software crisis are divided into two parts: first we consider the expansion and development of software engineering techniques to aid in resolving the AI-in-software engineering conundrum; we then consider the techniques, peculiar to AI, that will alleviate the problem — in all, it is intended to be the basis for a discipline for AI software. I make no claim to provide you with a usable discipline — I wish that I could. But such a discipline is some years off. The best that I can do now is identify the major problems and suggest some general strategies that will be important, I believe, within the discipline when it finally emerges.

The degree to which individual strategies belong to AI or software engineering is, of course, often a matter of debate. Thus whilst "generators" (see later) are primarily an AI development, the underlying idea called semicoroutines can be found in software engineering (Dahl, Dijkstra, & Hoare, 1972). Nevertheless, it is useful, if not definitive, to consider the following strategems as each springing from one of two sources.

In this chapter I shall discuss only the technical aspects of the problem. Social, ethical and moral questions do not surface until the next chapter. This is not to suggest that they are less important. But they are certainly more slippery and totally open to debate. Nevertheless the major concerns should be aired even in a book whose principal goals are unashamedly technological.

### 6.2.1 . Can software engineering keep AI in check?
Software engineering is a growing and thriving business. Is it an organism with sufficient robustness to absorb AI and its alien viruses and continue from strength to strength on the resultant hybrid vigour? Is software engineering rich enough in antibodies to effectively nullify the insidious aspects of AI?

Probably not, but it does possess a number of weapons that can give the more bellicose features of AI a hard time provided the system designer has sufficient tactical skill. Below we discuss logistic schemes for the implementation of effective tactics in the impending struggle. Modularity (including "structured programming") is the key strategem, the basis for the onslaught against the problems that AI introduces.

#### 6.2.1.1 *Modularity: a many-splendoured thing*
The whys and wherefores of modularity as a device for alleviating the software crisis have been discussed and illustrated in Chapter 2. The task now is to see what more modularity can do to avert a super software crisis.

Modular design and implementation of computer systems is a manifestation of the time-honoured principle of divide and conquer. As all successful empire builders have known, if you can split up the opposing hordes then you can beat them more easily — a viewpoint that suggests the other classic adage (slightly remodelled): if you don't join them you can beat them.

For the AI system designer the hordes in question are mobs of heuristics. The goal of a modular design is to isolate each heuristic. That seems straightforward enough: imprison each heuristic within a module and allow a minimum of interaction, always under close surveillance.

One obvious line of separation is the one between data structures and procedures. As an example, the heuristic compiler described in Chapter 3 (Partridge, 1975) used several heuristics that rearranged the data structures periodically on the basis of information collected during normal parsing. Thus the heuristics (such as, move the most frequently used structures to a higher level) were driven by the program's past experience — a quantity whose full range and scope is unknown and unknowable to the system designer. But constraints that the system designer can, and did, incorporate were:

(1)   Heuristic modifications were restricted to a certain data structure; the algorithm that processed this data structure remained unaltered.
(2)   Data structure modifications changed the details of a particular structure, but the "class" of the data structure remained unaltered — the abstract data type was invariant under the heuristic.

Within the heuristic compiler the language to be translated was defined in terms of a hierarchy of binary trees. The heuristics employed, moved branches between levels of the hierarchy, and inserted newly generated branches in the hierarchy. But the data structure was always a hierarchy of binary trees and the tree-processing algorithms were not altered.

Use of this type of strategy for implementing heuristically self-adaptive systems has several important advantages. Firstly, the system designer can, by means of conventional software engineering techniques (i.e. partial proofs and comprehensive testing), assure himself that the algorithms process the implemented class of data structure correctly.

Secondly, the modular design has encapsulated the necessary dynamics within a data structure; the processing algorithms are static. Further than that the capability for unforeseen self-modification is trapped within a particular class of data structure: a binary tree hierarchy. The class of data structure is thus also static; it will not change into a network nor a ternary tree. So the tried and tested algorithm–data structure relationship will remain invariant throughout the life of the system despite the fact that the system is fundamentally adaptive — it learns from experience.

O'Shea (1982), in describing the design of a self-improving tutor, stresses the need for machine learning in CAI and the need to "isolate" the various components of the system. The details are not available but, in general, the design appears to be consistent with my argument for both adaptability and modularity in AI software.

Remember our general discussion on the near-decomposability of intelligence; couple this with the customary refusal of AI problems to yield to clean modular designs, and we have a decidedly bleak outlook for the impact of modularity in AI. Ranged against this dispiriting prognosis are several more cheerful possibilities.

It may be that we have not as yet hit upon the right modules for cracking intelligence apart. It is also possible to design and implement a modular equivalent of a non-modular phenomenon at the cost of a larger size for the modular version. This increase in size — which itself increases complexity — imposes a practical limitation on the possibilities for modular simulations of non-modular processes.

It would be wise to separate AI modules from non-AI modules even if the AI modules themselves are rather intertwined. Such a separation will facilitate the application of different and more restrictive techniques to the potentially more disruptive and probably more dynamic AI modules.

*The case for AI apartheid*

In the absence of any principle to the effect that all modules should be created equal, the system designer is free to pursue a policy of 'apartheid' — separate development of AI and non-AI modules within a single system. And in particular there is also no stipulation that development within these two classes of modules should be in some sense equal (as with the invidious real-world application of this scheme 'separate' is not taken to imply 'equal').

It is appropriate to put more time, effort, and restrictions into the most likely insurgents, the AI modules. The differences in design methodologies (described in Chapters 2 and 4) clearly argue for apartheid in the design and development of AI software.

The strategy of choice is to first design, implement and test the non-AI modules, whilst providing some well-defined dummy modules to substitute for the as yet undeveloped AI modules. Having obtained a superstructure of well-defined, 'correct' software, we can slot in our first approximations to the AI modules and develop them incrementally using the run–debug–edit based paradigm of Chapter 4.

An appropriate metaphor here is that the non-AI modules form a skeleton on which we build the musculature of AI modules. This skeleton of conventional software can also function as a 'default system' when the AI modules fail, as they sometimes will (more on this later). The non-AI skeleton itself should constitute a minimally adequate solution so that the system does not crash when the AI modules fail; it just degrades gracefully to a conventional, non-intelligent system.

If we again consider the heuristic compiler, we can provide an example of this strategy. A context-free parser was constructed and tested; the parse structures generated were readily evaluated as correct or incorrect, and syntactically incorrect input was tagged as such. Clearly a conventional software engineering problem, and thus a robust and reliable system can be constructed.

The subsequent AI development phase involved first, opening up the problem: the parser had to accept *all* input as more or less correct and thus it had to generate an interpretation of every input string received. A discussion of the ill-structure introduced can be found in James and Partridge (1976). Ill- structured subproblems such as the trade-off between highly unlikely interpretations of input as correct versus much more likely interpretations if we assume that the input contains a very common error — i.e. correct but unlikely, or incorrect due to a likely error.

In retrospect I can see a lot of inefficiencies in the heuristic compiler that could have been avoided had the system known something about itself and about its task in general. If, for example, it had known which of its data structures were regular (self-knowledge), and which pattern-matching strategies could not succeed on all of the rest of the items in a regular data structure if they failed on the first item (meta-knowledge), then a lot of fruitless searching could have been avoided. The usefulness, or rather as I will argue, the necessity for meta- or self-knowledge is a point that we take up in the following chapter (although I will give preference to the term 'meta-knowledge' to designate all knowledge in the somewhat ill-defined level above basic knowledge).

Secondly, heuristics such as, 'highly unlikely interpretations assuming correctness of input can be replaced by highly likely interpretations that assume the presence of a common error', were implemented and inserted. These heuristics were then incrementally developed within the fixed framework of the tested and minimally adequate (with respect to the more ambitious AI problem) system previously constructed.

In reality we cannot expect system development to separate so neatly into a software engineering phase followed by an AI development phase. There will inevitably be some to-and-fro between these two methodologies as a result of interaction between modules. Nevertheless, software engineering before artificial intelligence is the order of events to strive for; the well-defined software should provide a test harness for the subsequent development of the AI modules. The first decisions made are the ones that should endure because they involve the best-understood features of the proposed system.

Another manifestation of this strategy of constructing solid foundations before attempting to build up the ill-understood components is the idea of rapid prototyping. This scheme for testing preliminary designs stems from a recognition that the 'all at once' approach to complex design will not work and that minimal commitment followed by some degree of evaluation is an efficient way to explore ill-understood domains.

Balzer, Cheatham, & Green (1983), whose suggestions are discussed in Chapter 7, advocate the execution of specifications, "prototyping", as a means of comprehensive evaluation before an implementation is contemplated. Kowalski (1984) offers Prolog as an executable requirements analysis language. He suggests that we use it to explore user requirements by trial and error.

The language Ada offers the possibility of compiling the abstract specifications of modules before the implementations of the modules have been constructed. This facility allows an examination of inter-module compatibility before any commitment is made as to how the modules will be implemented.

Sandewall (1978) describes how certain LISP environments will also support some prototype evaluation in terms of systems containing initially undefined functions. He sees this strategy as contributing to a method of program development called "structured growth".

A major aim of this book can be viewed as an attempt to draw together and describe a selection of program development strategies that may one day constitute a methodology of "structured growth".

### The need for 'iron curtains'

The system designer will be well-advised to throw an 'iron curtain' around each AI module. The degree to which, and means by which, an AI module can influence and be influenced by its environment should be both severely restricted and closely scrutinized.

The output of an AI module must be positively vetted; guilty until proved innocent is the axiom of inter-module interaction. Heuristics by their very nature do not always perform adequately. It is desirable that the inadequate behaviour be suppressed at birth (with, perhaps, some internal note of the event kept for use in subsequent 'maintenance' sessions).

Euthanasia, as always, is a dubious strategy for maintaining a vigorous system, but pruning a tree promotes health if done properly. There is the fundamental problem of evaluating the long-term merit of a heuristic result at birth. Apparently good results may eventually give rise to disastrous program behaviours, and vice versa. Given also that the value metric is seldom as simple as correct or incorrect, early decisions are by no means easy.

Nevertheless heuristic results should be closely monitored: the patently bad ones filtered out, and the dubious ones flagged as such. Here we see indications that some sort of 'decision agent' or 'referee' may have a role to play in controlling AI systems.

Decision agents have been posited by Papert (1980) within the context of the "society-of-mind" theory of intelligence. He argues for the "chaos and controversy of competing agents" rather than the "certitude and orderliness" of general logical principles.

I have suggested the need for "referees" (Partridge, 1981), these are active agents that can be guaranteed to provide at least some decision whenever the heuristic mechanisms fail. The justification for such active agents is that some decision (even a somewhat arbitrary one) is always better than no decision — a wrong result is better than no result, the former provides the impetus for removing the source of the error, the latter just leaves us wondering.

In an effort to contain the over-exuberance of heuristic modules, AI has developed the idea of a generator. "A generator is a co-routine that runs until it produces one item and then suspends itself" (Barr & Feigenbaum, 1982). In the context of the current argument, a generator is a module that can produce information which may, or may not, be able to satisfy the demand of the module that referenced the generator. If the information returned by the generator is inadequate (usually in the sense that it does not match some desired pattern sufficiently closely), then the generator may be referenced again and it will make another attempt to satisfy the demand.

Thus the mass spectrogram analysis program, DENDRAL, contains a module that generates possible molecular structures given a chemical formula. A mass spectrogram is synthesized from the generated structure, and it is compared with the actual mass spectrogram input. If the two mass spectrograms match sufficiently closely then a molecular structure has been found for the compound being analysed. But if the match is not sufficiently close then the generator is requested to generate another possibility. One heuristic within this generator examines the input mass spectrogram and identifies substructures that must be present in every candidate structure generated — by so doing, it reduces the space to be searched by the generator from that of all chemical structures consistent with the formula to one in which possible structures must also contain certain, specified substructures. The effects of the heuristics that employ the predicted-substructures restriction are contained within the molecular structure generator, and the quality of these heuristics can be estimated by examination of the candidate molecular structures generated.

We can see that the generator-technique can be used to isolate an heuristic complex as well as to exercise some quality control over the results generated. This is perhaps an appropriate point at which to address an obvious follow-on question. What if an appropriate result is never generated?

If the generator is searching an infinite space of possibilities, the module requiring the heuristic result will be left waiting indefinitely. If the generator exhausts its fund of possibilities without turning up a winner for the waiting module we may have a stalled system. In either case it is clear that if an adequate heuristic result cannot be guaranteed in all situations then some backup result, a minimally adequate default value, must be provided, or perhaps human assistance requested.

These default values can be built into the initial software engineering skeleton for the system; they can be in effect the dummy AI modules that facilitate initial construction of a robust and reliable skeleton. AI system development can then proceed by layering more sophisticated heuristic structures on top of the dummy modules, then should the heuristics fail to generate an adequate result the underlying default values will always be there.

The longer we allow a heuristic result to propagate through the system, interacting with other heuristics, the sooner we will run into the classical credit (or blame) assignment problem: where do we pin the blame for an inadequate outcome of a composite process. Which particular heuristic — or combination or heuristics — is to be held responsible? There is a need in production software to scrutinize heuristic results, in isolation, as early as possible, and to err on the side of caution. The caution to be exercised will be dependent upon both particular software applications and general system design— in particular is the program self-modifying or not?

The EH system could probably be allowed to explore more dubious behavioural possibilities than could a ballistic missile defence system. Obviously some areas of application would be more sensitive to results of questionable adequacy than others; the permeability of a module's interface should reflect both the fragility of the module itself and the module's potential for sabotaging the rest of the system.

Another function of the iron curtain around each AI module would be to restrict human access to the workings of the module. Restricted access is already a feature of software security techniques. The inclusion of AI modules in a system gives rise to several additional reasons for restricting human access.

First, the complexity, fragility, and possibly self-modifiability of AI algorithms means that any inexpert tampering will be much more likely to lead to general failure than to the desired behavioural modification. Secondly, assessing the adequacy of a modified heuristic is a complex, long-term, context-dependent process. Thus a casual modification, even if it does not wreck the module, is unlikely to be, in general, appropriate. Lastly unauthorized tampering will be particularly difficult to detect in a self-modifying and not completely predictable module. As we shall see, the long-term maintenance of AI modules is somewhat different and more complex than the customary process of software maintenance.

### 6.2.2  What can AI do to avert a super software crisis?

Nothing is all bad, not even AI. Although AI software is very largely a forthcoming event, AI research workers have for several decades been developing tools for managing the extra problems peculiar to AI; they have been attacking and scoring notable successes against the new complexity barrier that is AI.

In his Turing Lecture Dijkstra (1972) argued that hardware advances have naturally aggravated the software crisis: they have continually opened up the possibility for programming ever more complex problems. Dijkstra goes on to state that we should only consider programming problems with nicely factored solutions. We should get to know and master our limitations and in that way we will come to push these limitations back and back.

As you will have gathered much of AI is from a totally different universe; it is, to Dijkstra, not technically feasible. But man is with us, and AI is also with us (in spirit if not wholeheartedly in body) and for better or for worse we are going to have to live with it. A quote from Minsky's incoming presidential address to the American Association for Artificial Intelligence (Burstein, 1983) is appropriate here. Whilst suggesting that AI is perhaps the hardest current scientific problem with the exception of figuring out how the genetic system works, Minsky ventures the further suggestion that the complexity of genetic coding is "because it was programmed by no one who knew what they were doing... If there had been a Dijkstra then, we wouldn't have man, but we'd have some very neat animals."

Computers, as reliable logic crunching machines, are the tools that have allowed mankind to leap over one complexity barrier in his search for knowledge. But, as Dijkstra pointed out, on clearing the hurdle the programmers landed in a swamp — otherwise known as the software crisis. We are still struggling through this swamp and now the barrier of AI is before us. We may well find a firm path over the barrier and through the mire by wallowing in it rather than by constructing a solid run up through a mastery of our present limitations. Intellectual struggle and thrashing about in an ill-understood domain are the usual prerequisites for scientific advancement. Incremental progress based upon a steadily growing pile of well-understood units is not the stuff of scientific revolutions; and a revolution may be called for.

Optimistic floundering around may be a legitimate research activity provided the sorties into the unknown have some guiding rationale. But investigative and largely speculative research projects should not be dressed up and sold as finished products. We do first need to develop a ground plan of the new environment such that both the route and the final goal of any proposed trips are relatively well-understood in advance.

A thirst for knowledge and excitement is always going to lead scientists up and over the barrier; it is naive to expect otherwise. What we must guard against are claims that we are almost over the barrier when in reality we have only just approached it.

Winograd (1975) addresses the problem of the new complexity barrier presented by AI. He argues for the development of programming environments that will function as "a moderately stupid assistant" to the programmer. There is a spectrum of possibilities from extensive bookkeeping to advice on design decisions and automatic implementation of details.

In today's terminology he is talking about an expert programming system: a system with a body of knowledge, including meta-knowledge, about both programming techniques and the strengths and weaknesses of specific programming languages, and capable of generating plausible inferences for advising the programmer.

### 6.2.2.1 The program development environment

When faced with the impossible, help is needed. The pioneer AI programmers soon found that they were attempting something close to the impossible (as compared with software engineering, which is only very difficult). The AI response was to remove the myriad trivial system details from the concern of the programmer, by creating a program development environment, and thereby allow him to concentrate attention on the system essentials. The existence of a sophisticated program development environment can considerably reduce the complexity of the problem.

Consideration of this environment can be broken into three parts: the programming language; the multifarious but relatively straightforward processes of indexing, cross-referencing, and general keeping accounts of all system details; and lastly a heuristic advisory facet that accumulates knowledge about the goals and objectives of the target system. I shall use these three areas as foci for my discussion.

*The babel of AI languages*

Along with most other subfields of computer science, AI has not been tardy in its efforts to invent new programming languages to solve its own particular brand of problems. An AI programming language must support flexible, dynamic systems. Both data structures and algorithms should be modifiable at run time. In fact this convenient and useful division — data structure and algorithm — becomes a blurred line in AI: data structures need to be executed, and algorithms need to be manipulated as if they are data structures.

One of the early high level programming languages — LISP (McCarthy *et al.*, 1965) — is still very much the vernacular of AI. Though AI aficionados actually work with the extended dialects such as MACLISP (Touretzky, 1982) or INTERLISP (Teitelman & Masinter, 1981) — dialects plus extras that constitute two of the finest program development environments available. An earlier but comprehensive description of "the 'LISP' experience" is given by Sandewall (1978).

As an example of a LISP program we can specify a function that sums a list of values, say integers, and returns that sum as its result. Consider the following pseudo-code specification of such a function:

> function LISTSUM,
>   IF the list contains no values
>     THEN return zero as the function value
>     ELSE return the first list value added to
>     the sum of the rest of the list values as
>     the function value

The only slightly disturbing feature of this algorithm, especially to the non-recursive programmer, is the hint of circularity in the ELSE clause. The sum of a non-empty list is obtained by adding the value of the first element to the sum of the rest of the list. There are two reasons that together save the algorithm from endless circularity:

(a) The rest of the list (i.e. the list without its first element) is always shorter than the list it derives from.
(b) The THEN clause returns a result for the shortest possible list (i.e. the empty list).

Thus it is true that there is a circularity within the ELSE clause; the computation of the sum of a list of values is expressed in terms of the sum of a shorter list of values. But this circular, self-referencing, known as recursion, will eventually terminate when the rest of the list is empty, the function will then 'unwind'; it will compute the sum of the empty list, then the sum of the last list item, then the sum of the last two items, and so on until it obtains and returns the sum of all items in the list.

In LISP the body of this function, LISTSUM would be:

```
(COND((EMPTY LIST)O)
      ( T (PLUS(HEADOF LIST)(LISTSUM(RESTOF LIST))))))
```

if we assume appropriate definitions for the functions, EMPTY, PLUS, HEADOF, and RESTOF.

Recursion in LISP is the substitute for iteration in more conventional software engineering languages (although a conventional iteration mechanism is always also provided).

One of the most important features of the LISP language for AI purposes is the equivalence between executable code and data. In the above example we have a segment of executable code; the body of the function LISTSUM. It is also a list of items (a LISP list is delimited by one pair of parentheses).

```
(COND((EMPTY LIST)O)(T(PLUS(HEADOF LIST)
(LISTSUM(RESTOF LIST)))))
```

This list is somewhat complex in that it contains sublists that themselves contain sublists. As a list it is also a valid LISP data structure in which the list items, say the atom COND or the sublist ((EMPTY LIST)O), can be manipulated by other LISP functions.

Although all lists can be treated as data structures, only certain lists can be executed, namely those lists whose first element identifies a function and the rest of whose elements provide appropriate values for the parameters of the particular function identified by the first element.

As you can see the syntax of LISP is simple. For both executable code and data the only structure is a list of objects delimited with parentheses. In fact the syntax of LISP is too simple; it is so uniform that the inherent structure of a LISP program tends to elude the human perceptual mechanism. What the programmer's eye tells the programmer's brain is that a LISP program is a collection of identifiers that has been liberally sprinkled with left and right parentheses with much the same apparent order as stars in the sky.

But it's great for machines; that is to say, the syntactic simplicity and uniformity of program and data greatly simplifies the implementation of program and data as interchangeable structures.

The demand for dynamic capabilities in AI, run-time modification of both algorithms and data structures, quickly leads to incomprehensible programs. Dynamic systems suggest an interpreter rather than a compiler implementation. Interpreters with their closer proximity to the source code offer a more ready basis for an interactive and helpful programmer support environment than compilers do.

The scenario for AI program development is thus an arrangement of mutual benefit: desirable language characteristics make the programmer's task more difficult, but the easiest implementation strategy can readily support the addition of modules to ameliorate the programmer's lot.

Extended dialects of LISP are one important manifestation of AI development environments, primarily because of the vast library of support subprograms that consitute an important part of these LISP extensions. The chief reason for developing AI software on a LISP machine such as the Symbolics 3670 is not the fact that it directly executes LISP, but because of the support environment that comes with the machine; a major part of this environment is the 100 MIT-man-years of support functions.

Apart from a steady accumulation of support subprograms there has also been a development of AI-specific control mechanisms and data structures. The development and implementation of new language features gave birth to new AI languages; control structures such as pattern-directed invocation in which procedures may be invoked as a result of a pattern-matching operation rather than explicitly by name; data structures such as theorems and assertions that, when coupled with the theorem proving control structures, provide a ready implementation for knowledge storage and retrieval systems.

North America has been the spawning ground for most new AI languages, although POP-2 (Popplestone, 1968) and Prolog (Clocksin & Mellish, 1981) are notable exceptions.

Most AI languages are no longer with us; they exist only as exhibits in the museum of AI. The respective language manuals are material for the historian rather than the serious programmer. Language design in response to needs that were too specific seems to have been the root cause of the lack of longevity in AI languages.

Programming language design, in general, is an ill-understood art: Pascal seems to have been a good one, PL/I a poor one, and Ada remains an interesting open question, though in his Turing Lecture Hoare (1981) places Ada in almost the same class as the ill-fated PL/I. In general Hoare echoes Dijkstra's earlier described sentiments that computer scientists should operate only in areas that they clearly understand; this stricture rules out much of AI, almost by definition. With respect to language design Hoare's major point is that programmers are always surrounded by complexity and "if our basic tool, the language ... is also complicated, the language itself becomes .part of the problem rather than part of its solution." Hoare presents a cogent argument for simple, reliable programming languages and for avoiding applications that are not well understood. AI researchers are clearly less than fully in accord with Hoare and we shall examine their argument.

An interesting and useful set of principles of programming language design that reflect much of the current wisdom on this topic are given by MacLennan (1983).

Conniver and Planner, for example, were exploratory probes into the space of possible programming languages; they were directed at the area of AI applications. Much useful information was gained from them — information that was vital for mapping the space of AI programming languages which, of course, are part of the map of all programming languages. Although the map is by no means complete the original vehicles will not be used again. The information received will facilitate the design, implementation, and launching of the next generation of investigative devices into the of AI programming language space. Until much more information is collected and fitted together the quest for an argot of AI is a fundamentally speculative enterprise.

The search for non-AI programming languages is only slightly more directed because we possess more knowledge of the structure of this space due to relatively prolonged and extensive experimentation within it.

AI programming languages are the most recent descendants from the evolutionary line of man-machine communication. A characteristic trend within this evolutionary sequence is one of abstraction and thus a removal of detail that the programmer must be cognizant of (this also implies a loss of fine control which can be a drawback); from machine code, through assembly codes and high level languages, to AI languages we can clearly discern this trend of abstraction.

More conventional computer science has pursued a somewhat parallel course with the development of abstract data structures. Whether the abstraction capabilities implemented in say Ada and Modula-2 will have any direct impact on AI language research remains to be seen.

Before leaving the world of AI programming languages further mention must be made of Prolog. It is a European language that provides a neatly defined and efficiently implemented theorem proving capability; as an efficient inference engine it has a strong claim to be an essential ingredient in the management of knowledge bases for expert systems.

In Prolog the control structure and the declarative structure of a program are separated. A Prolog program specifies only the relationships that hold between the computational objects. How these relationships will be processed (i.e. what control structure will be used) is separate and part of the implementation of the language.

This separation has a number of attractive qualities (Prolog is a table-driven programming language; remember the benefits of table-driven mechanisms, Section 4.4.1.2). We can, for example, 'drive' the declarative structure either backwards or forwards: either deducing the implications of our program, or checking if a given statement is true with respect to the program. But some people would argue that this separating out of control has resulted in a loss of control. Nevertheless, Prolog represents an interesting new view of programming, and one that will undoubtedly be developed in the next few years.

Consider our earlier knowledge base coded as a Prolog program:

```
NEWPHEWOF(Y,X) :- UNCLEOF(X,Y).
HOBBIT(X) :- UNCLEOF(X,Y),HOBBIT(Y).
HOBBIT(bilbo).
UNCLEOF(frodo,bilbo).
```

This Prolog program is composed of four clauses which can be read in a right-to-left manner. Thus the first clause states that if the UNCLEOF X is Y then the NEWPHEWOF Y is X. The third clause is a fact that states that 'bilbo' is a HOBBIT. It should be apparent that this Prolog program is a straightforward implementation of the knowledge base that we discussed in Chapter 3.

If this is a program then what does the data look like? The user input to a Prolog program is questions, and the Prolog program decides the truth or falsity of these questions. Thus we might ask if the NEWPHEWOF 'bilbo' is 'frodo'.

?- NEWPHEWOF(bilbo,frodo).

We are asking the system to check or verify the above statement. Our input statement "unifies"with the conclusion of the first clause when Y is 'bilbo' and X is 'frodo'. In order to conclude the truth of our statement we must determine the truth of UNCLEOF(frodo,bilbo) — the condition from the first clause obtained by using the same substitution. The truth of this condition is given directly by the fourth clause, thus the system would output:

yes

In the other mode of using a Prolog program we can request the system to compute a result if possible. We might wish to know what objects are HOBBITs in this system. We would then input:

?- HOBBIT(Z).

The system will then attempt to find some value for the variable Z that makes HOBBIT(Z) true. Using clauses two,three, and four, it should then respond:

Z=frodo]

We can then ask if there are any more known HOBBITs. Using the third clause it should respond:

Z=bilbo

If we ask again the response should be:

no

There appear to be some interesting implications of these two modes — verify and compute — of using a Prolog program. Analysis (Guthrie, 1985) has shown that verification of a result is never slower than computing that result, and sometimes it is much faster. The research investigated the possibility of increasing software reliability by using a non-procedural (e.g. Prolog) program to check the result of a procedural computation. These analyses may also provide insight into the optimal use of forward- and backward-chaining strategies for knowledge base inferencing in expert systems.

A major reason for the current prominence of Prolog is the Japanese connection: the Japanese threat to dominate computer technology with "fifth generation" machines (see Feigenbaum & McCorduck, 1983) including a proposal that Prolog might form the basis of the associated programming languages, also to be developed. I expect that the outcome will be either a patois based on the best of both AI and non-AI languages or otherwise LISP will retain its role as the fundamental language of AI systems.

Prolog is also prominent in another AI programming languages venture: integrated multi-language systems. POPLOG (Sloman & Hardy, 1983) is such a system and it combines POP-II with LISP and Prolog. The most important reason for having such a system is that different tasks in a single system can best be served by different languages. So, for example, in the cognitive industrial robot described earlier the control algorithms may be best implemented in POP-II, and the knowledge base in Prolog.

*The super-secretary*

Developing a large computer program is, in some ways, rather like writing a book: if the finished work is to hang together it must exhibit a consistency of structure and technique. A big difference is that the human editor, the guardian of consistency, will provide the author, in a more or less user-friendly manner, with all relevant comments at a first reading. The comments will not only be the specific inconsistencies found but higher level, abstract comments will also be given to guide both the specific changes indicated and subsequent expansion of the manuscript. By way of contrast the typical computer system will provide the programmer only with cryptic, very specific, piecemeal comments on the inconsistencies within a program: a certain variable is undeclared, a type conflict of operands in an expression, a referenced subprogram cannot be found, etc. A program development environment can (as indeed some do) function much more like a friendly editor in his purely technical role. The computer system can maintain complex, cross-referenced, indexes of all the program identifiers. Such accounting can be used, apart from a purely error-trapping role, as a source of information and guidance for the programmer.

This super-secretary can issue warnings about suspicious and potentially troublesome constructs: as for example the use of the same identifier to name two different objects, the selection may be legal but perhaps likely to lead to future confusions.

The system can make available the details of any part of the overall program under development such that the programmer can check on earlier design decisions as an aid to the design of some current module of interest. It should not be necessary for the programmer to plough laboriously through his previously designed modules looking for specific constructs. Nor should it be necessary to have to get a complete system up and running before the simple, syntactic inconsistencies are automatically brought to the programmer's attention.

But there is only so much information that can be made available to the programmer with certainty and on the basis of simple indexing and cross-referencing of programmer-specified constructs.

Teitelman (1972) has described and implemented "the programmer's assistant", the general function of which is to make it possible for the human programmer to say to the computer "do what I mean" instead of "do what I say", and "undo what I just tried — it did not work".

The latter sentiment could clearly only be nurtured, and thus bear fruit, in an AI program development environment. The censorious methodology of software engineers could view this implication of code hacking only with horror — a grotesque suggestion that must be disposed of as quickly and quietly as possible.

Apart from the above described concordance listings, Teitelman suggested:

(i)   a sophisticated structure editor;
(ii)  a debugging package;
(iii) a "prettyprint" facility for producing structured symbolic output;
(iv)  a program analysis package for producing a readily comprehensible picture of the flow of control between procedures;
(v)   forgiveness for errors (both spelling errors and errors of thought);
(vi)  a mechanism for undoing the results of previous operations to investigate an alternative path.

Items (i) to (iv) are now common features of LISP program development environments (see for example the LISP for the IBM PC, IQLISP(1983)). To some extent they almost have to be: the extreme simplicity and uniformity of LISP syntax and semantics tends to yield programs of surpassing opacity. Lost In Superfluous Parentheses may not be the source of the acronym LISP but it can quickly become all too appropriate when the human programmer is deprived of his support environment.

In addition to (i) through (iv), items (v) and (vi) are now features of the INTERLISP program development environment. Notice that item (v) clearly starts within the super-secretary's domain (with spelling correction) but it also extends beyond and well into the realm of AI itself (with correction of errors of thought). The point where this forgiveness feature crosses into AI, our last area of program development environments, is also roughly the point up to which it is currently implemented in the INTERLISP environment.

To provide really high-quality assistance the program development environment must have some AI. This appears to be a viciously circular argument: viz., to construct AI systems we need a program development environment that possesses some AI. In reality the circularity is unhelpful but not an insuperable problem. There is no logical necessity for AI in the program development environment, but it would be advantageous.

In practice we have incremental development of AI systems and AI system development environments. Any level of AI (or indeed none at all) in a program development environment can lead to AI systems that in turn can lead to more powerful AI program development environments, and so on .... Let us now look at the possibilities for AI in program development environments.

*A moderately stupid assistant*

As mentioned earlier Winograd (1975) argues the case for a program development environment that functions rather like a moderately stupid assistant. The reason for qualifying the assistance to be provided as moderately stupid is perhaps twofold. First, the human programer wants to be clearly in charge, the more creative and cognitive aspects of program development are to be kept within the human preserve. Second, it will by now come as no surprise to discover than even moderate stupidity must be founded largely upon AI. So moderate stupidity is both a useful and a realistically attainable goal; a brilliant assistant is a dubious objective from both viewpoints.

Winograd suggests that "the key to future programming lies in systems which understand what they are doing". He is saying that the system must have meta-knowledge. In the next chapter I will argue that meta-knowledge is a (perhaps, the) critical attribute of systems to support the full potential of commercial AI effectively. Winograd then outlines four ways in which such a system could help the human programmer.

(i)  Semantic, as well as syntactic, error checking could be a feature of such a system, thus eliminating many errors before the program is ever run. Static semantic errors and even implications for the dynamic semantics could be brought to the programmer's attention.

(ii)  Answering questions such as, "Is variable X global to any other subprogram?", will be based upon the super-secretary's cross-referenced indexes. By way of contrast a useful answer to the question, "What are the relative merits of structuring module Y in two different (and given) ways?", will require a sophisticated AI ability. The question-answering system will need to draw plausible inferences based upon its knowledge of the context for module Y (derived from a model of the program under construction) both in detail and general. In short, the development system must understand the particular aims and aspirations of the programmer.

(iii)  The system should be capable of filling in trivia without bothering the programmer with the actual details automatically supplied. The programmer might decide to expand a set $S$ by two elements. It should not be necessary to clutter the programmer's thinking with the particular implementation chosen at some earlier stage. "Expand set $S$ by two elements", is the command issued and the system takes care of the details.

(iv)  Finally Winograd would like to see his moderately stupid assistant perform as an expert at debugging programs; not the tracking down and analysis of errors (that would require more than a moderately stupid assistant) but the ability and knowledge to apply debugging strategies (such as tracing and backtracking) on the basis of high-level human directives. Thus the human programmer could ask, "Where was the value of $Z$ last changed?", and the system could run and trace an execution (perhaps a symbolic execution) of the program in order to answer the question.

Winograd certainly paints a picture that is attractive to the AI programmer. Unfortunately most of his suggestions still constitute more of a wish list than a description of any implemented system. Nevertheless, this is the direction of program development environments of the future (for reasons that are developed in the following chapter), and such systems will have a vital role to play in the development of AI in software engineering.

As the reader is no doubt aware — especially after our discussion of the essential methodological differences between AI and software engineering (Chapters 2 and 4) — sophisticated program development environments just had to be a product of AI rather than software engineering. For successful AI system development they are almost a necessity; for software engineering, especially the captious formal school, certain aspects of such environments are anathema. Interactive, incremental design and development of AI systems at a machine-executable level are fundamental to AI. Code hacking is an abomination, beyond the pale of the software engineering design methodology.

Programming language development environments will play a major part in the assault on the complexity barrier that derives from AI in software engineering. Such programming environments have been a goal of AI researchers for many years, big strides have been made towards the objective, but many good ideas remain unimplemented. The environment necessary to fully support AI program development will itself have to contain significant AI — it takes AI to make AI.

Although much real work lies ahead in order to demonstrate the viability of many of the more adventurous proposals, the program development environment is an important weapon in the campaign to avert a super software crisis. Such environments are moreover primarily a contribution from the world of AI.

If such tools are available for AI program construction, why not have analogous systems to assist the AI-program maintenance engineer? The answer is that we will need, and must have, program maintenance environments. Such AI-system support has received little attention primarily because we are still squarely in the system development phase of AI; after-sales service is a future problem that will be tackled in due course. But in this book we are attempting to anticipate (and thus forestall) the future problems of AI in software engineering. So let us examine both the proposed need for a program maintenance environment and some likely characteristics of such an environment.

### 6.2.2.2 The program maintenance environment

I have argued that a moderately stupid assistant will be a great help when constructing an AI program or, for that matter, any program. Why not employ much the same chap to assist in the continuing maintenance of AI programs?

Remember that a machine learning capability means that each copy of an original program will become an individual — no two copies are likely to remain identical, each will adapt to its own particular context. Also recall (from Chapter 4) that AI programs can seldom be correct and thus finished products in a way that non-AI software can and should be.

The original software, as released, will have an at least adequate performance within some range of expected application environments. Neglecting, for a moment, the possibility of machine learning, each particular application environment will be a unique approximation to the incompletely specified function that the program was designed to accommodate. Actual performance adequacy will vary from application to application, and adequacy can only be assessed (if it can be satisfactorily assessed at all) by prolonged observation of performance.

To some extent the idiosyncrasies of particular applications can be accommodated by an initial fitting and tuning of the general program. But because of the unknown and ill-defined aspects of an AI application, and the dynamic nature of AI application environments, any initial tuning is both unlikely to be perfect and likely to change in adequacy over time.

If a machine learning capability (which will not be perfect, remember Section 6.1.2) is then also included in the application software (and as discussed earlier there are good reasons for believing that adaptability is a necessary prerequisite of high quality AI software), the adequacy of a program will, by design, change over time. Given this scenario we can see that the maintenance of AI software will involve a service component.

Even if there are no known errors to fix and no upgrades to install, maintenance of AI software may be necessary to check upon the current level of performance adequacy and its recent history of change (for example, is it steadily degrading?). Perhaps AI software will need to be serviced after every so many hours of usage, to examine newly learned features and fine tune them to the particular application. AI programs should then be regularly serviced and tuned just like a complex piece of machinery such as a car.

To some extent such software will tune itself, but in the absence of perfect learning periodic checks to remove learned errors and to rectify any progressive degradation (due to the accumulation of imperfect modifications) will be needed.

The analogy between AI software with imperfect learning and complex machinery is in terms of the inevitable degradation of performance over time — i.e. they will both wear out. The physical wear of machinery is analogous to the cumulative lack of fit between imperfect modifications and the changes in the system's environment.

A perfect technology could presumably eliminate physical wear, but perfect technology is probably of much the same order of likelihood as perfect learning.

If we consider the likely size, complexity, and self-modifiability of sophisticated AI software the task of the program service engineer becomes daunting, to say the least. But when we recall the similarity between development and maintenance of AI software, a possible solution suggests itself: provide the maintenance engineer with a program maintenance environment.

Again we can see an analogy with the maintenance and servicing of modern cars. Once the mechanic could check performance and fine tune a car by ear and an innate ability to empathize with internal combustion engines. But today's much more complex, fuel-efficient, metal monsters require the mechanic to have the necessary maintenance environment to do a good job. A computer-controlled complex of sensors and probes provides the current performance measure, and by following a well-defined sequence of adjustments the mechanic can fine tune performance as measured by the instrument complex. The AI software maintenance engineer performing a routine service will also need complex test and evaluation equipment to do a good job.

Rudimentary program maintenance environments already exist. Sets of test programs and test data are typically used to evaluate the current status of hardware–software combinations. One example of more advanced research is described by Nieper & Boecker (1985) as "Making the invisible visible: tools for exploratory programming." They introduce the notion of a "software oscilloscope" that can be used to display, and thus aid visualization of, relationships among data and control structures that are otherwise invisible within a program.

The effective maintenance of AI software will require a drastic enhancement of such test and evaluation facilities to produce program maintenance environments with much the same level of sophistication as that outlined earlier for the development environments. The maintenance environment must provide tools with which the engineer, a stranger to the system, can test, evaluate, and tune system performance just by following a well-specified sequence of operations.

A useful maintenance environment would provide low-level, detailed information on the state of various aspects of the system being serviced. Then consultation of the programmed manual would enable the engineer to perform appropriate adjustments.

A maintenance environment that functions as a moderately stupid assistant, on the other hand, would run detailed checks on the basis of general directives from the human engineer. For example, "please check the clean-counter-top heuristic", might be the engineer's request. The system would then report back in terms of general statements such as, "the clean-counter-top heuristic is a complex heuristic composed of the following unitary heuristics.... Please indicate which investigative strategy you would like to apply."

Investigative results would similarly be returned to the engineer who could then issue general directives for a modification that the maintenance environment would implement in detail.

"The results of applying investigative strategy 37 indicate that counter-tops are only cleaned over a breadth of 28 inches. The kitchen has a counter-top that is 32 inches wide." To this somewhat better than moderately stupid reply the human engineer can then respond with, "Please modify the clean-counter-top heuristic to include counter-tops up to 32 inches wide."

The maintenance environment would then translate this last directive into the details of program code modification, perhaps just changing some program constant, say, max-counter-width from the standard value of 28 to the local requirement of 32. Clearly a trivial change; it could perhaps have been a much more complicated series of changes — say, adjustment of probabilities and probability thresholds to effectively move the wider counter-tops into an "expected" or "normal" category with respect to the relevant heuristics. But the point is not how complex or how simple the necessary implementation change turns out to be, it is the fact that the maintenance engineer can successfully effect the necessary change without having to know the actual implementation details.

Apart from the problems of constructing such a helpful program maintenance environment, there is the further problem of the sources of necessary information. Clearly the AI system users will be one source of information. In the above example the owners of the Expert Housecleaner could well have initiated the query about counter-top cleaning by telling the engineer that their new counter-tops were not being cleaned satisfactorily. The maintenance system itself might then have caught the inconsistency between the upper bound on counter-top width in its counter-top cleaning heuristic and its knowledge of actual counter-top widths within this particular house.

But, in general, the information necessary for adequacy judgements must be accumulated over a period of time. The system must accumulate empirical data on its own behaviour, this is descriptive meta-knowledge. As we shall see later such self-knowledge appears to be crucial for non-trivial machine learning as well as a source of valuable information for the maintenance engineer; these two functions are, after all, much the same: either the system modifies itself or some outside agent does the modifying. The AI system itself should maintain history files of its day-to-day performance in order to maximize the effectiveness of the program maintenance environment.

Such files might contain traces of all self-modification and the results of heuristics that proved to be particularly effective or ineffective (if such evaluations can be made by the system, otherwise user input might supply the necessary feedback). The problem here is one of selecting what to store; we need all potentially useful performance data without losing the really important information in oceans of trivia.

A further point to note is that the AI system and its maintenance environment must intermesh; the AI system must accumulate performance data in such a way that the maintenance system can use it, and the maintenance system must "understand" the AI system in detail to be able to function successfully as a go-between with the AI system and the human engineer. The necessary, almost symbiotic, given the evolutionary growth paradigm, relationship suggests that AI software and maintenance tools should be designed and developed together as a coherent group. Alternatively, the AI software is developed within a pre-existing environment as suggested in the following chapter.

The upshot of this largely speculative argument is that, in practice, AI software will have to be developed and released in conjunction with appropriate software tools for maintaining and monitoring system performance in the long run. And at an even more general level, the concept of a program maintenance environment should be developed along the lines of program development environments.

Finally, the dynamic nature of AI systems coupled with the incompletely specified aspects of AI problems means that AI system maintenance will include a service component. Servicing an AI program is checking and fine tuning the dynamic harmony between the AI system and its particular application environment given that both are likely to change over time. Change in the application environment may only be transformation of ill-defined aspects of the general incompletely specified function to well-defined ones, as a result of long-term observation of the specific application. Software servicing to correct the accumulated mismatches of imperfect learning is yet another feature that distinguishes AI software from non-AI software.

### 6.2.2.3  *Programs that can tell a tale*

If you have a problem, tell somebody about it. This is not an introduction to non-directive therapy nor a rerun of the ELIZA syndrome, but another AI technique to help avert a super software crisis — self-explaining programs.

Weinberg (1971) foresaw this development when he wrote that currently flow-charting programs are the only manifestation of machine help for understanding programs, "we must use more imagination in getting the machine to tell its story in as many alternative ways as possible."

When an AI system behaves unexpectedly there are several classes of possibilities:

(a)  There is what we might term a traditional bug in the logic or code that causes the control sequence, and thus output, to be other than that intended; it is thus unexpected.

(b)  The program has followed the intended algorithms but because of an unforeseen combination of possibilities the program output was a surprise; the output may be adequate, inadequate, or of uncertain adequacy.

The usual procedure at this point is to roll up one's sleeves and pore over the listings in an attempt to rationalize the unexpected output. If you are lucky there is a trace facility available. A traced rerun of the program will produce a mass of detailed data that can considerably aid the programmer's quest for an interpretation of the unforeseen output. The drawbacks of tracing are: if the trace is too selective then crucial details are likely to be missing, whilst in an indiscriminate trace the important details are awash in trivia and have to be laboriously identified and fished out. A 'smart' tracing facility would obviously be useful.

Why not let the program tell you why it did what it did? The ability to explain itself or justify its behaviour is an integral part of expert systems in AI.

Apart from being a maintenance aid, a self-explaining capability is a key strategy for developing confidence in the adequacy of an AI system. An unexpected result coupled with a rational explanation adds much needed credibility to the result. It is not at all rare for a human expert, say a diagnostic physician, to revise her own diagnostic strategy on the basis of an unexpected but adequately explained diagnosis from a computer expert system.

A self-explaining capability is necessary to allay the suspicions with which most people, quite rightly, treat computerized experts. This point brings to the fore a major by-product of expert systems research: the human expert can often refine and improve her expertise as a result of interaction with a computerized expert. By-product might be the wrong term here: the improvement in understanding of the human skill might be the major practical benefit, since precious few of the computerized experts have, as yet, emerged completely from their cosy research environments to perform as practical software products.

*Self-explaining traces*

Knowledge-based systems can be particularly amenable to the addition of a self-explaining capability. Each fact and rule is uniquely labelled; F1, F2, ... for the facts and R1, R2, ... for the rules. Then a justification list is also associated with each fact and rule.

A justification list is a list of the facts and rules that can be used to explain the fact or rule to which it is attached. The axioms of the system may be indicated as such by, say, an empty justification list (or trace list, as it is sometimes argued is a more appropriate name, see later).

Consider once again the usual knowledge base, but with some extra features:

(F1(HOBBIT BILBO) () )
(F2 (UNCLEOF FRODO BILBO) () )
(R1(IFTHEN (UNCLEOF X Y) (NEPHEWOF Y X)) () )
(R2 (IFTHEN (AND (UNCLEOF X Y) (HOBBIT Y)) (HOBBIT X)) () )

This knowledge base is again composed of four entries, two facts, F1 and F2, and two rules, R1 and R2. But now each entry consists of three parts: a label, a fact or rule, and a justification or trace list (all four justification lists are empty because the four entries are all given as true initially).

As before, the facts specify properties of specific objects, thus F1, "BILBO is a HOBBIT", or relationships between specific objects, thus F2, "BILBO is the UNCLEOF FRODO". The rules specify what facts can be inferred if some condition is satisfied, thus R1, "if Y is the UNCLEOF X, then X is the NEPHEWOF Y". The query "Is BILBO a HOBBIT?", becomes can we prove (HOBBIT BILBO) true with respect to the above knowledge base? Fact F1 states that this is indeed true, so having found the match between this first fact and our statement to be proved, the output is:

*Yes, BILBO is a HOBBIT. [The computer output is denoted by an initial *]

"Why?" [This question is answered by using the trace that was con-
structed whilst proving the truth of the query, namely the list (F1).]
   *BILBO is a HOBBIT is a given fact.
"Is FRODO a HOBBIT?"
*Yes, FRODO is a HOBBIT. [This query is proved to be true on the
basis of rule R2 and facts F1 and F2, thus the associated trace list is (R2
F2 F1).]
   "Why?"
   *Using rule R2:
      If Y is the UNCLEOF X, and Y is a HOBBIT then X is a
HOBBIT,*
   and the given facts:
      BILBO is the UNCLEOF FRODO (F2),
      and BILBO is a HOBBIT (F1),
   it can be proven that,
      FRODO is a HOBBIT.

This taxonomic fact newly discovered may now be added to the knowledge base. The addition might be:

(F3 (HOBBIT FRODO) (R2 F2 F1))

This implication from the original knowledge has a non-empty trace list;
the new fact is stored with its pedigree, so that if it is used within a future
proof it can thus contribute its parentage to the overall explanation of
whatever is proven. The associated trace list is also used to guide subsequent
modifications of the knowledge base. If BILBO is later found to be an Orc
with hairy feet then all the facts inferred from F1 (i.e. with F1 in their trace
list) will have to be re-examined.

*Self-justifying programs*
The association of trace or justification lists with each fact and rule in an
appropriate knowledge base, and the construction of a list of such traces to
accompany each attempt to evaluate a query provides a ready basis for self-
explaining systems. The final requirement is a translation module to transform a trace list into an English-like explanation.
   It is argued that such traces and resultant explanations are just an outline
of what the program did and not justifications at all; the term "justification
list" is a misnomer with implications that go way beyond the realities of the
structure.
   Swartout (1983), for example, claims that explanations generated from
the above described trace mechanism cannot tell why what the system is
doing is a reasonable thing to be doing. The knowledge necessary to produce
an authentic justification, rather than an explanation, was used to generate
the program but is not available within the resultant code.
   The XPLAIN system under development by Swartout works in conjunction with an automatic programmer that generates a program by refinement

from abstract goals. By examining the refinement structure created by the automatic programmer, XPLAIN provides justifications of the code.

It should be made clear that these more ambitious goals for a self-explaining capability introduce a severe increase in difficulty over and above the trace-type explanation. This being the case such a justification ability is in general still firmly within the research domain, but it does point to the future potential of the self-explaining system.

The user of an advisory AI system might well demand a justification in terms of system goals and objectives to buttress any less than obvious advice that the system offers. The maintenance engineer, on the other hand, would probably gain more insight into the state of the system being serviced if the system provides trace explanation to accompany its output.

Clearly the appropriateness of a system-generated explanation is a case of running the right horse for the course; appropriateness is a complex, context-dependent quality that needs to be dynamically adjustable to individual user requests if the self-explaining technique is to be used to full effectiveness — a case of tightly-coupled context sensitivity.

Nevertheless, a straightforward, trace-type, self-explaining capability is both currently feasible and a useful first step in applying this AI technique to alleviate the problems that AI engenders within software engineering.

*Automatic abstraction of specifications*
As discussed in Chapter 4 the development of an AI program is the process of evolving ever more adequate approximations to an incompletely specified function. Each successive implementation embodies a specification of the approximation to the ill-defined target problem.

As every software engineer knows the way to the heart of a program is through the specification (provided it is an implementation of that specification). If an AI program (or indeed any program) can automatically abstract and output its own de facto specification then the system is likely to be much easier to handle.

Whilst it is currently far-fetched to hope that a program can produce a highly abstract specification of itself (although as discussed above, Swartout appears to be aiming in this direction), it is quite feasible to generate low level specifications automatically. Such a specification is the high level code stripped of all the implementation-specific details.

Modern programming languages, in supporting both data structure abstraction and control abstraction bring this automatic abstraction goal nearer. Ada (Barnes, 1983) for example, offers extensive syntactic and semantic support for the rigorous separation of the abstractions of an algorithm and data structures from their necessary implementation details.

Careful system development with well-considered decisions as to how to distribute new code between implementation and specification will support the development of algorithms that can, purely on the basis of syntactic structure, strip out of a program both the algorithmic and the data structure abstractions.

Thus, for example, a package in the Ada language contains an explicit syntactic demarcation of specification and implementation. Just as importantly this syntactic differentiation is supported by a semantic one. The syntactic distinction provides the basis for an abstraction algorithm and the semantic constraints ensure that the syntactically prescribed decisions have been honoured.

We have already briefly considered the potential benefits of abstraction mechanisms as a route to 'designing for change' in AI (Chapter 4). Abstraction mechanisms are also used to 'hide' information and thereby promote modularity and so reduce complexity.

I am now suggesting that in AI it will be useful to use the available information hiding techniques as a route to information losing in addition to the more conventional uses — abstraction is information losing, we abandon the least significant information (either discard it outright, or reduce it to the essential distillate by generalization).

The 'package' is an information-hiding mechanism in Ada; I shall use it as an example. A package has two parts: a public or specification part, and a private or implementation part. The specification part constitutes the abstract specification of the package; it specifies all that a user can know about, and hence use in, the package. The implementation part contains an implementation of the abstract specification; it is not accessible to the package user.

The programmer can in effect delineate all code as either 'specification' or 'implementation'. As you will recall from Chapter 4 the terms 'specification' and 'implementation' are not absolutes; they are relative terms. Thus in practice the situation is likely to be more complicated. A series of levels of specification-implementation demands a more discriminating decision process than the binary choice required for two absolute categories.

Notice also that an AI-system programmer intent on supporting a specification abstraction algorithm may well elect to distribute code rather differently than if the goal was conventional software documentation. Code in a specification position (e.g. a package specification in Ada) will be preserved by an abstraction algorithm. Code that is implementation detail to a software engineer may well embody some structure whose preservation is considered important for the AI-system maintenance engineer. It is not obvious that the best structure to abstract for understanding the AI in the system (heuristics and dynamic structures in general) is the same as the best structure to support conventional software maintenance of the system (a point that I stressed in Chapter 5).

The following rather crude knowledge base is coded as an Ada package. As constructed it comprises a collection of rules and mechanisms for adding, accessing, and removing rules. The semantics of Ada ensures that use of this knowledge base is limited to the three mechanisms listed as procedure and function specifications at the beginning of the package. All code from the reserved word PRIVATE to the end of the package is inaccessible to users of the package.

```
PACKAGE knowledge-base IS
```

```
TYPE rule IS PRIVATE;
PROCEDURE putrule (condition, action:string);
FUNCTION nextrule RETURN rule;
PROCEDURE remove-rule (item:rule);
PRIVATE
TYPE rule IS
RECORD
   condition:string;
   action:string;
END RECORD;
END knowledge-base;
PACKAGE BODY knowledge-base IS
   TYPE ruleset IS array (1..max) OF rule;
      knowledge:ruleset;
      nextspace:integer:=1;

         .
         .
         .

      PROCEDURE putrule (condition, action:string) IS
      BEGIN
      knowledge(nextspace):=(condition, action);
      nextspace:=nextspace+1;
      END;

         .
         .
         .

   END knowledge-base;
```

Clearly construction of an algorithm that strips out package specifications is a viable proposition. With the current example and some minor linguistic transformations we obtain the following specification:

The knowledge base is composed of rules, the following operations on the knowledge base are possible:

  (i)  rules can be constructed from a condition part and an action part;
 (ii)  the next rule can be obtained;
(iii)  rules can be deleted.

It should be apparent that conventional top-down software design in which high-level descriptions become subprogram references can and do also begin to support the algorithmic stripping out of specifications uncluttered by particular implementations (in this case the bodies of the subprograms referenced). The specification-generation algorithm can peel layers off the hierarchical design. Thus hierarchical design in Fig. 2.3 of Chapter 2 would yield, say, the high level description:

> the ball and receptacle located;
> the located ball is picked up;
> the ball is placed in the receptacle.

if we neglect all structure below the second level.

It should also be clear that Ada by no means solves all of the problems obstructing development of an algorithmic specification generation technique. But it does provide at least a glimpse of the possibilities for using information hiding mechanisms as a route to automatic information losing. Rajlich (1985) illustrates the uses of Ada to support a number of different paradigms for design and implementation in conventional software engineering. He distinguishes between software design paradigms (such as top-down), and life cycles (the sequence of stages through which a piece of software passes). He does consider the "incremental life cycle", but for him it is "characterized by the use of one language for both design and implementation." This idea is clearly in accord with my suggestions for a disciplined, incremental, system development paradigm for AI. But when he states that this "incremental life cycle poses the possibility if verifying incomplete designs," and that "code written for one step will remain valid for all remaining steps," we see that he is dealing solely with conventional software engineering problems; AI problems fall largely outside of his discussions.

My general point here is that one direction of emphasis in modern programming language design is towards abstraction: both syntactic and semantic features to differentiate between the abstract specification of algorithms and data structures, and particular implementations of these specifications.

The degree to which a given language fails to support specification-implementation differentiation is likely to be directly proportional to the extent to which the necessary specification generation algorithm is an AI algorithm (rather than a provable, non-heuristic algorithm). Even so, with respect to the potential for automatic abstraction of specifications the best languages currently available probably still leave this problem squarely in AI territory.

Although there is as yet little research in this direction, it appears to be a useful and not impossible technique for facilitating the maintenance of AI systems. But it does require organized cooperation between the language used, the AI-system programmer, and the abstraction algorithm. The programming language must contain differentiation mechanisms, the programmer must use a consistent differentiation strategy, and the abstraction algorithm must "understand" the interaction between the other two components. We need a coherent collection of strategies and they must be applied with discipline.

In an adaptive AI system the programmer may have to confront the extra complication of meta-level mechanisms for the correct placement of system structures. A self-modifying program has to contain a strategy for distributing a particular modification between specification and implementation sections of the system.

In this chapter I have described a collection of strategies (some well-understood and immediately implementable, others much more nebulous and thus currently research problems in their own right) that together might begin to constitute a discipline for developing AI software on the basis of the best that the two conflicting methodologies appear to offer. A major point is that neither methodology has all the answers: the run–debug–edit cycle is typically applied with deplorably little constraint and control; the software engineering paradigm puts an emphasis on form (i.e. an initial RFS that is both complete and consistent, and the suggestion that software can be "correct") that is inappropriate for AI applications. In the long run a comprehensive and more thoroughly integrated paradigm to support commercial AI will be required. This problem is taken up in the next chapter.

# 7

# A plan for the revolution and a few words of caution

*The unpredictability of the world makes intelligence
necessary; the predictability makes it possible.
Together they ensure that it comes with no guarantees.*

Now is the time both to outline and to further justify my prognostications for harnessing the full potential of AI in practical software, and to air some associated societal questions.

The grand plan for realizing the best of intelligent behaviour within practical computer software is based on an attempt to merge the two paradigms (the subjects of Chapters 2 and 4) into an harmonious whole. This may strike the reader as somewhat perverse after I have invested so many words in proclaiming their differences and essential incompatibilities.

But the merger will, of course, constitute something of a new paradigm. Furthermore the suggestions are largely beyond the state of the art and thus necessarily somewhat speculative. In an effort to minimize the science fiction, the speculations are firmly grounded in at least state-of-the-art research if not in thoroughly tried-and-tested techniques.

My approach to the necessary merger of the AI and conventional software engineering methodologies is via a few fairly well-defined steps. I shall attempt to establish the validity of each step within the next few sections — one step per section.

In summary I shall argue that intelligent behaviour, in general, is fundamentally context-sensitive, and that the context-sensitivity is both complex and dynamic. This, in turn, implies the existence of a sophisticated self-adaptive ability in implementations of intelligence; it is certainly true of the only implementation we know of, that is, *Homo sapiens* (and also of most other forms of life).

A prerequisite of non-trivial learning is meta-knowledge; the system must know something of what it knows and doesn't know, and it must also understand, at some level, its goals and potential ways of achieving them.

And from context-sensitivity to the need for meta-knowledge there is a basic need for outside knowledge, lots of it. Intelligence is also knowledge based, but this is well known and accepted so I shall not labour it.

A sophisticated support environment, "from the cradle to the grave", is the proposed way to manage the complexity of AI software — a high level of complexity that is inevitable despite the extensive applications of the earlier-described techniques such as controlled modification. The necessary support environment, I shall argue, must also be based on knowledge of the encapsulated AI software — the system as a whole needs self- or meta-knowledge.

## 7.1   CONTEXT-SENSITIVE FUNCTIONS

As introduced in Chapter 1 and developed repeatedly throughout the book, the characterization of AI problems in terms of functions means that we must come to terms with the fact that these functions are context-sensitive. Natural language is perhaps the most forceful example: natural-language communication is both an important goal for commercial AI, and a highly context-sensitive problem.

J. R. R. Tolkien, author of *The Hobbit* and *The Lord of the Rings*, was (initially at least) primarily interested in languages. He started to invent languages (pseudo-natural languages, not formal languages), and he quickly discovered that one could invent no more than the most superficial aspects of a language without a context — natural languages are not context-free phenomena.

He developed the context of Middle-earth just to support his interest in inventing languages. As his authorized biographer, Carpenter (1977) says of Tolkien, "He was going to create an entire mythology. The idea had its origins in his taste for inventing languages. He had discovered that to carry out such inventions to any degree of complexity he must create for the languages a 'history' in which they could develop ... The existence of these languages was a *raison d'etre* for the whole mythology."

Context-sensitivity was raised, in Chapter 1, as a feature of AI that helps to distinguish AI that is currently viable in practical software, and AI that is not. The critical test, I argued, was how context-free or loosely-coupled to its context an AI problem is. Tightly-coupled context-sensitivity characterizes the empty set of practical AI software.

Another useful dimension along which we can view context-sensitivity is with respect to its tendency to change — at the crudest level, is it static or dynamic? I shall argue below that many AI problems are characterized by tightly-coupled and dynamic context-sensitivity. Then a need to take complex and dynamic relationships into account for decision making leads us inexorably on to a need for machine learning.

To some extent context sensitivity can be internalized in the function and we have a context-free, but larger, function. The knowledge encapsulated by AI implementations is internalized context.

The most realistic approaches to intelligent CAI, for example, include a model of the user. The most important context sensitivity in this problem is that between the machine and the human being under instruction — the system user. By generating and maintaining a model of each user the computer system has internalized the crucial context sensitivity of the problem.

Apart from the problem of maintaining up-to-date models or knowledge of the relevant aspects of an AI program's domain (i.e. machine learning, the topic of the next section), an important question in AI is: how much context do we need to internalize?

It all depends on the scope of our AI system. It is clear that a useful level of AI can be achieved in limited domains as a result of an internalization of a severely limited collection of knowledge; expert systems exhibit some AI on the basis of a narrow domain-specific knowledge base.

What is not clear is: how much can the AI in expert systems be upgraded and extended (e.g. to include a sophisticated explanation component) within the current framework for such systems — inflexible and highly limited context sensitivity?

If we are aiming for a more general AI system, not necessarily one with the full capabilities of you or me, but say an expert system that takes people into account — their aims, objectives, hopes and fears, all with respect to the particular expertise of the AI system — then the context sensitivity must be both broadened and made dynamic.

You and I have internalized a model of the world within which models of specific subworlds are developed to differing degrees dependent upon their relative importance in our lives. We can behave sensitively, and thus have a basis for intelligent responses, to a wide range of phenomena. It is clear that our intelligence is founded upon a lot of knowledge; it is also clear that we do not know anything approaching all that there is to know. But what we do have is the ability to learn and dynamically internalize new knowledge (develop a new or expanded context sensitivity), whenever it is in our interest to do so.

In principle the state of any given person's knowledge at a given time could be fed into a computer and the computer system could behave just as intelligently as the original person although it has no learning capability whatever. But for how long would it remain intelligent? The answer depends upon how static or dynamic is the knowledge upon which the intelligent behaviour is founded.

Expertise in, say, pure mathematics could be expected to endure for long periods of time; the basic knowledge is well established and not subject to major changes. But intelligent interaction with respect to current affairs, or with any given individual, is liable to degrade rapidly — both contexts are dynamic. Out-of-date knowledge will soon reduce this static system to a pathetic anachronism.

So we'll just update the system's knowledge whenever necessary — every day, or every hour, or even every minute — there is still no necessity for machine learning? I think that there is, but this is an argument for the next section. I shall first finish off this section by focusing the discussion on current practical AI, natural-language interfaces and expert systems, the major source of apparent counterexamples to my thesis.

Domain-specific knowledge may be relatively static, as in the above example of pure mathematics. The implementor of an expert system , who spends an inordinate amount of time modifying the system's knowledge base, might well want to challenge that statement. But compared to knowledge of the empirical world (who and what are where, and doing what), knowledge of chemical structure, and knowledge of geological formations, and knowledge of the associations between symptoms and diseases, are decidedly static.

The fact that even with these static knowledge bases the knowledge engineer is largely preoccupied with modifying the knowledge base is a danger signal for the way knowledge-engineer intervention will escalate when more dynamic contexts are attempted, if we fail to incorporate self-adaptivity.

A state-of-the-art report on AI (Waltz, 1983) states that "reasonably good" natural-language processing is currently available only in, "static contexts, and limited, well-structured domains of applications."

In describing XSEL, a front end to the R1 expert system, McDermott (1982) singles out the context-free nature of XSEL's three main tasks. He says, "The most striking characteristic of these subtasks is that for all three the decisions to be made are relatively independent both of prior and of subsequent decisions." And although a significant amount of knowledge is required to achieve performance adequacy, "the fact that the component selection task can be recognition driven [i.e. context free] makes XSEL conceptually quite simple."

The explanation task, he continues, is quite different. In reference to the knowledge-based programs of recent years, he says, "for the most part, these programs do not treat explanation as a task that requires intelligence." As a first approximation to the user-context sensitivity necessary for good explanations, XSEL has five kinds of information from which to generate an explanation. The adequacy of this fixed, five-point, discrete approximation to the continuum of user context remains to be seen.

My argument is not that such discrete simulations cannot support the rich and continuous context sensitivity within user-and-system interaction — such would be one of the well-known Dreyfus fallacies. What I am saying is that however sophisticated the discrete approximation becomes it will need to be self-adaptive in order to exhibit the explanation capabilities of an average human being. Again we return to the question of: are the capabilities of an average human being necessary? Clearly, in some very practical sense, they are not, but to achieve anything like the full potential of AI a surprising amount of such capabilities will be necessary.

An analogous argument based on the reasoning capabilities of current expert systems is given by Wos, Overbeek, Lusk, & Boyle (1984). They state, in their text on automated reasoning, that current expert systems rely largely on "focused reasoning" (i.e. reasoning with known procedures that can be well-controlled). They argue that "unfocused reasoning" (i.e. no well-defined procedure is known that will directly yield the answer) must be used or else we will overlook many possible applications. In their words, "many significant applications will require unfocused reasoning."

Returning to the specific limitations of system rigidity, Boden (1984), for example, also discussing expert systems, states that, "Current systems are relatively simple and inflexible, and restricted to very narrow domains. They can be incrementally improved, but only up to a point." She also sees machine learning as a pressing problem for the future. "If a program cannot learn for itself, its development is limited by the time and ability of the programmer to provide it with new information and ideas."

Clearly Boden's ideas are supportive of my argument although she does not seem to view machine-learning as playing quite the same unique and crucial role as I do. Nevertheless, this brings us onto the question of the need for, or necessity of, machine-learning in AI. I will argue that it is a necessity in practice if not in principle; the alternative is a severely limited application of AI as practical software.

## 7.2   THE CRITICAL ROLE OF MACHINE LEARNING

"To be blunt, an AI program that doesn't learn is no AI program at all" (Schank, 1983). I wouldn't go that far (and neither would he at other times, I suspect), but even neglecting the hyperbole, Schank is clearly with me in spirit. Although we agree on the importance of learning, I am happy with the term AI software as applied to adequate implementations of complex, open-ended problems even though they make no pretensions to learn.

And although not so dramatic, my point is somewhat harder to substantiate: I would agree with Schank that, "Learning is, after all, the quintessential AI issue." But it does not necessarily follow that commercial AI must involve machine learning. The result of a learning behaviour can always, in principle at least, be simulated by periodic updating of the system by some outside agency.

In practice we are already witnessing a renewal of interest in machine learning as a strategy for alleviating the problems generated by the knowledge bases used in expert systems — problems of both construction and maintenance of large and complex, but relatively static, collections of information. We find this point made in the review of AI chaired by Waltz (1983), and in almost every other mention of the knowledge-acquisition problem.

Michie (1982), for example, in his review of the state-of-the-art in machine learning sees a practical need for machine learning in terms of increasing programmer productivity. He then focuses on a semi-automated scheme for knowledge acquisition — this scheme, he calls structured induction, I have considered earlier.

Waltz's committee cite, "the ability to learn from experience", as one of a small number of "important characteristics that such machines would have to have before AI could be said to have succeeded" (Waltz, 1983). They do not single out machine learning as I would, but to my mind the other characteristics that they list — such as, common sense, and the ability to deal appropriately with natural language input — all imply a prerequisite machine learning ability. This would seem to cast the machine learning characteristic in a more fundamental role than they appear to accord it.

From his long perspective on the AI scene, Samuel (1983) singles out natural-language communication and learning as the two basic problems of AI. He goes on to say "that the desired progress in man–machine communication will not be made until it is treated as a learning problem . . . In fact, I look on learning as the central problem of AI research." So it seems that I am in good company with my extreme view.

I think that it is clear that, in practice at least, there is general agreement that machine learning is an important research problem that still needs to be solved to some reasonable degree. It is not clear that such general agreement could be found to support my claim that machine learning is perhaps one of the two most fundamental problems to be solved in AI (the other is meta-knowledge, discussed later).

I would like to make the claim that non-trivial machine learning is actually necessary in principle before we will see the full potential of AI in commercial software. But such in-principle arguments are difficult to make; it all depends on your principles.

Consider two possible implementations of an intelligent dialogue capability: one system embodies non-trivial machine learning, the other utilizes an external agent to update its knowledge whenever necessary.

The computer system must typically respond to the user after learning something (trivial or complex) from the user's previous communication. A system based on the in-principle objection to the necessity of machine learning will have to entertain the possibility of the external agent updating the computer's knowledge during the analysis of every user utterance!

But if your basic principle is that, 'nothing is impossible,' then an in-practice argument for the crucial role of machine learning is the best that can be produced, in principle.

Let me list three reasons why I believe that machine learning will be necessary in commercial AI:

(1) Everyone is different, if AI is to behave even reasonably intelligently in its interaction with people, it cannot neglect this fact.
(2) Any one person is different at different times; a major role of commercial AI is to impart knowledge to people, if it does not respond to the changes it induces it will be a failure — it will not be AI.
(3) The empirical world is a rapidly and subtly changing place (apart from the people in it); an AI system to remain an AI system must keep abreast of the relevant changes, if a human external agent does this job for it, most of the practical justification for AI is eliminated.

The above points provide us with a characterization of the limits of non-adaptive commercial AI: it is those problems that involve neither people nor any other aspect of the empirical world, except in a very subsidiary role. This is clearly a characterization that is closely akin to the earlier ones based on loosely-coupled context sensitivity and static contexts.

The possibility of having a knowledge-based AI system that behaves intelligently without a self-adaptive capability will only be viable in the domains of relatively static knowledge. That restriction largely excludes intelligent interaction with people and the domains of everyday expertise such as house cleaning. It is a limitation to intellectual expertise in largely theoretical domains — there's clearly lots of scope for such AI there, but it is also far short of the full potential of AI.

Remember that I am not arguing that commercial AI cannot go any further without non-trivial machine learning. There may be decades of useful and exciting expansion of the applications of non-learning AI. I am making the case that without sophisticated machine learning our options will always be limited; large and important sections of potential AI application will be excluded, and the full potential of AI as practical software will not be achieved.

Even if we can agree that sophisticated adaptivity will be necessary in commercial AI that still leaves the question of, to what degree will the system have to be self-adaptive? From our review of approaches to machine learning in Chapter 3, you may recall that a given need to assimilate information may be implemented in many ways. In particular there is a spectrum of possibilities from totally automated discovery to a fairly trivial ability to accept from a human tutor mentally predigested information. This latter possibility does not really qualify to be called non-trivial machine learning, but there are many strategies, intermediate between these two extremes, that do qualify.

It may be possible to implement the necessary sophisticated adaptivity in terms of a fairly simple program, and a smart and dedicated human tutor — and this is a valid approach to take when researching the problem. But for commercial AI it falls foul of all of the previous arguments for the necessity of machine learning — i.e. human beings will be doing all of the difficult work, and this onerous task will be different for every individual copy of the software.

For non-trivial machine learning a lot of knowledge concerning the program's organization and goals and objectives must be available some-where — either in the program itself or in the human tutor. The main point underlying the necessity for machine learning is that no human being has to maintain, at his finger-tips, all of this knowledge about the program (and remember, each copy of the program is an individual) such that he can accurately modify it at the drop of a new significant fact.

So although the necessity for machine learning does mean that the machine and not the human should indeed be shouldering the burden, it is again not at all clear how far we can go with AI into dynamic contexts by sharing the load to some extent. Indeed, as mentioned before, the real power of AI may reside in an intimate man–machine relationship — a symbiotic superintelligence. But I do not believe that this partnership will work if all of the learning and adaptation has to come through the organic partner.

As the reader should now be well aware, commercial AI presents formidible complexity problems and the necessity for machine learning just adds to them. The requirement that the machine bears the burden of the learning is a specific measure to lessen the complexity that the associated humans have to manage.

Nevertheless there is a fundamental problem of complexity: conventional software engineering can be very complex, all indications are that sophisticated AI software will be orders of magnitude more complex.

## 7.3   SUPPORT ENVIRONMENTS AND THE MANAGEMENT OF COMPLEXITY

Man is the tool-using animal; where other organisms just dabble, *H. sapiens* has dived in, deep. We have devised tools to extend our natural abilities whenever the need arose, and cognitive needs are no exception. But the successful utilization of one tool can quickly lead us onto the need for another — computers and the subsequent software tools are one such example that we have already discussed.

A general strategy for managing the complexity of commercial AI is to develop and use the necessary tools — typically software packages to take care of some of the complexity for us. Neither AI nor conventional software engineering have been slow to do this.

The methodologies described in Chapters 2 and 4 are different and so, not surprisingly, although there is much commonality, there are some differences in the kinds of software tools that have come from AI and from software engineering. Throughout the book I have drawn attention to such tools. McDermott, designer of the R1 expert system, claims that the tools developed to support AI "are quite different from the tools developed for use in well-structured domains; in particular, they are intended to be used to implement continuously evolving programs"(McDermott, 1982).

An integrated collection of software tools becomes a programmer's support environment. In the previous chapter we examined the desiderata for support environments for both program development and for program maintenance, in AI.

I pointed out that there is a substantial gap between the generally accepted desirable characteristics of an AI support environments, and the support environments implemented to date. And the reason was: it takes AI to make AI. In other words, we are ensnared in an unhelpful circularity.

A support environment of the quality required will have to be based upon AI but we need such a support environment to help us implement this AI. The result is that progress is slow; it is nevertheless the way of the future, I believe. We are going to need extensive help from AI to surmount the complexity barrier of AI.

AI as a research enterprise is complex; add non-trivial machine learning and it becomes much more complex; add the need to produce usable and maintainable AI software and the complexity of the overall endeavour goes up again; add also concrete, as opposed to abstract, AI and complexity goes up yet again.

Charniak, Riesbeck, & McDermott (1980) deal exclusively with "abstract" AI — "programs which only deal with abstractions" — and explicitly eschew "concrete" AI — "programs which must deal with the real world".

This concrete–abstract distinction is another view of the empirical-world problem raised earlier to support my argument for the necessity of machine learning. If we must take some aspects of the empirical world into account, then we must program to minimize the adverse effects of Murphy's Law — the theme of which is, if it can go wrong it will go wrong. As an example consider the famous GPS (General Problem Solver) system — abstract AI — and the cognitive industrial robot introduced earlier — potentially concrete AI.

In the midst of solving the "monkey-and-bananas" problem (described by Slagle, 1971), GPS, with complete confidence, could apply the "get bananas" operator and 100 per cent of the time the goal of "the contents of the monkey's hand are the bananas" was achieved. There was, of course, no monkey and no bananas — the program worked only with abstractions.

By way of contrast the cognitive industrial robot, in a similar situation, executes the "grasp-ball" function. But then it must check to determine if indeed the ball is now in its hand. An empty hand signals the need for an enquiry that will result in the invocation of some corrective plan.

Fig. 7.1 is a development of the cognitive industrial robot described in Chapter 4. This figure is a development of Fig. 4.2. The extra complexity of the problem is forced upon us by the move from a purely abstract AI application (I could not actually apply the scheme in Fig. 4.2 to a concrete situation with a real robot, it would just keep grinding to a halt) to the possibility of an application in the empirical world.

The increase in complexity is primarily due to the fact that all certainty has gone; everything is probabilistic with no guarantee that the probability functions are either simple or easily discoverable. The direct result of this uncertainty is that logical truths in the abstract version (e.g. grasp-ball implies ball-in-hand) have had to become checks (T1, T2, and T3) that some condition does indeed appear to hold. Thus the assertions of true conditions on the right of Fig. 4.2 become checks for the truth of these conditions in Fig. 7.1.

A second jump in complexity then occurs because we must now provide a module to analyse the causes of any check that fails, and to initiate an appropriate recovery strategy. Each recovery strategy must reroute control to some (usually) earlier part of the process and establish the appropriate context to restart normal processing.

It is true that the analysis and recovery function (box 7) could simply request operator intervention, but then the abstract AI would have been transformed into concrete non-AI. That is not to say that operator interven-

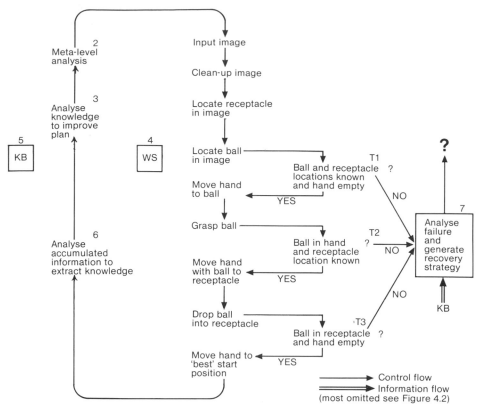

Fig. 7.1 — A specification for a 'concrete' version of the cognitive industrial robot of
Fig. 4.2

tion should never be requested — that is absurd. What I am saying is that an important aspect of bringing the full potential of AI to bear in practical software is the ability to deal with a modicum of the perturbations that are an intrinsic feature of the empirical world.

I don't think that the magnitude of the discontinuity between abstract and concrete AI can be overemphasized. The assertions in Fig. 4.2 follow logically from the abstract framework upon which the system is built (and such an approach is the epitome of good program design in formal software engineering) — they must be true, if the algorithm is correctly constructed.

The necessary truth of these conditions renders any checking of them superfluous and a waste of time and space (after the algorithm has been 'proved' correct). But in a concrete application these necessary truths become logical pit traps (if the algorithm falls into one it will never get out). What was the basis for the reliability of the algorithm becomes its downfall.

Concrete AI based on abstract AI would appear to be threatened by the "Titanic effect" of De Millo, Lipton, & Perlis (1979): viz., if the ship (algorithm) is by definition unsinkable (proved correct) then of course it is pointless to go to the trouble and expense of life boats, etc. (error checks, etc.). But then when it does sink (algorithm crashes), due to the fact that the empirical world isn't constrained by formal definitions, the results may be catastrophic (more on the theory of catastrophe very soon).

Now any AI-system designer worth his salt will of course recognize that the concrete application will necessitate the addition of numerous checks and traps. But after-the-fact patching with such checks is not the same as preparing for them from the beginning, and designing the system to deal with the inherent uncertainties right from the start.

This is another source of the 'first step fallacy' discussed with respect to artificial micro-worlds in Chapter 4. In this case the fallacy is that if we can solve the neater abstract problem, then we have also essentially solved the scruffier concrete version (the real problem). In my opinion the two versions are likely to require fundamentally different solutions, and the 'real' AI is mostly to be found in the concrete version.

I get a strong feeling (and one that should be familiar to every software engineer who has seen his simple and clean, perfect-case, algorithm buried and lost under a mass of error-traps) that a lot of the intelligence in intelligent behaviour, as opposed to abstract intellectual behaviour, is invested in dealing with the unexpected but inevitable problems that the empirical world brings along with it. Concrete AI cannot avoid these problems; abstract AI can.

An interesting aside concerns the implications of sophisticated machine learning, not necessarily perfect learning; if we can reach this goal then much of the complexity crumbles away. A basic system can be implemented. Then it need only be exposed to appropriate environments (perhaps carefully controlled environments), and it will develop into the required AI system. This situation appears to contain a complexity hump such that if we can master the level of complexity necessary to reach the top of the hump (i.e. successful implementation of sophisticated and fully-automated learning), then the complexity for the human designer will suddenly plummet.

In Fig. 7.2 I have graphed some speculations concerning the relationship between the complexity of the software task as perceived by the humans who perform it (designers and developers, and maintenance engineers), and the quality of machine learning that can be reliably produced.

For both classes of task it seems that the complexity will steadily increase as we add imperfect learning abilities to the software. But once the quality of machine learning rises to the point where the amount of useful information that the system can assimilate outweighs the problems due to imperfect learning we can expect a downward trend in task complexity. It also seems that the system developer will benefit more, and earlier in the sequence, than will the maintenance engineer (remembering that maintenance is after-delivery development and it is after installation that most of the relatively uncontrolled learning will occur).

But there will come a point when the maintenance process also starts to decrease in complexity due to a 'sophisticated' learning ability when the benefits far outweigh the problems.

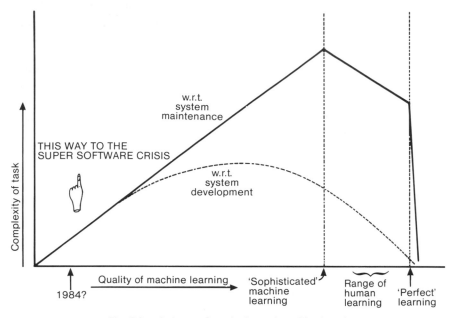

Fig. 7.2 — Software Complexity and machine learning

Finally if something like 'perfect' learning is attained (and it is not clear that it is attainable even in principle) then the maintenance costs associated with learning should disappear.

The dramatic discontinuity at the point of 'perfect' learning is reminiscent of the behaviours described by catastrophe theory (see Thompson, 1975): as one parameter of a system (in this case quality of learning) is slowly varying there is a sudden snap change in the value of some other previously steadily varying parameter (system complexity). The interesting point is that the result of the snap change is usually 'catastrophic' (bridges suddenly collapse, and dogs turn round and bite you instead of continuing to run away). But in our example the sudden change is not catastrophic, on the contrary, we would be delighted to reach this point with an AI software system — is this the first example of 'triumph theory'? (Incidently Thompson's paper has the wonderful title of "Experiments in Catastrophe", clearly an AI paper I thought when I first unearthed a reference to it.)

Sadly it is all purely academic speculation for the foreseeable future; decidedly imperfect learning is what we will have to contend with for a long time yet.

The recognized needs for intelligent support environments, if not the implemented systems themselves, are now commonplace. In the last chapter we developed the idea of a maintenance support environment. We have seen the incompatibilities between the two program development methodologies. The impact of this mismatch will be in the long-term use and maintenance of AI software.

We may well be able to construct an adequate AI program but the chances of successfully maintaining it in a user environment are minimal. And if the program can learn in a non-trivial way the probability of successful maintenance will take another dive.

I have discussed some techniques that will contribute to the production of more maintainable AI software — for example, controlled modification and abstraction of underlying representations. But I have also argued for the necessity of machine learning; a feature that can only aggravate the maintenance headache.

What more can be done to make after-sales service and maintenance reasonably possible for sophisticated commercial AI? The suggested answer is that program maintenance environments must be developed. Several components of such an environment were described and illustrated in the last chapter.

The idea of a maintenance environment is not totally new. Sussman, Holloway, & Knight (1980) in describing their plans for a support environment to aid in the design of digital integrated systems, state that, "What is needed is a computer aided design tool which can help an engineer deal with system evolution from the initial phases of design right through the testing and maintenance phases. We imagine a design system which can function as a junior assistant." But as for maintenance we hear no more.

In the introduction to a collection of papers on software engineering environments, Hunke (1981) justifies stressing maintenance as a separate phase on a par with specification and design on the basis that half of the effort spent on a software product is expended after the first delivery. He also states that maintenance has been disregarded for a long time by researchers.

Attention and discussion have in general been focused on program development environments; after all, first things first, we need an adequate implementation before we need worry about maintaining it. In addition there are a lot of similarities between design and development, and maintenance for AI software. Remember that within the incremental development paradigm of AI there is no RFS to aim for; it is more a case of attaining sufficient adequacy such that further development can be done, and may be done best, in the application environment.

The general function of this environment, which encapsulates the AI software from birth till death, is that of a filter. The environment should act as a sieve between the humans (designers, users, maintenance persons) and the AI program facilitating a two-way transfer of meaning whilst filtering off the individual representation structures and processes. But it is not a rigid kitchen colander, it should be more like a subtly context-sensitive organic membrane: it will dynamically open and close to allow the passage of whatever is the appropriate type and chunk size of information. Thus although it will generally filter off implementation detail (those used by the humans as well as those used by the program), it should, on demand, be capable of communicating, say, concrete knowledge representation structures to the maintenance person.

In a discussion attendent to the meeting that generated the book, *The AI Business* (Winston & Prendergast, 1984), Harris, speaking with reference to today's very low level AI products, was concerned by the shortage of people with sufficient AI expertise to support the products being marketed. This problem will only increase as more of the full potential of AI is realized in commercial products. Support environments of the type described should do much to lessen this problem.

Fig. 7.3 is a schematic illustration of the complete life-cycle environment

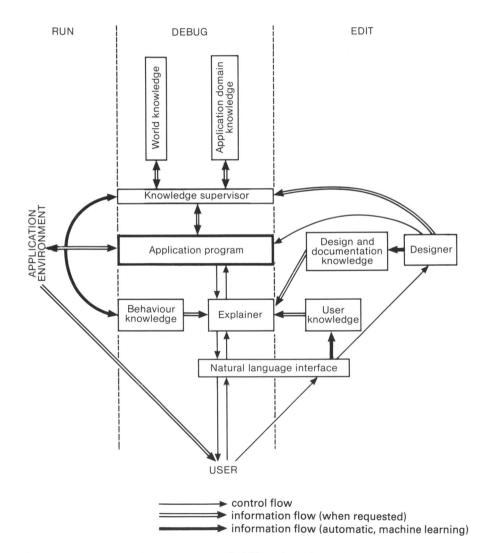

Fig. 7.3 — A complete life-cycle environment

that I advocate. The actual AI software — the application program — is almost completely encapsulated in the environment. The only direct access it has outside the environment is to those aspects of the empirical world that it was designed to deal with. Thus the cognitive industrial robot will interact directly with the appropriate industrial environment and an intelligent compiler will deal directly with user programs.

But the interaction with all humans is mediated by intervening modules — the natural language interface and, in the figure, either the "explainer" or the "designer" module.

The figure is drawn to emphasize the design, development, and maintenance function of this environment. To the user of a 'completed' system it could certainly function much more simply: he or she issues instructions to the application program; the application program executes; and the user obtains some resultant information, directly by observing the program's interaction with the application environment and indirectly from the program via the "explainer" module and natural language interface.

The reader should be aware that although Fig. 7.3 is complex (perhaps too complex) it is certainly far simpler than the reality is likely to be. I have, for instance, not connected all of the knowledge bases together for reasons of simplicity that I would also justify as a reasonable first approximation.

By analogy with the differences between perfect and imperfect learning we might expect a similar situation with perfect and imperfect complete life-cycle environments. A 'perfect' complete life-cycle environment would presumably allow any reasonably intelligent person to construct and use AI software. He would characterize an ISF as best he could by interacting in his preferred language with the computer system — all the time prompted and guided by the system. Together, it is perhaps feasible (just about) that they could construct a first approximation to the required AI software and then interactively develop it to achieve adequacy. Finally our developer could become a user of his software and do some maintenance and servicing whenever necessary.

But, back in the real world, we must deal with imperfect environments. In order to diminish somewhat the daunting complexity of the task we should probably consider design, development, and maintenance as one set of functions, and use of the software to be a separate function. These two classes of system interaction might be supported by rather different environments, although the knowledge accumulated by either type of environment should be usable by the other one.

What we gain by such a division is that the more complex processes (design, development, and maintenance) are paired with the humans who could reasonably be expected to possess significant technical expertise in computer software (system designers and maintenance programmers). We thus have an opportunity to get started with a simplified version of the design, development, and maintenance environment by relying on a certain level of necessary technical expertise on the human side of the interface. For the user environment we cannot reasonably do this, but the problem is much simpler anyway.

The essential requirement of the design, development, and maintenance environment is that it can extract and store all the necessary knowledge about the application programs in a form acceptable to the user environment — that is still a formidable problem. Nevertheless, it is a problem that can be tackled in an incremental manner: any knowledge of the application software that can be applied to ease the problems of human interaction with the software will be a gain. Luckily there is no requirement that the whole problem must be solved before it is of any use.

Fig. 7.3 clearly illustrates a wish, a vague wish at that, and while I cannot map out anything approaching a detailed design for such an environment I can offer some general ideas, but first let's look at some similar suggestions from other people.

With a philosophy akin to that of the SAFE system to be described later, Winograd (1979) argues that the nature of programming has changed fundamentally. He also sees a concentration of activity at the ill-structured end of the software design spectrum.

He argues for highly automated environments that will allow the programmer to escape from the low-level intricacies of the task, "higher level programming systems can provide the means to understand and manipulate complex systems . . . A programmer's use of a higher level system will be highly interactive."

Integrated programming environments are, as he says, not a new idea, and although they contain many useful components, they are far from achieving the goals that he discusses.

In all Winograd appears to be advancing a viewpoint that is in some ways quite similar to the one that I am advocating. He is concentrating on large and complex conventional software but he neglects formal specification and mathematical abstraction in favour of specifying and understanding program behaviour.

Wasserman & Gutz (1982) also suggest that the nature of programming is changing. They see a move to integrated development environments, in the short term. In the long term they envisage more drastic changes, such as environments with "local intelligence" that also address the need for system maintenance.

Again they are applying the "environment paradigm" to conventional software, and they predict that one result of these changes will be that "software developers will be able to attack a large number of application areas which could not previously be addressed effectively."

I can interpret this last quote (I'm not sure that they do) to include AI software. If the sophisticated, complete life-cycle, environment paradigm, that I advocate, ever materializes then AI software will have become conventional software. But then conventional software and the methods of constructing it will be very different from what we know today.

Smoliar & Barstow (1983) argue that excessive concern with programming languages and relative neglect of programming environments is a misguided distribution of effort. They view the role of programming languages as internal representations to be manipulated by software development tools. Programming languages "are for communication between machine facilities, rather than between people and machines." I agree with this view, but we will have to upgrade considerably and integrate current software tools before we see programming languages slip from their current key position in man's efforts to use computers as a problem-solving tools.

## 7.4   META-KNOWLEDGE COULD BE A KEY

"Know thyself" is a popular injunction in some circles and one that, I believe, we can usefully lay on AI systems. The support environment should know all that there is to know about the AI software that it encapsulates — the system as a whole should have self-knowledge. From another viewpoint, the system should know what is knows and what it doesn't know, it should know about the structure and content of its basic knowledge — i.e. it should have meta-knowledge.

In modern parlance the support environment is an AI program expert system; it knows all about AI software in general and it knows the details of the particular piece of software that it happens to be wrapped around.

How did it get this knowledge? The general knowledge clearly has to be constructed only once for a collection of individual AI software products. But what about the product-specific knowledge? If the big problem was to build it into the specific program anyway, why is it advantageous to have to build it into a support system?

The answer is that the support environment has also mediated the design and development of this particular piece of AI software. The support environment is in just the right position to acquire all it wants of the design, development, and implementation information about the specific software developed. We don't have to extract the design knowledge from the finished program and build it into the environment; the environment assimilates the necessary information during the process of design and development — it is, after all, the channel through which all of this information passes. It is an "active" channel, it requests, accepts, rejects, filters, and generally controls exactly what and how design and development information is presented to the system.

The TEIRESIAS program (Davis & Lenat, 1982) was designed as an interface between a domain expert and an expert system. It allows the domain expert to input knowledge without knowing the implementation details and it generates, from the expert system's behaviour, explanations at a level acceptable to the domain expert. The point that I want to make with this example is that the use of "allows" in the previous sentence is somewhat misleading. TEIRESIAS closely controls the information flow; it induces the domain expert to provide the necessary knowledge in a form that it finds acceptable.

Provided that the domain expert is not uncomfortable with the style of interaction required, all is well. The interface or the environment controls the interaction but if that control is sufficiently flexible and user-friendly it is not a problem for the user. And for the environment it is a great asset, for knowing within certain limits what information it will get, and in what form, obviously facilitates processing of that information to extract whatever it needs.

The work of Swartout (1983), described earlier, is an example of a concrete research project that fits right into this general paradigm.

The SAFE system (Balzer, Cohen, & Goldman, 1982) encompasses a general effort to automate the design of software at the informal end of the software design spectrum — that is, the type of software that most closely resembles AI. The aim is to capture the entire development and maintenance process and support it with software tools. The entire history of the system's evolution will occur, and be recorded, within the integrated environment.

The researchers view their suggestions as an alternative software paradigm particularly relevant in the current era of cheap hardware and expensive people. They are applying AI-based techniques to conventional software development hence they insist on the critical role of formal specifications. They describe an incremental approach to specification development in which a first formal specification is successively elaborated by the developer into the "initial" specification — a process very like my interpretation of the program development paradigm of AI, especially when we add the fully automated environment in both cases.

They also propose automatic transformation from specification to implementation hence they can afford to concentrate their efforts on the specification. This might be another way to avoid implementation clutter in the run–debug–edit paradigm except that some of this clutter is specification detail that we wish to explore.

Fig. 7.4 is an illustration of a "new paradigm" for software development

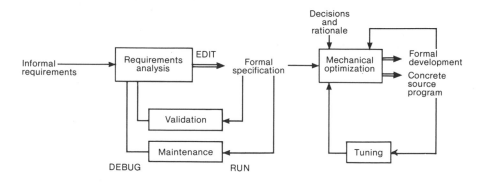

Fig. 7.4 — The "new paradigm" for software engineering and the run–debug–edit cycle (from Balzer, Cheatham, & Green, "Software Technology in the 1990's: Using a New Paradigm," *IEEE Computer*, pp. 39–45, 1983, ©IEEE, with permission)

in the spirit of the SAFE system. Balzer, Cheatham & Green (1983) claim that, "This radical approach to software switches the noncreative aspects of maintenance and modification from man to machine."

This proposal clearly falls within my general rubric of reducing the complexity of the task by moving the burden onto the machine. The major difference is that they suggest shifting "the current informal, person-based software paradigm to a formalized, computer-assisted software paradigm." The crucial difference concerns their intention to formalize the paradigm.

It is true that any progress in automation, whether my complete life-cycle environment or the scheme in Fig. 7.4, must involve a certain amount of formalization — every piece of software embodies a formal specification. But the features that will be formalized within these two suggested paradigms will be different — formalization per se is not necessarily an improvement. We have to examine the resultant costs and benefits of the specific formalization envisaged.

In the paradigm of Fig. 7.4 the authors are aiming for a formal specification of the problem, and it is this specification that is the subject of the run-debug-edit cycle — maintenance is performed on the specification rather than the implementation, and implementations are automatically generated from specifications.

There are, of course, a number of problems with this scheme, as the authors are the first to admit.

First, there is the problem of the "operational" nature of the specification: the specification must be executable, it must serve as a prototype of the implemented system. In addition, the specification must be readily understandable to the system users, for they will maintain the specification themselves by generating the new or revised capability requirements. This all seems to be quite reasonable: the user understands the specification, he can tentatively revised it to serve some different need, and then he can check it, and, if necessary, incrementally develop it via the prototyping facility. The user does not have to deal with and hence understand the implementation.

But how does the user translate performance inadequacies, or desired changes conceptualized in terms of program behaviour, into specification changes? The authors do not seem to address these points.

Second, there is the problem of automated implementation of the specification. The authors admit that completely automated implementation is not a real possibility "because of the wide gap between high-level specification languages and implementations" (i.e., the PLIG, discussed earlier); they suggested that a person should make a number of the necessary decisions as part of the input into the implementation process.

The authors then expand their argument for man–machine cooperation into suggestions for an "automated assistant". This assistant records the development history of the project and maintains "the corporate memory of the system evolution." The view we now get of this "new paradigm" is very like that described in my complete life-cycle environment.

The differences between these two proposals seem to be:

(a) The degree of emphasis put on AI: for me it is both the product of the paradigm, and an essential prerequisite for achieving the desired support environment; they do not mention it explicitly, the product of their paradigm is conventional software.

(b)  The relationship of specification to implementation: I view the implementation as the fundamental object that we have to deal with, although I want to work through abstracted representations such as the de facto specification; in the "new paradigm" the formal specification is the fundamental object and this places demanding constraints on acceptable specification languages as well as requiring fairly complete automation of the implementation process.

Arguing against my suggestions, and proposing an alternative that is based on the "new paradigm", Mostow (1985) has pointed out how difficult "decompiling" (inferring function from form) actually is. He suggests that "it seems much easier to support the implementation process [by automating the transformation from specification to implementation] than to invert it." The rebbutal (Partridge, 1985a) is based upon a contention that AI problems are largely specified and evaluated in a performance mode. Hence "decompiling" (to infer specification change from behaviour) is unavoidable — Chapter 5 is devoted to "decompiling" issues in an attempt to begin to attack this notoriously difficult, but unfortunately unavoidable, process.

The reader should note that the "new paradigm" becomes very similar to the current software engineering paradigm if we consider a conventional high-level programming language, such as Pascal, to be the specification language, and machine code to be the implementation language. From this perspective we now see the run–debug–edit cycle (or incremental system development) in its normal place. And we can view Balzer's, Cheatham's & Green's "new paradigm" as an attempt to push the current paradigm back to a position yet more removed from implementation details by means of higher-level programming languages (their high-level specification languages) and the then necessary higher-level compiler.

Remaining with this point of view a little longer, we can see that both paradigms (theirs and mine) require advances in machine-executable specification languages: I require support for the automatic abstraction of a specification, whilst the "new paradigm" demands that the executable language itself be both readily comprehensible to the system user and (largely) automatically implementable. In summary, I believe that the formalization required by the "new paradigm" will be difficult to produce (i.e. a formal specification language with all the necessary attributes), and it will not clearly solve some fundamental problems (e.g. behaviour-driven system modification).

A final observation on the "new paradigm" is that in AI (which is my domain of interest and not explicitly that of the "new paradigm"), where numerous fine details can be vitally important, it is not at all clear that the concept of executing abstract specifications ("prototyping") will be sufficient in itself to evaluate the adequacy of that specification.

Giddings (1984) recognizes that even in conventional software engineering the problems tend to be domain dependent (DD) rather than domain independent (DI). He proposes a nested and cyclic version of the conventional software engineering design methodology for developing DD software. "Rather than implementing a solution one is really refining a sequence of imperfect prototypes over an extended time," he claims, and I for one am liable to agree.

Giddings continues to suggest the use of a "problem-solving environment ... to increase the probability that effort invested in one prototype will be effectively utilized in successive prototypes," and again I am more or less in agreement with him. But then he proposes that the environment implements a formal model of the particular universe of discourse. It is at this point where we really part company. Certainly a formal basis for the environment is attractive, but is it possible?

My doubts as to the possibility of this approach are focused by Giddings' three hypotheses about human problem solving, hypotheses that, he claims, simplify his proposal.

These three hypotheses can be summarized (quite fairly, I think) as a belief that human problem solving strategies are both algorithmic and few in number. The truth of these hypotheses is one thing but finding the actual algorithms is quite another. And work in AI to date (and AI is the major field that studies human algorithmic problem-solving strategies), far from uncovering any of these few but powerful algorithms, has in fact leant more and more towards the view that human problem-solving is much more likely to be as large and intricate collection of complex, special-purpose strategies.

Hayes-Roth, Waterman & Lenat (1983), in the context of expert systems development, maintain that as programs grow ever more complex, "The program itself must assume more and more of the burden of understanding its own behaviour, documenting and justifying itself, and even modifying itself." They discuss this approach to the complexity problem in a chapter entitled, "Reasoning about reasoning", and they seem to favour the term "meta-knowledge" but they advocate that systems that know about themselves are the way of the future.

They also say, "the most potentially significant and innovative characteristic of an expert system is believed to be that of self-knowledge, knowledge about its own operation and structure. Although currently the use of self-knowledge is somewhat simplistic . . . the potential for its application is remarkable."

Chapter 28 in Buchanan & Shortliffe (1984) is called "Meta-Level Knowledge"; it focuses on the meta-knowledge used by TEIRESIAS in its efforts to substitute for the knowledge engineer and facilitate incremental development of MYCIN by domain experts.

Chapter 29 is an analysis of three classes of meta-knowledge: strategic — strategies for using basic knowledge in problem solving; structural — a knowledge of the structure of the domain of expertise, similar to the need for 'deep' knowledge discussed earlier; and support — information relevant for understanding a basic knowledge structure (i.e. credibility support), and thus usable to generate explanations of the system's behaviour.

They also mention in this book the compounding of problems that results from automatic knowledge acquisition in a system that contains meta-knowledge. The problem is that as basic knowledge is changed as a result of some learning mechanism then meta-knowledge must also be modified to appropriately reflect the lower level changes.

The use of an environment to control and mediate basic learning is the route to the answer to this problem. The environment should direct basic learning as a result of a need identified at a meta-level (to the knowledge being learned). Thus when the basic-level information has been assimilated the meta-level knowledge that initiated the learning in the first place is also updated accordingly. That seems simple enough, which is a good indication that it is probably wrong or at least grossly oversimplified.

The problems are of two types. First, we do see again a need for the environment concept, but we don't yet see any more clearly how to construct it. Second, it is quite likely that meta-knowledge other than that in control of the learning will need to be updated. The goal of maintaining a totally self-consistent, many-levelled, self-adaptive knowledge base is a very lofty goal — perhaps an impossible one, after all the best systems known (i.e., you and I) don't do it.

EURISKO (Lenat, 1982) is an implemented research project that attempts to exploit meta-knowledge — it tries to discover better heuristics in some given domain. EURISKO is an environment that monitors the performance of a domain-specific program; considered as a whole we have meta-knowledge as a basis for machine learning.

Not surprisingly successful machine learning must be based on meta-knowledge: the system needs to know, what it knows, what it doesn't know, what it can and can't do, and why — that is, meta-knowledge. So with meta-knowledge as a basis for both machine learning and for managing the inevitable complexities of AI software we have, I believe, unearthed a fundamental problem; it may be that meta-knowledge is another problem that must be solved (to some reasonable degree) before AI will advance much further into the harsh world of practical software.

In an article that deals provocatively with the potential scope and limitations of AI, Minsky (1982) considers the question: could a computer be conscious? He argues not only that it could be, but that "it might turn out that, at some point, we have to make computers more self-conscious, just in order to make them smarter!" This is clearly supportive of my claims for the necessity of self-knowledge, except that I maintain that self- or meta-knowledge is both a fundamental and an immediate requirement for the progress of AI into practical software.

Until the time when we can hand all of the details of the AI software development and maintenance process over to some perfect, complete life-cycle environment, I envisage the development and subsequent usage of AI software to be a cooperative man–machine process (see for example, the benefits of such cooperation in mathematical reasoning, Wos, 1985). The program-development expert system and the human programmer work together to build the AI software. On completion, the program-development expert system's knowledge of the particular piece of software is automatically transferred to a program-maintenance expert system. This maintenance or support system will work with the various people who need to interact with this software in its application environment. As suggested earlier this latter system might be bifacial: a simplified version of the complex maintenance function to be used only by a competent maintenance programmer; and a sophisticated version of the simpler 'use' function to interact with users that may well possess no technical expertise in computer science.

The program maintenance environment functions as an intelligent buffer between the AI software and the humans who must interact with it. Being a natural extension of the development environment that fostered the software as it was developed, it is clearly the best place to maintain the knowledge of the software at all levels of detail. As the repository of knowledge about the application program it should be able to function admirably as a mediator between users and the user program - hiding details when desirable and yet supplying them when asked to do so.

## 7.5   THE SOCIAL IMPLICATIONS OF COMMERCIAL AI

It is with some considerable trepidation that I am venturing into this non-technical domain. But my feeling of inadequacy is precisely the reason why I think that I should try to say something significant about the social implications of commercial AI.

The technicians in any field are always too ready to brush aside any discussion of social implications. It is 'non-scientific', or not the concern of a scientist, or undecidable anyway, or uncontrollable even if you could decide what is right — the individual reasons are many and varied.

But if anybody has some control and foresight with respect to the forthcoming AI revolution it should be us — the technicians. It is therefore incumbent upon us to develop some collective social responsibility for what we are doing, or trying to do — the following is a small offering on my part.

When the full potential of AI is available as practical software we will witness a major revolution in society. Currently, despite their undoubted benefits in many applications, computers are often viewed, with justification, as a major force contributing to the gradual erosion of the 'humanness' with which humanity is treated.

If computers are to continue spreading and infiltrating even more aspects of our lives then we need to be surer about the ways in which we apply them. It is no longer so much a question of can a computer fill some role in our society, the concern is: in what way should the computer play the role?

Many initial computer application projects have been focused on just getting the computer to do something regardless of exactly how it does it. Some of the results have been disastrous in terms of destroying, in many people's minds, all possibility of computers enriching our lives.

AI applications will, in general, be encroaching on an especially sensitive area — the domain of intelligent behaviours, the special preserve of humanity. Some people will view AI as an invasion of the last bastion of humanity, and something that must be prevented at all costs. And based upon many examples of the dehumanizing applications of computers to date, they have a point, I think.

But the future need not mirror the past, we should learn from it and do better. AI, if developed and applied correctly, embodies a unique potential for the application of computers that treat individual people as individual people. It is in fact an opportunity to reverse many of the 'mass-production', dehumanizing aspects of our society.

Mass-production and mechanization in general are with us and here to stay. But AI holds the promise of transforming the implications of the terms "mechanism" and "automation" from the current ones of "inflexible" and "dehumanized" to something more like "responsive" and "personalized".

But whilst the potential societal benefits are great, so are the dangers. Weizenbaum (1976) expounds at length on some of the dangers of AI for society. He has a lot of good arguments but I don't think that the questions are as readily decidable as he tries to present them to be.

Sloman's (1978) book on the interactions between AI and philosophy contains a lot of valuable academic discussion, but from our current perspective it is more important for its "attempt to publicise an important, but largely unnoticed, facet of the computer revolution: its potential for transforming our ways of thinking about ourselves."

That the computer should treat us as individuals is not strictly necessary for AI (although I have argued that it is necessary for future development), but it does appear to be the central question with respect to whether AI will enrich or impoverish our lives.

Even if some humans do behave intelligently and yet treat us as if we are not individuals, they are still employing a lot of dynamic, context-sensitive responses. What we notice is a lack of the highly sophisticated individual treatment that one human being typically accords another.

An intelligent, but crudely personalized, static computer system will, by comparison, make the average uninterested physician (for example) appear to be supersensitive to one's individual foibles.

It can, and is, argued that however sensitive and responsive AI systems become they are not people, they are machines, and therefore can only contribute a dehumanizing influence to our lives. But given that machines are here to stay I would maintain that good AI is preferable to no AI.

An Erewhonian rejection of computer technology is not going to happen and I, of course, don't think that it should; there is always the danger of throwing out the inestimable potential benefits with the bath water when we outright reject a complete domain of human endeavour just because we see some bad mixed in with the good. The sensible response is not wholesale rejection but careful exploration from which we develop understanding; we then have a basis for a judicious selection from the known range of possibilities.

There are no answers; there are very few indications of the possibilities for the long-term impact of AI. But that is no excuse for practitioners to refuse to think about the problem. We should be prepared and encouraged to offer our hopes, fears, and just speculations (see for example, Boden, 1984).

The resultant discussion, however non-technical and lacking in constraints, is our best hope for foreseeing the dangers, and foreseeing them with sufficient time to avoid them.

AI research, especially in the USA (where most of it is done), has always been heavily funded from military sources. AI as weapons research worries a lot of people, as I think it should. But, of course, the issues are not clear-cut.

Weapons research may result in discoveries that support undoubted societal benefits; if non-military research produces results with military applications, those applications will be pursued.

Perhaps the future is brighter in that we are currently witnessing an efflorescence of commercial AI ventures, so some growing proportion of AI-research support will not be directly military. But it will likely be short-term-applications driven and that could lead to societal problems as well. I have discussed these problems at more length elsewhere (Partridge, 1985b).

Boden's (1977) simile of the AI researcher as Mickey Mouse in the Disney production of the Sorcerer's Apprentice is currently all too appropriate. Most of us are dabbling (perhaps hacking is a more fitting term) in domains that we do not understand and can only barely control, at best. Luckily computer programs, unlike magic spells, stubbornly refuse to "take-off" and do endless unforeseen things as a result of an ill-understood change; mercifully they almost always just grind to a halt.

# 8

# Some problems and some conclusions

"Nothing moves faster than a bandwagon in a vacuum."

anon.

In this brief, final chapter I shall consider some of the major objections to my arguments and then summarize my beliefs. The objections have been either stated by the various reviewers of earlier incarnations of this book, or voiced by the disruptive elements in the audiences that have listened to my talks.

## 8.1 THE SPIV PARADIGM IS JUST A STRAW MAN

In Chapter 2 I offered the SPIV paradigm (Specify–Prove–Implement–Verify) as a caricaturization of the formal approach to software engineering. And although no practising software engineer would consider such a simple, linear scheme, it does, I claim, characterize the under-lying mindset. Let us first take a few quotes that suggest to me that the SPIV paradigm itself is in fact more awesome than strawsome in its credibility. Then I shall select some practical viewpoints that clearly derive from, or hanker after, a SPIV-like paradigm despite their iterative and approximate natures.

First the formalists:

"the only problems we can really solve in a satisfactory manner are those that finally admit a nicely factored solution." (Dijkstra, 1972)

"A lack of clarity in specifications is one of the surest signs of a deficiency in the program it describes, and the two faults must be removed simultaneously before the project is embarked upon." (Hoare, 1981)

"The difference between the 'old program' and the 'new program' is as profound as the difference between a conjecture and a proven theorem." Dijkstra in (Gries, 1981)

— Certainly not straw men, and also I admit not a clear statement of the SPIV paradigm, but the primacy of complete prior analysis followed by formal specification and verification of the final product is there — and that is what I am advancing with the SPIV mnemonic.

The practising software engineer does not aim so high, it is true, but the aim is in much the same direction. The general trend is to crowd the unavoidable iterative process of approximation at the front end, and then to take off on a SPIVish route once a satisfactory specification has been obtained.

Kowalski (1984), for example, in his presentation of Prolog and a "new technology" for software design, describes an iterative trial-and-error process for "analysing the knowledge that lies behind the user requirement." But once we have a formal specification the situation is different: "Good programmers start with rigid, or at least formal, software specifications and then implement them correctly first time round — never get it wrong." Similarly, the "new paradigm" discussed in the previous chapter and illustrated in Fig. 7.4 offers much the same viewpoint: there is a process of approximation designed to generate a formal specification which then 'locks in' the subsequent design and implementation. The point is not so much that real software engineering is not done in the SPIV manner, but that SPIV-think sets up an ideal to which much homage is paid. If this formal paradigm is not impossible in principle (and I don't see many arguments for this impossibility, although I believe it to be so) then it must be viewed as the ultimate goal of all software methodologies, for it does seem to embody the best of all possible worlds. And conversely, any existing methodology is, by hypothesis, inferior. What is more it is inferior to the degree that it fails to approach the formal paradigm. Of course, this puts the run–debug–edit-based paradigms, which don't even pretend to start with a formal specification, galloping away with the inferiority ratings. It leaves the software engineers apologizing for their shifting specifications and undertaking to shape up requirements analysis in order to achieve more stability with their specifications. This may, or may not, be the right way to proceed, it depends upon the degree of inherent dynamic ill-structure in the problem.

## 8.2   EXPLORATION OF APPROXIMATE SPECIFICATIONS IS SOFTWARE ENGINEERING AS MUCH AS IT IS AI

This objection leads on naturally from the previous one. The objection is that the practical software engineer knows that he is exploring an approximate specification in just the same manner as I have portrayed the AI system developer. In reality software engineering is no more well-structured than AI. So where is the difference?

My point is not that AI and software engineering problems can be characterized as ill-defined and well-defined, respectively. Clearly requirements analysis in software engineering also generates an approximation to some ISF, although it is typically more finely and completely specified than in AI. But the key difference is not degree of approximation, it is in the *use* of the specification (and this brings us right back to the SPIV-type basis again). In software engineering the specification is the keystone that locks the iterative program development loop in place. That is not to say that there is no development outside this loop. A major thrust in software design methodologies is to maximize development outside of this loop and thereby transform it into something more closely approximating a SPIV-type sequence of steps. Outside of the development loop we have reanalysis of requirements and as a result respecification of the RFS. But then the RFS becomes once again a complete and well-defined statement of all that the system designer need consider.

The RFS may be somewhat of a moving target, but it moves in well-specified discrete steps. It is otherwise totally static. Contrast the AI system designer's task: the specification is typically ill-defined, incomplete, dynamic, and is largely a performance-mode description — it is by its very nature a moving and an ephemeral target. AI system development is the exploration of the dynamics and ill-structure of the problem in an effort to discover an adequate, but probably still dynamic (remember the need for machine learning), approximation.

To return once more to Humpty Dumpty, who appears to have had some interesting insights into natural language before his untimely demise: after asserting to Alice that his words mean what he chooses them to mean she questioned his authority to so invent meanings. The fragile egg replied, "The question is which is to be master — that's all." In software engineering the RFS is master, in AI it is the context often in the form of the empirical world. For a performance-mode description, which is typical of AI problems, can be viewed as a description of the effects that the system being described has on the empirical world, its context (in particular, the instances of humanity within it).

So, for example, natural language understanding can be described in terms of what a person would be likely to say to achieve certain effects, and what they would be likely to reply or do in response to other people and things. AI problems are often characterized in terms of their interactions with their context. We can and do generate abstract specifications (for instance, to account for the observed phenomenon of natural language understanding), and such endeavours can be a useful source of guidance to the system developer. But ultimately it is the real world phenomenon that is the basis for system evaluation — it is the master.

### 8.3   COMMERCIAL APPLICATION IS DIFFERENT FROM DESIGN AND DEVELOPMENT

At this point the reader may say, "ok, I can accept what's been said, more or less, but the arguments all refer to the initial development of AI products. Once an adequate approximation has been found then the techniques of practical software engineering can be used to generate a robust and reliable product. The finding of adequate approximations may be ill-defined, etc., but once found the subsequent application to commercial environments is the conventional process."

My response is that a static AI system is almost a contradiction in terms (intelligence is fundamentally adaptive), and until such time as we can program perfect learning (if such a thing is possible) the development and long-term usage of AI software will not be markedly different. Application and usage of AI software will resemble development in a way that is quite foreign in conventional software engineering.

## 8.4   THE EPILOGUE

In conclusion, as promised in the preface, I have not solved many problems associated with the development of the full potential of commercial AI. What I do claim to have done is to have explained a lot of the problems that will be associated with the development of the full potential of commercial AI. I have also constructed an overall picture of what the full potential of AI may be and what the problems of transforming it into commercial software are.

I have also explored some routes to solutions of these problems and I have described some of the major hurdles along the way. Let me now summarize what I have done and what I believe its significance to be.

I have argued that meta-knowledge is a problem area that is a crucial one for realizing the full potential of AI as practical software. The general paradigm for AI software involves an encapsulation of particular application programs within a sophisticated, life-cycle, support environment, and a necessary component of this environment is knowledge about the application program — i.e., meta-knowledge.

In fact we don't explicitly encapsulate the AI program within a support environment; it is both developed and used within this environment — in a real sense, it only exists and functions intelligently within this environment. The environment is the interface between the AI program and humanity; it is like a spacesuit around some alien being that enables survival and communication in a non-comprehending world.

At the moment we are not in any position to design and implement the necessary environment, but we can begin, and have already begun, as some of the examples demonstrate, to work on the components of this environment — components such as those described in Section 6.2.2.3.

The idea of the design, development, use, and maintenance of the AI software all within this support environment appears to expand the problem of developing such an environment. But eventually we will experience a simplification because a system that controls design and development will have all of the necessary information for also directing the use and maintenance of the software.

Secondly, I have argued for non-trivial machine learning as a necessity for the progress of commercial AI. I have also espoused a belief in the necessity for meta-knowledge in implementations of machine learning. Machine learning is largely an unsolved problem, and as such it will place a severe limitation on the potential for commercial AI.

Thirdly, I have made concrete suggestions, with examples, of techniques that will contribute to a discipline of incremental AI program development. In general I have argued that the 'all at once' philosophy characteristic of the formal science of software engineering, far from providing an exemplar to aim for, is not appropriate for AI: we need, for example, principles of "structured growth" in contrast to those of "structured programming". In a paper entitled, "The Challenge of Open Systems", Hewitt (1985) argues for what I take to be, in effect, a run–debug–edit-based paradigm for "developing the intelligent systems of the future." He discusses the problems of continuous change and evolution, and the need to accommodate necessarily incomplete information, which implies, he says, exploration rather than searching — the traditional approach in AI. I have stressed the need for principles of abstraction and both described and illustrated a number of possible uses. I have also outlined a possible further use for the software engineering principle of information-hiding: that of automatic information-losing. The development and use of principles tailored to the special problems in AI will itself alleviate some of the complexity problems facing the AI software developer. It will thus also facilitate the incremental development of AI programs that begin to exhibit the characteristics necessary for practical software. The alternative situation that AI software may engender, I have termed a super software crisis. Although somewhat alarmist, and not altogether accurate, it is a term that conveys my beliefs.

The conventional software crisis is still going strong. The introduction of AI can only aggravate the situation. 'Aggravate' is too weak a word when you consider the possibilities for sloppy self-adaptive mechanisms and the absence of any definitive RFS. 'Magnify beyond recognition' may well be a more accurate description of the result of introducing the complexities of AI without the necessary extra discipline — hence the term 'super software crisis'.

Fourthly, I have taken a number of different-looking approaches to the problem of demarcating the set of AI problems that will not fit into the conventional software development paradigm. It is, of course, for this set of problems that I claim we will need a disciplined run–debug–edit-based paradigm if we are ever to realize the full potential of AI in practical software. I have looked at context-sensitivity, performance-mode description, inherent dynamic ill-structure, analytic intractability, and concrete versus abstract problems in an attempt to expose the essential characteristics of this AI set. Whilst these views are by no means all equivalent, they do tend to overlap considerably. I have searched for multiple viewpoints in order to better characterize what I believe to be a nebulous but nevertheless quite real essence of AI. There is a large body of phenomena that we have not yet come close to recreating artificially, especially in a form suitable for commercial exploitation.

Does this essence disappear as we make progress in AI? Have I effectively defined the essence as that which is not yet programmed? If so I have taken an inordinately long route to arrive at a common but vacuous criticism of AI. Clearly I do not think that I have fallen into that particular trap. In fact I strongly suspect that the first artificial systems that begin to exhibit something like the full potential of AI will do little or nothing to lessen the mystery and the apparent ill-structure of intelligent behaviour unless we first make considerable progress towards a better understanding and mastery of our programmed artifacts.

AI, with all it has potentially to offer, has not yet crossed the Rubicon of large-scale practical application, but it will, and when it does it needs to be fully prepared to manage the empire it seizes.

To borrow the bones of a couple of sentences from John Fowles: AI as practical software is but a pot. It holds whatever we put in it, from the greatest evil to the greatest good.

It is the responsibility of the computer science community to attempt to foresee the implications of the revolution it is about to initiate, to foresee and direct events toward the latter option insofar as that is possible.

# References

Alexander, C. (1964) *Notes on the Synthesis of Form,* Harvard University Press: Cambridge, Mass.

Anderson, J. R. (1982) Acquisition of Cognitive Skill, *Psychological Review*, **89**, 4, pp. 369–406.

Arbib, M. A. (1972) *The Metaphorical Brain,* Wiley: NY.

Balzer, R., Cheatham, T.E., & Green, C. (1983) Software Technology in the 1990's: Using a New Paradigm, *IEEE Computer,* November, pp. 39–45.

Balzer, R., Cohen, D., & Goldman, N. (1982) Specification Acquisition From Experts, in Annual Technical Report, Information Sciences Institute, University of Southern California, pp. 33–41.

Barnes, J. G. P. (1983) *Programming in Ada,* Addison-Wesley: Reading, Mass.

Barr, A., & Feigenbaum, E. A. (1981) *The Handbook of Artificial Intelligence,* vol. 1, Kaufman: Palo Alto, CA.

Barr, A., & Feigenbaum, E. A. (1982) *The Handbook of Artificial Intelligence,* vol. 2, Kaufman: Palo Alto, CA.

Bazjanac, V. (1974) Architectural Design Theory: Models of the Design Process, in *Basic Questions of Design Theory,* W. R. Spillers (ed.), North-Holland: Amsterdam, The Netherlands, pp. 3–19.

Ben-Shakhar, G. (1980) Habituation of the Orienting Response to Complex Sequences of Stimuli, *Psychophysiology,* **17**, 6.

Boden, M. A. (1977) *Artificial Intelligence and Natural Man,* Basic Books: NY.

Boden, M.A. (1984) Impacts of Artificial Intelligence, *AISB Quarterly,* no. 49, pp. 9–14.

Boehm, B. W. (1984) Verifying and Validating Software Requirements and Design Specifications, *IEEE Software,* January 1984, pp. 75–88.

Bramer, M. A. (1982) A Survey and Critical Review of Expert Systems Research, in *Introductory Readings in Expert Systems,* D. Michie (ed.), Gordon & Breach: London, pp. 3–29.

Brooks, F. P. (1975) *The Mythical Man-Month,* Addison-Wesley: Reading, Mass.

Buchanan, B. G., & Shortliffe, E. H. (1984) *Rule-Based Expert Systems,* Addison-Wesley: Reading, Mass.

Bundy, A. (1983) The Nature of AI: a Reply to Ohlsson, *AISB Quarterly,* no. 47, pp. 24–25.

Bundy, A. (1984) Superficial Principles: an Analysis of a Behavioural Law, *AISB Quarterly,* no. 49, pp. 20–22.

Bundy, A., & Silver, B. (1982) A Critical Survey of Rule Learning Programs, *Procs. of ECAI,* pp. 151–157

Burleson, C., Partridge, D., & Lopez, P. D. (1985) Significant Events as a Basis for Cognitive Robotics, *Procs. 18th Systems Sciences Conf.,* Hawaii, pp. 168–175.

Burstein, M. H. (1983) National Conference on Artificial Intelligence, *AISB Quarterly,* no. 46, pp. 13–15.

Carbonell, J. R. (1970) AI in CAI: An Artificial Intelligence Approach to Computer-aided Instruction, *IEEE Trans. on Man-Machine Systems,* **MMS-11,** pp. 190–202.

Carpenter, H. (1977) *Tolkien,* Allen & Unwin: London.

Cerri, S. A. (1984) The Intersection of AI and Education, *AISB Quarterly,* no. 49, pp. 15–19.

Chandrasekaran, B., & Mittal, S. (1983) Deep Versus Compiled Knowledge Approaches to Diagnostic Problem-Solving, *Internat. J. Man-Machine Studies,* **19,** pp. 425–436.

Charniak, E., Riesbeck, C. K., & McDermott, D. V. (1980) *Artificial Intelligence Programming,* Lawrence Erlbaum Associates: NJ.

Clancey, W. J. (1979) Transfer of Rule-based Expertise through a Tutorial Dialogue. Rep. No. STAN-CS-769, Computer Science Dept., Stanford University. Summarized in Barr & Feigenbaum (1982).

Clocksin, W. F., & Mellish, C. S. (1981) *Programming in PROLOG* Springer-Verlag: NY.

Coleman, D. (1979) *A Structured Programming Approach to Data,* Springer-Verlag: NY.

Collins, A., Warnock, E. H., Aiello, N., & Miller, M. L. (1975) Reasoning from Incomplete Knowledge, in *Representation and Understanding,* D. G. Bobrow & A. Collins (eds.) Academic Press: NY, pp. 383–415.

Dahl, O. J., Dijkstra, E. W., & Hoare, C.A.R. (1972) *Structured Programming,* Academic Press: London.

Davis, R., & Lenat, D. B. (1982) *Knowledge-Based Systems in Artificial Intelligence,* McGraw-Hill: NY.

De Millo, R. A., Lipton, R. J., & Perlis, A. J. (1979) Social Processes and Proofs of Theorems and Programs, *Communications of ACM*, **22**, 5, pp. 271–280.

Dijkstra, E. W. (1972) The Humble Programmer, *Communications of ACM*, **15**, 10, pp. 859–866.

Dijkstra, E. W. (1976) *A Discipline of Programming*, Prentice-Hall: Englewood Cliffs, New Jersey.

Eisenberg, J., and Hill, J. (1984) Using Natural-Language Systems on Personal Computers, *BYTE*, January 1984, pp. 226–238.

Feigenbaum, E. A., & McCorduck, P. (1983) *The Fifth Generation* Addison-Wesley: Reading, Mass.

Fodor, J. A., (1983) The *Modularity of Mind*, MIT Press: Cambridge, Mass.

Fogel, L. J., Owens, A. J., & Walsh, M. J. (1966) *Artificial Intelligence Through Simulated Evolution*, Wiley: NY.

Freeman, P. (1977) The Nature of Design, in *Tutorial on Software Design Techniques*, 2nd edition, IEEE Computer Society, P. Freeman and I. Wasserman (eds.), pp. 29–36.

Gaschnig, J. (1982) Prospector: an Expert System for Mineral Exploration, in *Introductory Readings in Expert Systems*, D. Michie (ed.), Gordon and Breach: NY.

Giddings, R. V. (1984) Accommodating Uncertainty in Software Design, *Communications of ACM*, **27**, 5, pp. 428–434.

Gries, D. (1981) *The Science of Programming*, Springer-Verlag, NY.

Groves, P. M. & Thompson, R. F. (1970) Habituation: a Dual-process Theory, *Psych. Rev.*, **77**, 5.

Guthrie, L. (1985) Some Results on Evaluating and Checking Functions in a Language Designed for Redundancy, PhD Thesis, Dept. Computer Science, New Mexico State University.

Hayes, P. J. (1979) The Naive Physics Manifesto, in *Expert Systems in the Electronic Age*, D. Michie (ed.), Edinburgh University Press: Edinburgh, pp. 242–270.

Hayes-Roth, F., Waterman, D. A., & Lenat, D. B. (1983) *Building Expert Systems*, Addison-Wesley: Reading, Mass.

Hewitt, C. (1985) The Challenge of Open Systems, *BYTE*, April, pp. 223–242.

Hoare, C. A. R. (1981) The Emperor's Old Clothes, *Communications of ACM*, **24**, 2, pp. 75–83.

Hofstadter, D. R. (1979) *Gödel, Escher, Bach: an Eternal Golden Braid*, Basic Books: NY.

Hunke, H. (1981) (ed.) *Software Engineering Environments*, North-Holland: Amsterdam, Netherlands.

IQLISP (1983) *IQLISP reference manual*, Integral Quality, P.O. Box 31970, Seattle, WA 98103, USA.

James, E. B., & Partridge, D. (1973) Machine intelligence: the best of both worlds? *Internat. J. Man-Machine Studies*, **4**, pp. 23–31.

James, E. B., & Partridge, D. (1976) Tolerance to Inaccuracy in Computer Programs, *Computer Journal*, **19**, no. 3, pp. 207–212.

Johnston, V. S., Partridge, D., & Lopez, P. D. (1983) A Neural Theory of Cognitive Development, *J. Theor. Biol.*, **100**, 3, pp. 485–509.

Korf, R. E. (1980) Toward a Model of Representation Changes, *Artificial Intelligence*, **14**, pp. 41–78.

Kowalski, R. (1984) Software Engineering and Artificial Intelligence in New Generation Computing, The SPL-Insight 1983/84 Award Lecture.

Kuhn, T. S. (1962) *The Structure of Scientific Revolutions,* University of Chicago: Chicago, IL.

Langley, P. (1983) Learning Search Strategies through Discrimination, *Internat. J. Man-Machine Studies*, **19**, pp. 513–541.

Lehman, M. M., and Belady, L. A. (1985) *Program Evolution, the process of software change,* Academic Press: NY.

Lenat, D. B. (1982) The Nature of Heuristics, *Artificial Intelligence* **19**, pp. 189–249.

Lenat, D. B., & Brown, J. S. (1983) Why AM and Eurisko Appear to Work, *AAAI-83 Conference,* Washington, D.C., pp. 236–240.

Levesque, H. J. (1984) The Logic of Incomplete Knowledge Bases, in *On Conceptual Modelling,* M. L. Brodie, J. Mylopoulos, & J. W. Schmidt (eds.), Springer-Verlag: NY, pp. 165–186.

Linger, R. C., Mills, H. D., & Witt, B. I. (1979) *Structured Programming,* Addison-Wesley: Reading, Mass.

MacLennan, B. J. (1983) *Principles of Programming Languages,* Holt, Rinehart & Winston: NY.

McCarthy, J., *et al* (1965) *LISP 1-5 Programmer's Manual,* 2nd edition, MIT Press: Cambridge, Mass.

McCarthy, J. (1984) We Need Better Standards for AI Research, *The AI Magazine,* **5,** 3, pp. 7–8.

McDermott, D. (1976) Artificial Intelligence Meets Natural Stupidity, *SIGART Newsletter,* No. 57, pp. 4–9.

McDermott, J. (1982) XSEL: a Computer Sales Person's Assistant, in *Machine Intelligence 10,* J. E. Haycs, D. Michie, & Y-H. Pao (eds.), Ellis Horwood: Chichester, UK, pp. 325–337.

Medress, M. F. (1978) Speech Understanding Systems, *Artificial Intelligence 9,* pp. 307–316.

Michalski, R. S., Carbonell, J. G., & Mitchell, T. M. (1983) *Machine Learning,* Tioga: Palo Alto, CA.

Michalski, R. S., & Chilausky, R. L. (1980) Learning by Being Told and Learning from Examples: an Experimental Comparison of the two Methods of Knowledge Acquisition in the Context of Developing an Expert System for Soybean Disease Diagnosis, *Policy Analysis and Information Systems,* **4,** No. 2, pp. 125–160, June.

Michie, D. (1982) The State of the Art in Machine Learning, in *Introductory Readings in Expert Systems,* D. Michie (ed), Gordon and Breach, London, pp. 208–229.

Michie, D. (1983) transcription of a lecture, UCLA, 9th March.

Miller, G. A. (1966) Thinking Machines: Myths and Actualities, *The Public Interest,* **2,** pp. 92–97, 99–108.

Minsky, M. (1970) Form and Content in Computer Science, *Journal ACM*, **17**, 2, pp. 197–215.

Minsky, M. (1981) A Framework for Representing Knowledge, in *Mind Design*, J. Haugeland (ed.), MIT Press: Cambridge, Mass., pp. 95–128.

Minsky, M. (1982) Why People Think Computers Can't, *The AI Magazine*, Fall, 1982, pp. 3–15.

Mostow, J. (1985) Response to Derek Partridge, *The AI Magazine*, **6**, 3, pp. pp. 51–52

Mylopoulos, J., & Levesque, M. J. (1984) An Overview of Knowledge Representation, in *On Conceptual Modelling*, M. L. Brodie, J. Mylopoulos, & J. W. Schmidt (eds.), Springer-Verlag: NY, pp. 3–17.

Naur, P., & Randell, B. (eds.) (1969) Software Engineering, Brussels 39, Belgium: NATO Scientific Affairs Division.

Newell, A. (1977) Reflections on Obtaining Science through Building Systems, *Procs. 5th International Joint Conference on AI*, MIT, pp. 970–971.

Newell, A., & Simon, H. A. (1976) Computer Science as Empirical Inquiry: Symbols and Search, *Communications of ACM*, **19**, 3, pp. 113–126.

Nieper, H., & Boecker, H.-D. (1985) Making the Invisible Visible: Tools for Exploratory Programming, Dept. Computer Science, University of Colorado, Boulder, CO 80309.

Ohlsson, S. (1983) Mechanisms, Behaviour, Principles: a Time for Examples, *AISB Quarterly*, no. 48, pp. 24–25.

Ohlsson, S. (1984) AI Principles: the Functions of Scientific Laws, *AISB Quarterly*, no. 50, p. 36.

O'Shea, T. (1982) Intelligent Systems in Education, in *Introductory Readings in Expert Systems*, D. Michie (ed.), Gordon & Breach London, pp. 147–176.

Papert, S. (1980) *Mindstorms*, Basic Books: NY.

Parnas, D. L. (1979) Designing Software for Ease of Extension and Contraction, *IEEE Trans. on Software Engineering*, **SE-5**, 2, pp. 128–138.

Partridge, D. (1975) A Dynamic Database which Automatically Removes Unwanted Generalization for the Efficient Analysis of Language Features that Exhibit a Disparate Frequency Distribution, *Comp. J.* **18**, 1, pp. 43–48.

Partridge, D. (1976) The Informed Guessing Machine and Ill-structured Problems, *Proceedings of the Milwaukee Symposium on Automatic Computation and Control*, pp. 331–336.

Partridge, D. (1978) A Philosophy of 'Wicked' Problem Implementation, *Proceedings of AISB/GI Conference*, Hamburg, pp. 238–247.

Partridge, D. (1978a) A Syntactic View of Semantic Networks, *Internat. J. Man-Machine Studies*, **10**, pp. 113–119.

Partridge, D. (1981) "Computational Theorizing" as the Tool for Resolving Wicked Problems, *IEEE Transactions on Man, Systems, and Cybernetics*, **SMC-11**, no. 4, pp. 318–322.

Partridge, D. (1981a) Information Theory and Redundancy, *Philosophy of Science*, **48**, 2, pp. 308–316.

Partridge, D. (1984) What's in an AI program? *Procs. European Conf. on AI*, Pisa, Italy, pp. 669–673.

Partridge, D. (1985) Input–Expectation Discrepancy Reduction: a Ubiquitous Mechanism, *Procs. 9th International Joint Conference on AI*, UCLA, pp. 267–273.

Partridge, D. (1985a) Rude vs. Courteous, *The AI magazine*, **6**, 4, p. 28–29.

Partridge, D. (1985b) The Social Implications of AI, in *AI: Implications and Applications*, M. Yazdani (ed.), Chapman Hall: London.

Partridge, D., Johnston, V. S., & Lopez, P. D. (1984) Computer Programs as Theories in Biology, *J. Theor. Biol.*, **108**, pp. 539–564.

Popplestone, R. J. (1968) The Design Philosophy of POP-2, in *Machine Intelligence 3*, D. Michie (ed.), Edinburgh University Press: Edinburgh, pp. 393–402.

Pylyshyn, Z. W. (1978) Computational Models and Empirical Constraints, *The Behavioral and Brain Sciences*, **1**, pp. 93–127.

Quinlan, J. R. (1982) Semi-autonomous Acquisition of Pattern-based Knowledge, in *Introductory Readings in Expert Systems*, D. Michie (ed.), Gordon & Breach, London, pp. 192–207.

Rajlich, V. (1985) Paradigms for Design and Implementation in Ada, *Communications of ACM*, **28**, 7, pp. 718–727.

Rescorla, R. A., & Holland, P. C. (1976) Some Behavioural Approaches to the Study of Learning, in *Neural Mechanisms of Learning and Memory*, M. R. Rosenzweig and E. L. Bennett (eds.), MIT Press, Cambridge, Mass.

Ross, D. T. (1977) Guest Editorial — Reflections on Requirements, *IEEE Transactions on Software Engineering*, **SE-3**, 1, pp. 2–5.

Ross, D. T., & Schoman, K. E. (1977) Structured Analysis for Requirements Definition, *IEEE Transactions on Software Engineering*, **SE-3**, 1, pp. 6–15.

Sacerdoti, E. D. (1982) Practical Machine Intelligence, in *Machine Intelligence 10*, J. E. Hayes, D. Michie, & Y. H. Pao (eds.), Ellis Horwood: Chichester, UK, pp. 241–247.

Samuel, A. L. (1963) Some Studies in Machine Learning Using the Game of Checkers, in *Computers and Thought*, E. A. Feigenbaum and J. Feldman (eds.), McGraw-Hill: NY, pp. 71–105.

Samuel, A. (1983) AI, Where has it Been and Where is it Going? *Proceedings IJCAI-83*, Karlsruhe, W. Germany, pp. 1152–1157

Sandewall, E. (1978) Programming in an Interactive Environment: the LISP Experience, *Computing Surveys*, **10**, 1, pp. 35–71.

Schank, R. C. (1982) *Dynamic Memory*, Cambridge University Press: Cambridge, UK.

Schank, R. C. (1983) The Current State of AI: One Man's Opinion, *The AI Magazine*, Winter/Spring 1983, pp. 3–8.

Schvaneveldt, R. W., Durso, F. T., Goldsmith, T. E., Breen, T. J., Cooke,

N., Tucker, R. G., & De Maio, J. C. (1985) Measuring the Structure of Expertise, *Internat. J. Man-Machine Studies*, **23**, pp. 699–728.

Simon, H. A. (1962) The architecture of complexity, *Procs. of the Amer. Phil. Soc.* **106**, 6, December, pp. 467–482.

Simon, H. A. (1981) Prometheus or Pandora: The Influence of Automation on Society, *IEEE Computer*, November, pp. 69–74.

Slagle, J. R. (1971) *Artificial Intelligence: The Heuristic Programming Approach*, McGraw-Hill: NY.

Sloman, A. (1978) The Computer Revolution in Philosophy, Humanities Press: Atlantic Highlands, NJ.

Sloman, A. & Hardy, S. (1983) POPLOG: A Multi-Purpose Multi-Language Program Development Environment, *AISB Quarterly*, no. 47, pp. 26–34.

Smoliar, S. W. & Barstow, D. (1983) Who Needs Languages and Why do they Need them?, *Procs. ACM Principles of Programming Languages Conf.*, pp. 149–157.

Sokolov, E. N. (1963) *Perception and the conditioned Reflex*, Pergamon Press: NY.

Steiner, G. (1975) *After Babel: Aspects of Language and Translation*, Oxford University Press: London.

Sussman, G., Holloway, J., & Knight, Jr., T. F. (1980) Computer Aided Evolutionary Design for Digital Integrated Systems, *Proceedings of AISB-80 Conference*, Amsterdam.

Swartout, W. R. (1983) XPLAIN: A System for Creating and Explaining Expert Consulting Systems, *Artificial Intelligence Journal*, **21**, 3, pp. 285–325.

Swartout, W., & Balzer, R. (1982) On the Inevitable Intertwining of Specification and Implementation, *Communications of ACM*, **25**, 7, pp. 438–440.

Tausworthe, R. C. (1977) *Standardized Development of Computer Software*, Prentice-Hall: Englewood Cliffs, NJ.

Teitelman, W. (1972) "DO WHAT I MEAN": The Programmer's Assistant, *Computers and Automation*, (April), pp. 8–11.

Teitelman, W., & Masinter, L. (1981) The INTERLISP programming environment, *IEEE Transactions on Computers* **C-14**, 4, pp. 25–35.

Thompson, J. M. T. (1975) Experiments in Catastrophe, *Nature*, **254**, 5499, pp. 392–395.

Touretzky, D. S. (1982) *A Summary of MacLisp Functions and Flags*, 4th edition, Carnegie-Mellon University Computer Science Department: Pittsburgh.

Turing, A. M. (1950) Computing Machinery and Intelligence, *Mind*, **59**, pp. 433–460.

Waltz, D. (1983) Artificial Intelligence: an Assessment of the State-of-the-art and Recommendations for Future Directions, *The AI Magazine*, Fall, 1983, pp. 55–67.

Wasserman, A. I., & Gutz, S. (1982) The Future of Programming, *Communications of ACM*, **25**, 3, pp. 196–206.

Weinberg, G. M. (1971) *The Psychology of Computer Programming,* Van Nostrand Reinhold: NY.

Weizenbaum, J. (1965) ELIZA — A Computer Program for the Study of Natural Language Communication Between Man and Machine, *Communications of ACM,* **9,** 1, pp. 36–45.

Weizenbaum, J. (1976) *Computer Power and Human Reason,* Freeman: San Francisco, CA.

Wielinga, R. J. (1978) AI Programming Methodology, *Procs. AISB/GI Conf.,* Hamburg, pp. 355–374.

Wilks, Y. (1976) Natural Language Understanding Systems within the AI Paradigm: a Survey and some Comparisons, in *Artificial Intelligence and language comprehension,* Washington, D.C.: National Institute of Education, pp. 79–120.

Winograd, T. (1972) *Understanding Natural Language,* Academic Press: NY.

Winograd, T. (1975) Breaking the Complexity Barrier Again, *SIGPLAN Notices,* **10,** 1, pp. 13–30.

Winograd, T. (1979) Beyond Programming Languages, *Communications of ACM,* **22,** 7, pp. 391–401.

Winston, P. H. (1975) Learning Structural Descriptions from Examples, in *The Psychology of Computer Vision,* Winston, P. H., (ed.) McGraw-Hill: NY.

Winston, P. H. (1977, 1984 2nd edition) *Artificial Intelligence,* Addison-Wesley: Reading, Mass.

Winston, P. H., & Prendergast, K. A. (1984) *The AI Business,* MIT Press: Cambridge Mass.

Wirth, N. (1971) Program Development by Stepwise Refinement, *Communications of ACM,* **14,** 4, pp. 221–227.

Wirth, N. (1973) *Systematic Programming: An Introduction,* Prentice-Hall: Englewood Cliffs, NJ.

Woods, W. A. (1975) What's in a Link: Foundations for Semantic Networks, in *Representation and Understanding,* D. G. Bobrow and A. Collins (eds.), Academic Press: NY, pp. 35–82.

Wos, L. (1985) Automated Reasoning, *The American Mathematical Monthly,* **92,** 2, pp. 85–92.

Wos, L., Overbeek, R., Lusk, E., & Boyle, J. (1984) *Automated Reasoning,* Prentice-Hall: Englewood Cliffs, NJ.

Yourdon, E. (1975) *Techniques of Program Structure and Design,* Prentice-Hall: Englewood Cliffs, NJ.

# Index